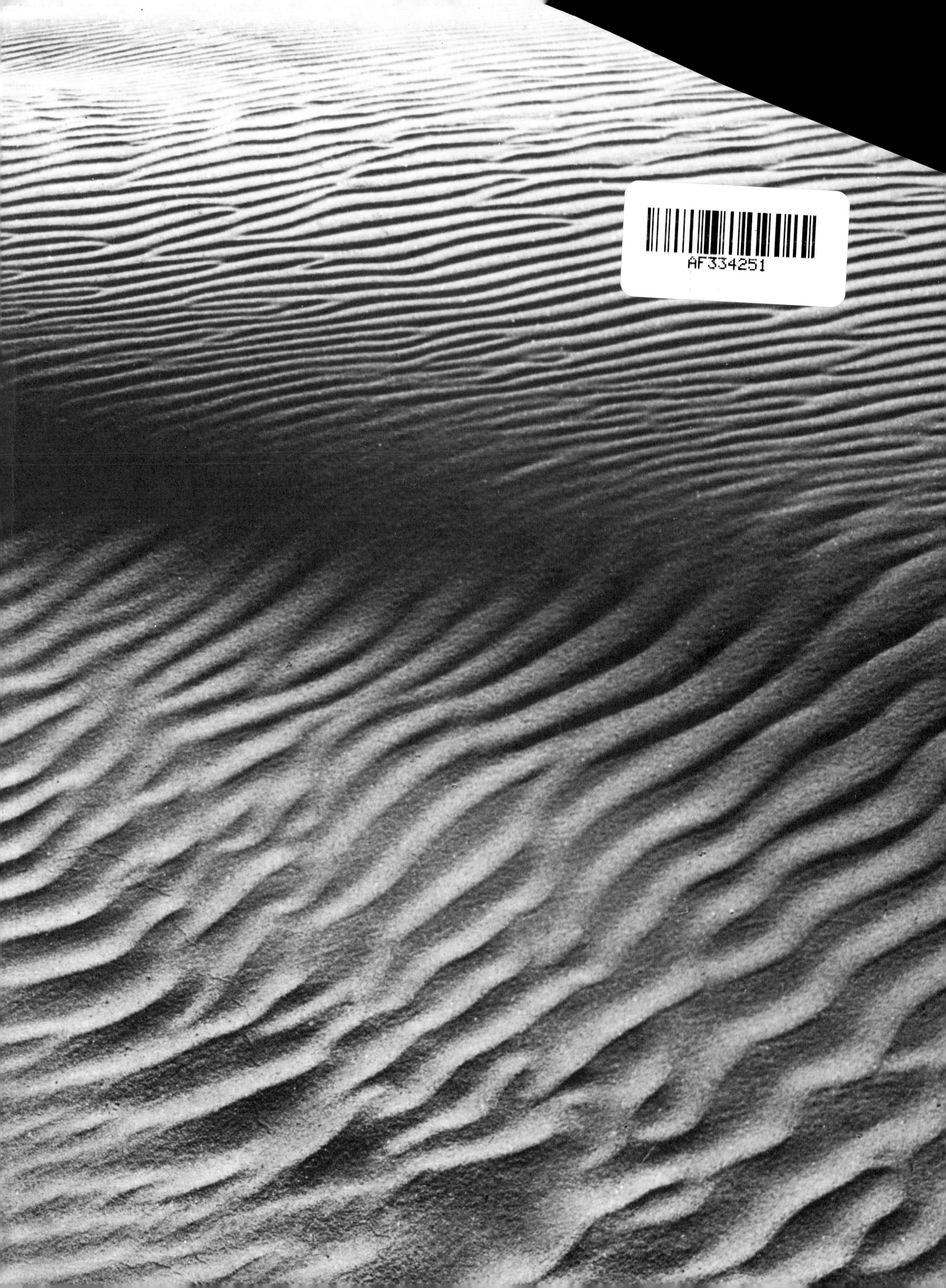
AF334251

To Mike and Family,
with many thanks for your hospitality
and the good times!
Love,
Cheryl.

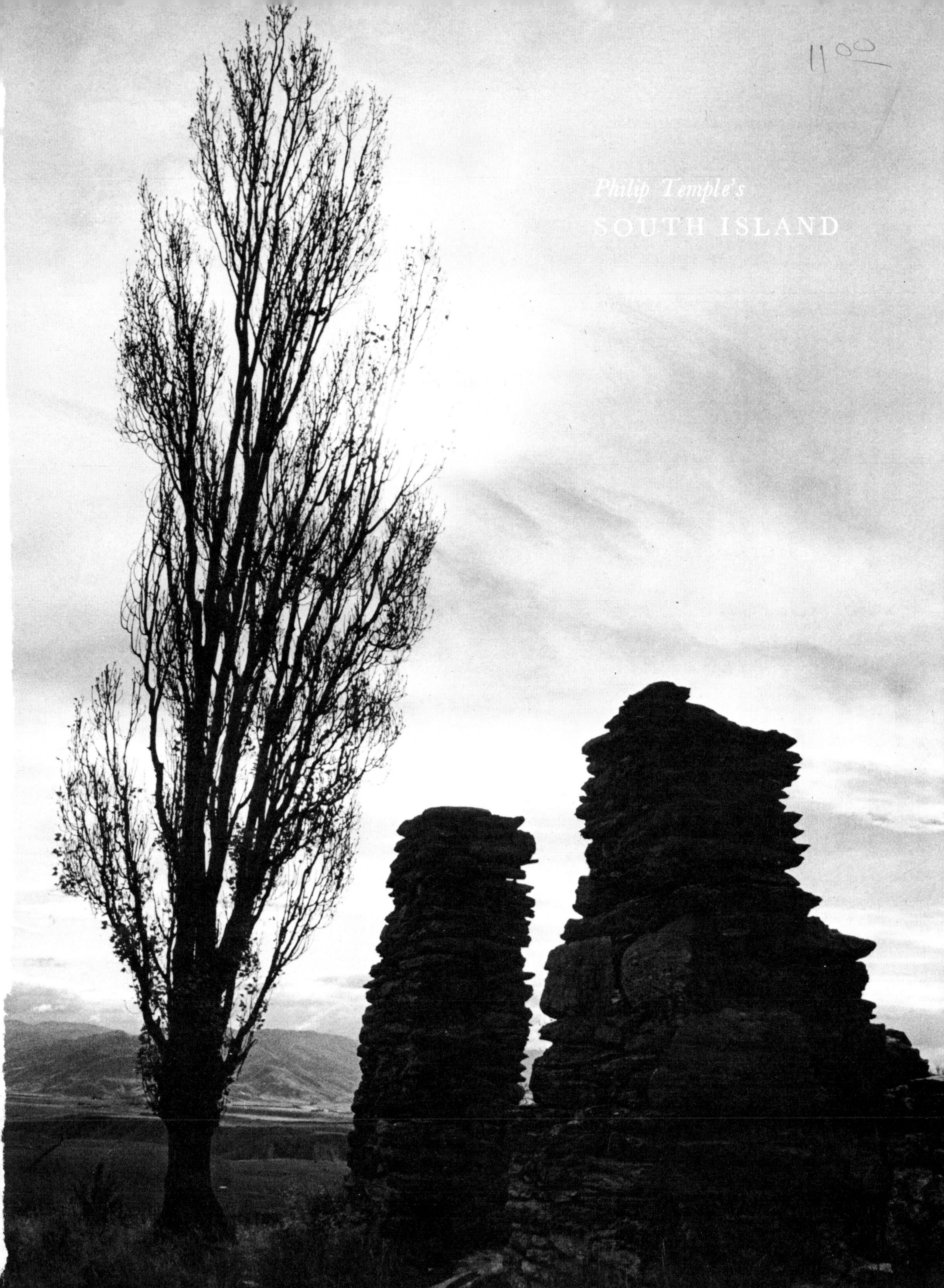

Philip Temple's
SOUTH ISLAND

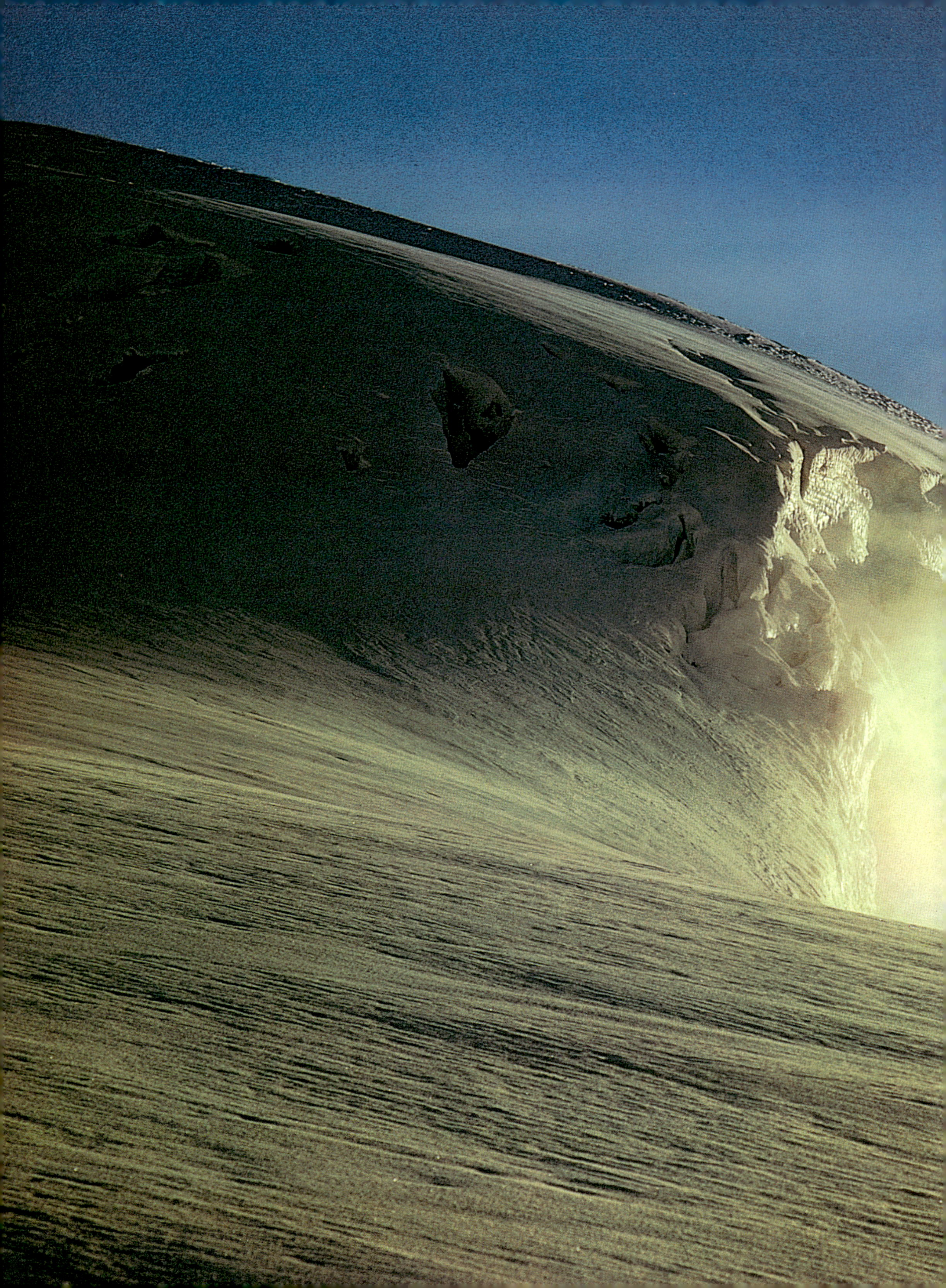

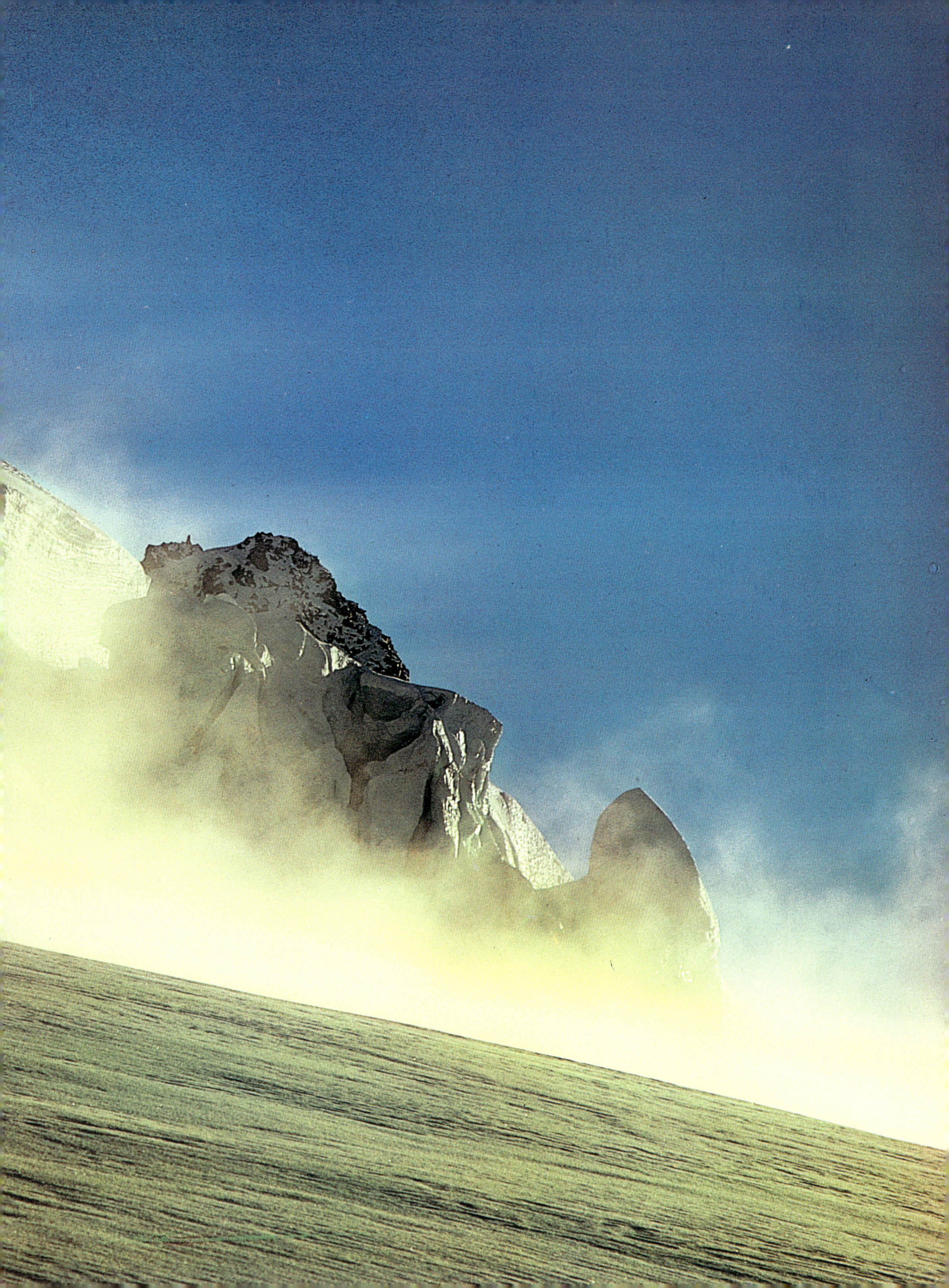

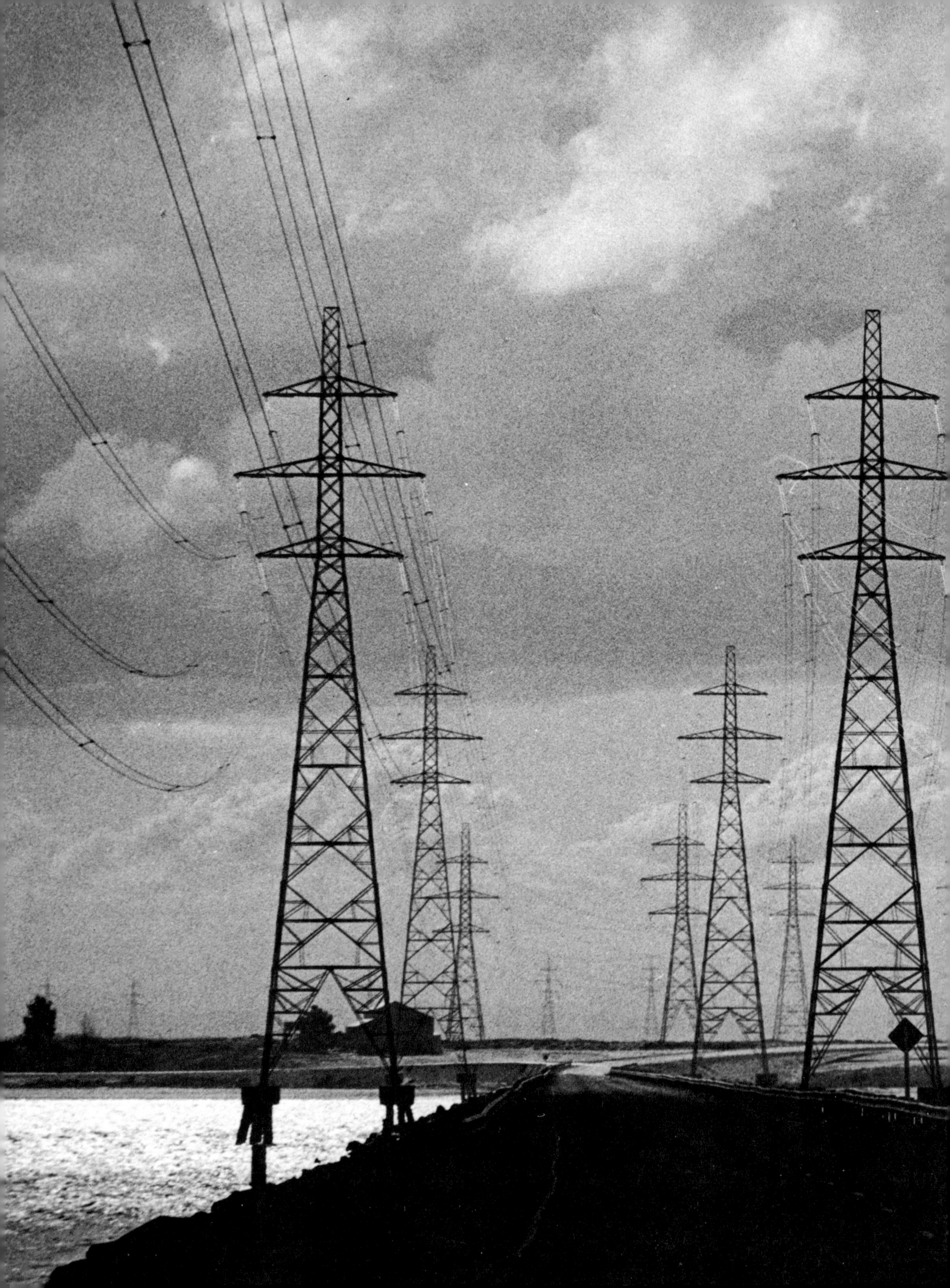

Philip Temple's
SOUTH ISLAND
OF NEW ZEALAND

WHITCOMBE AND TOMBS

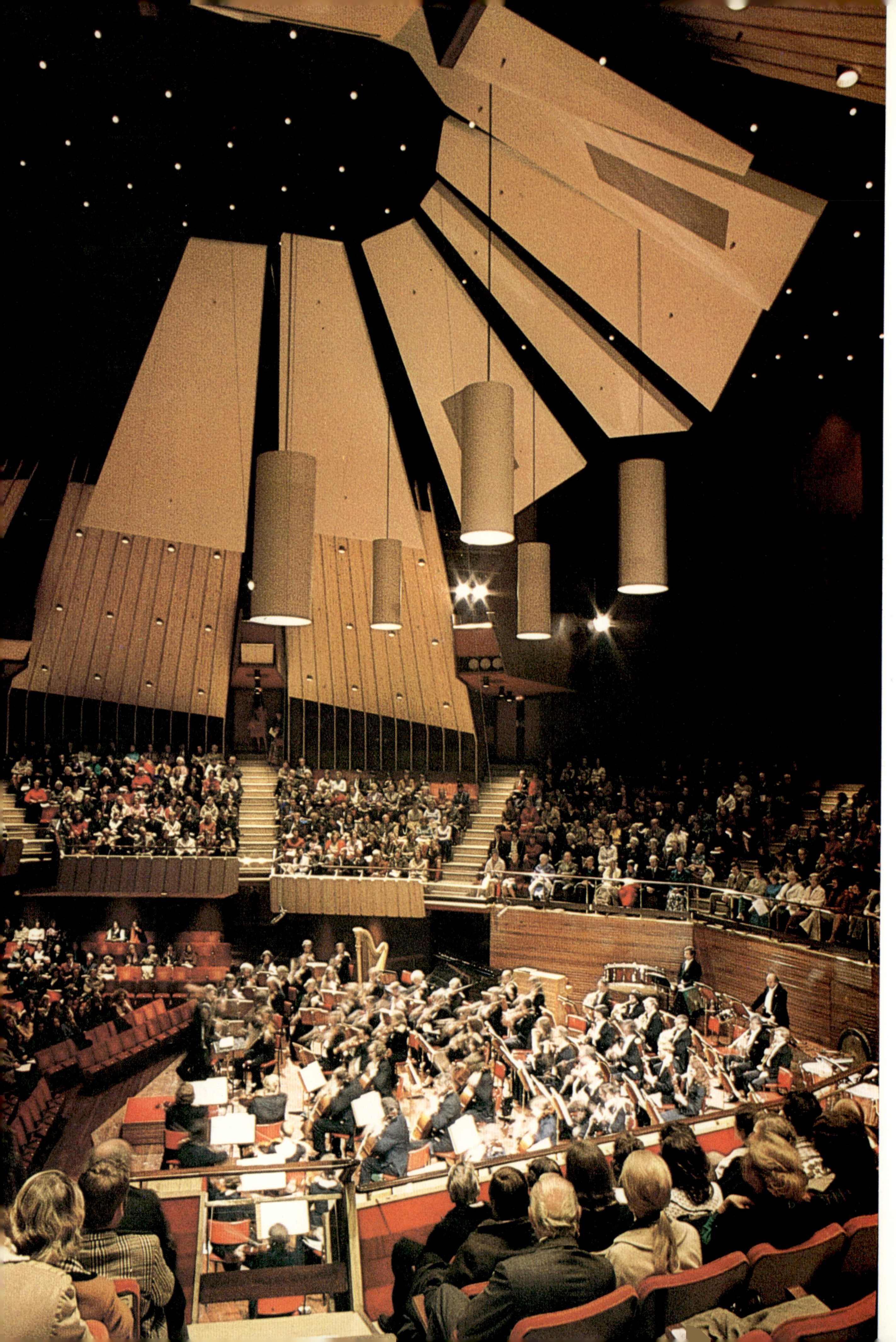

CONTENTS

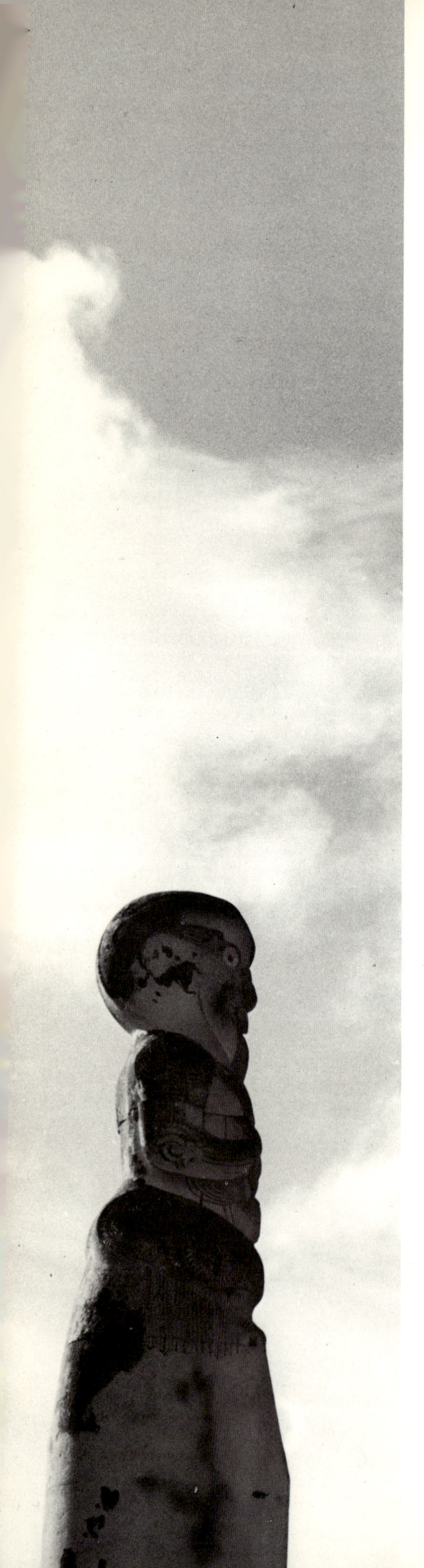

COMPANION VOLUMES BY PHILIP TEMPLE

Mantle of the Skies: The Southern Alps of New Zealand (1971)

Christchurch: A City and its People (1973)

Patterns of Water: The Great Southern Lakes of New Zealand (1974)

NOTE: Commentaries on the photographs appear on pages 148-52. A foldout list has been provided on page 151 for ready reference to location of photographs

FIRST PUBLISHED 1975

© 1975 PHILIP TEMPLE

PUBLISHED BY WHITCOMBE AND TOMBS
A DIVISION OF WHITCOULLS LIMITED
CHRISTCHURCH, NEW ZEALAND

ISBN 0 7233 0417 3

DESIGNED BY PHILIP TEMPLE

COLOUR SEPARATIONS AND PRINTING AND BINDING IN JAPAN
UNDER THE SUPERVISION OF JOHN WEATHERHILL INC., TOKYO

THIS book is a personal impression, in pictures and prose, of the South Island of New Zealand. Scenes and people portrayed, and topics dealt with in the text, may well be seen as illustrative of New Zealand as a whole. But, as far as is reasonable, I have placed emphasis — through depiction of natural and urban landscapes and through the story of settlement and development — on the South Island's distinct form and character.

Beyond the introductory group of photographs, sections depict urban scenes and life; rural landscape, work and recreation; and a final sequence of pictures illustrates the distinctive qualities of South Island landscape. The photographs show the island as it can be seen today. The text is devoted almost entirely to yesterday, to themes of settlement and growth, often as related by early settlers and commentators. Together, photographs and text create a more rounded impression than might be achieved by either alone.

The book is dedicated not only to South Islanders but to all those who find some measure of identity with the island's superb landscape and its inimitable human associations.

PHILIP TEMPLE

THE SOUTH ISLAND...

Mountain, river,
sea and city,
a story of sheep and gold

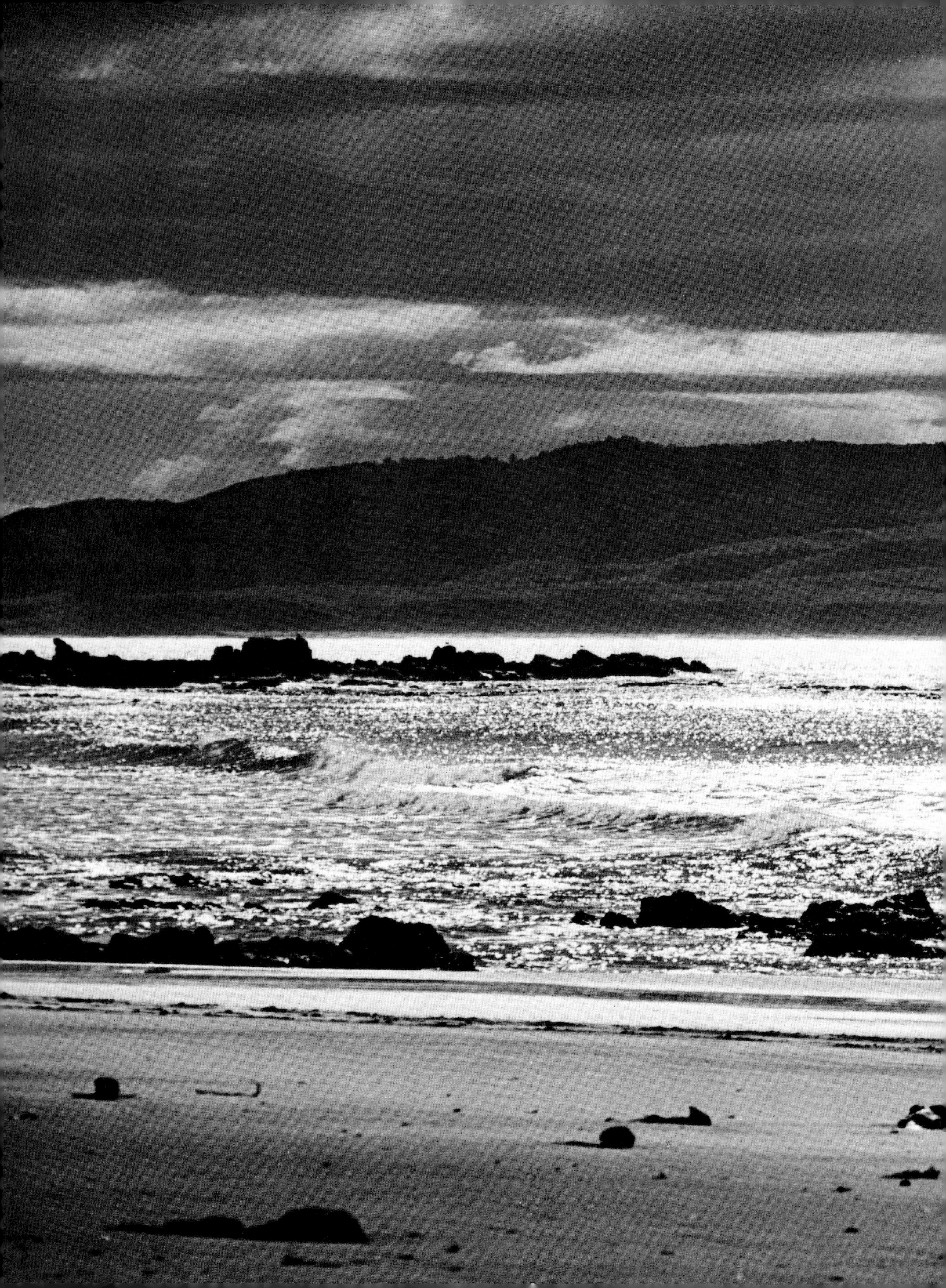

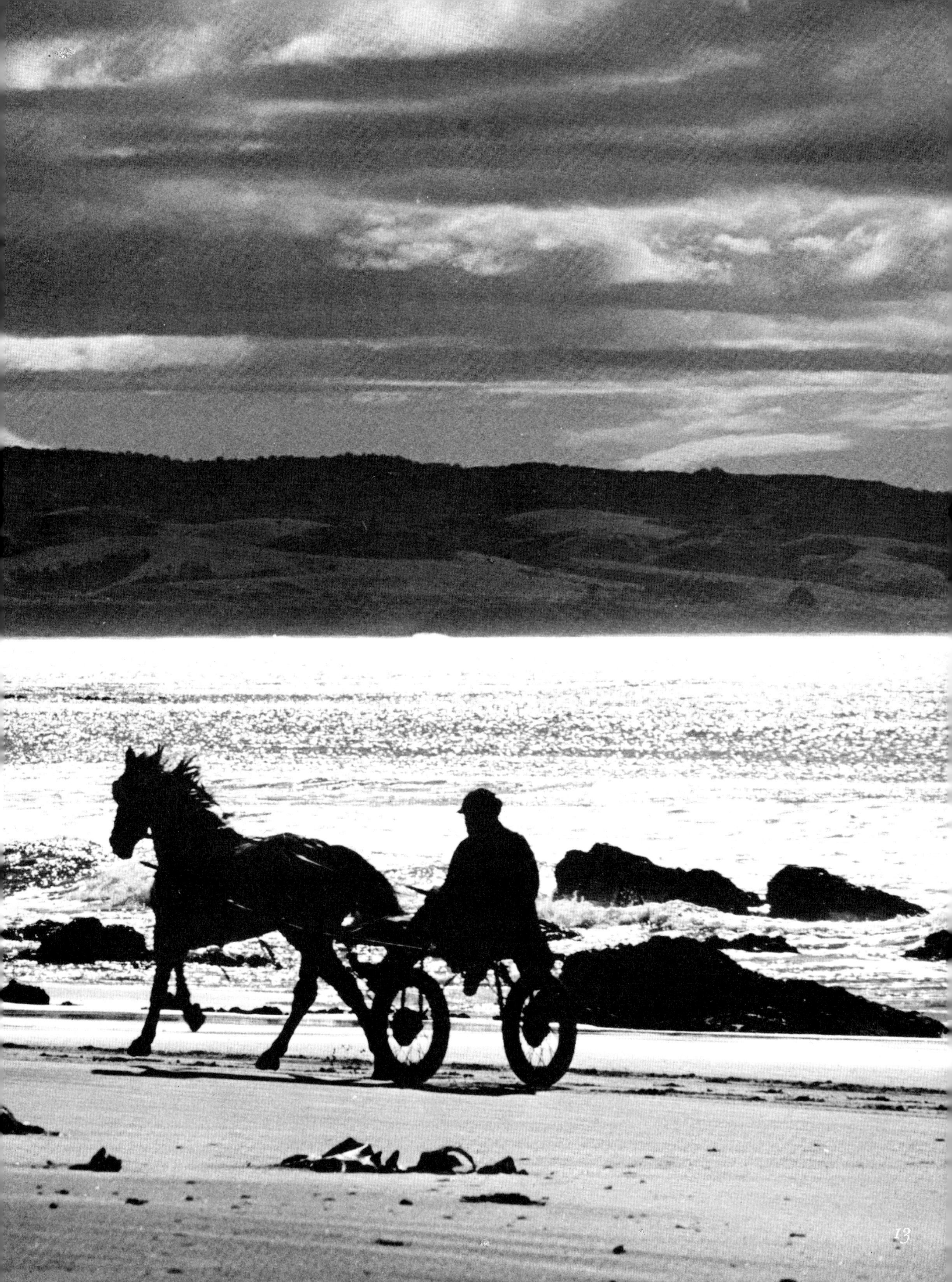

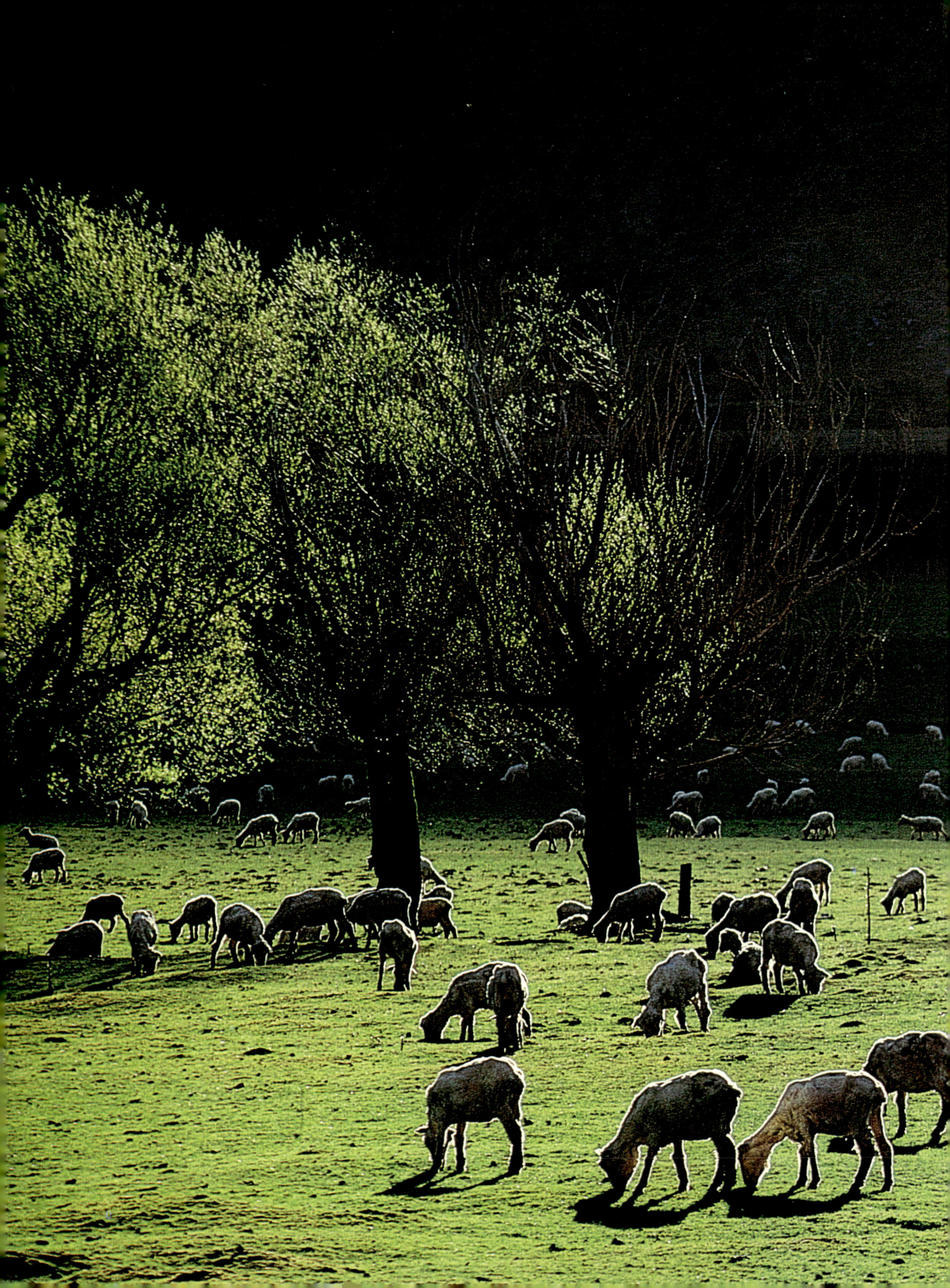

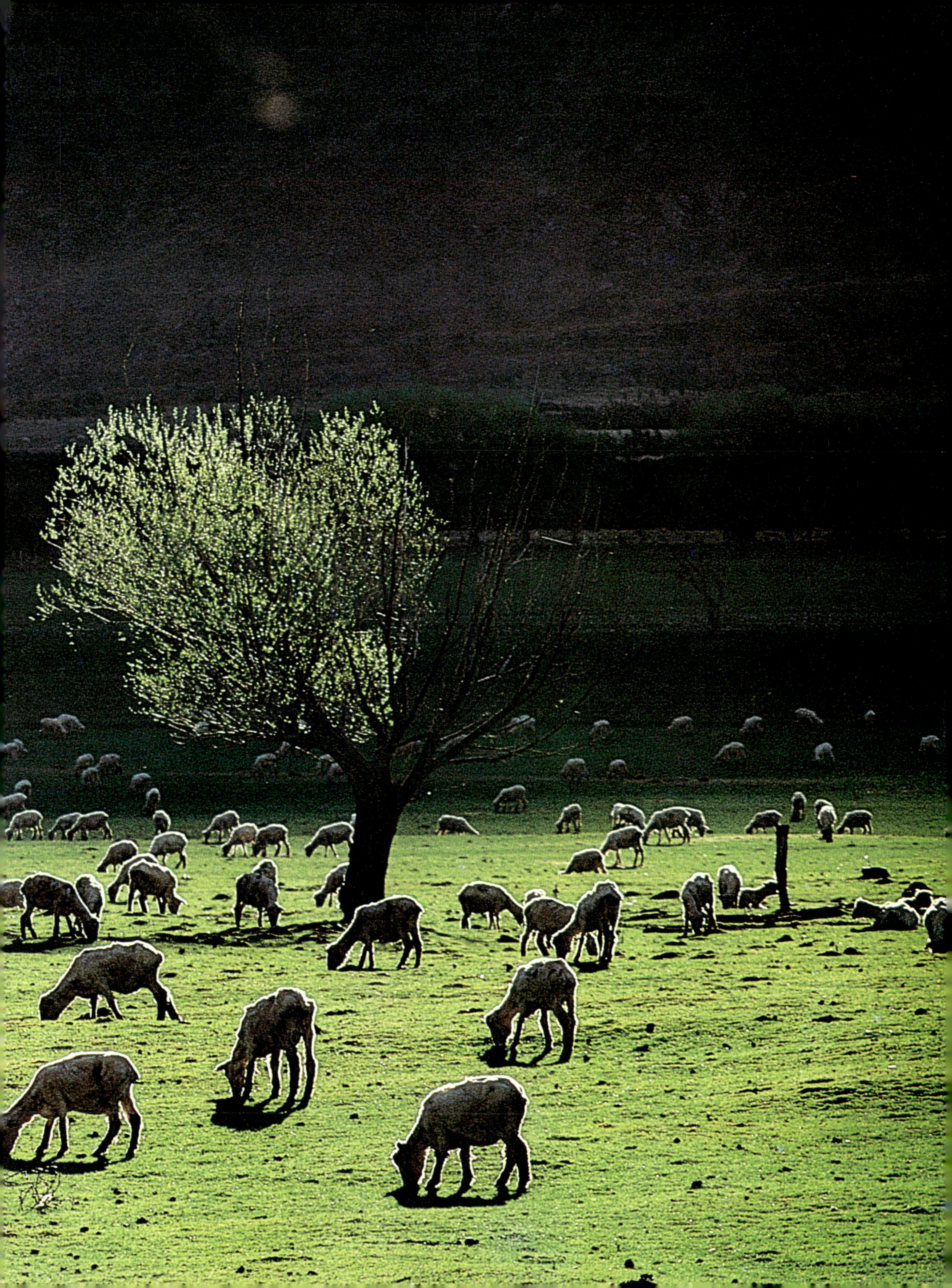

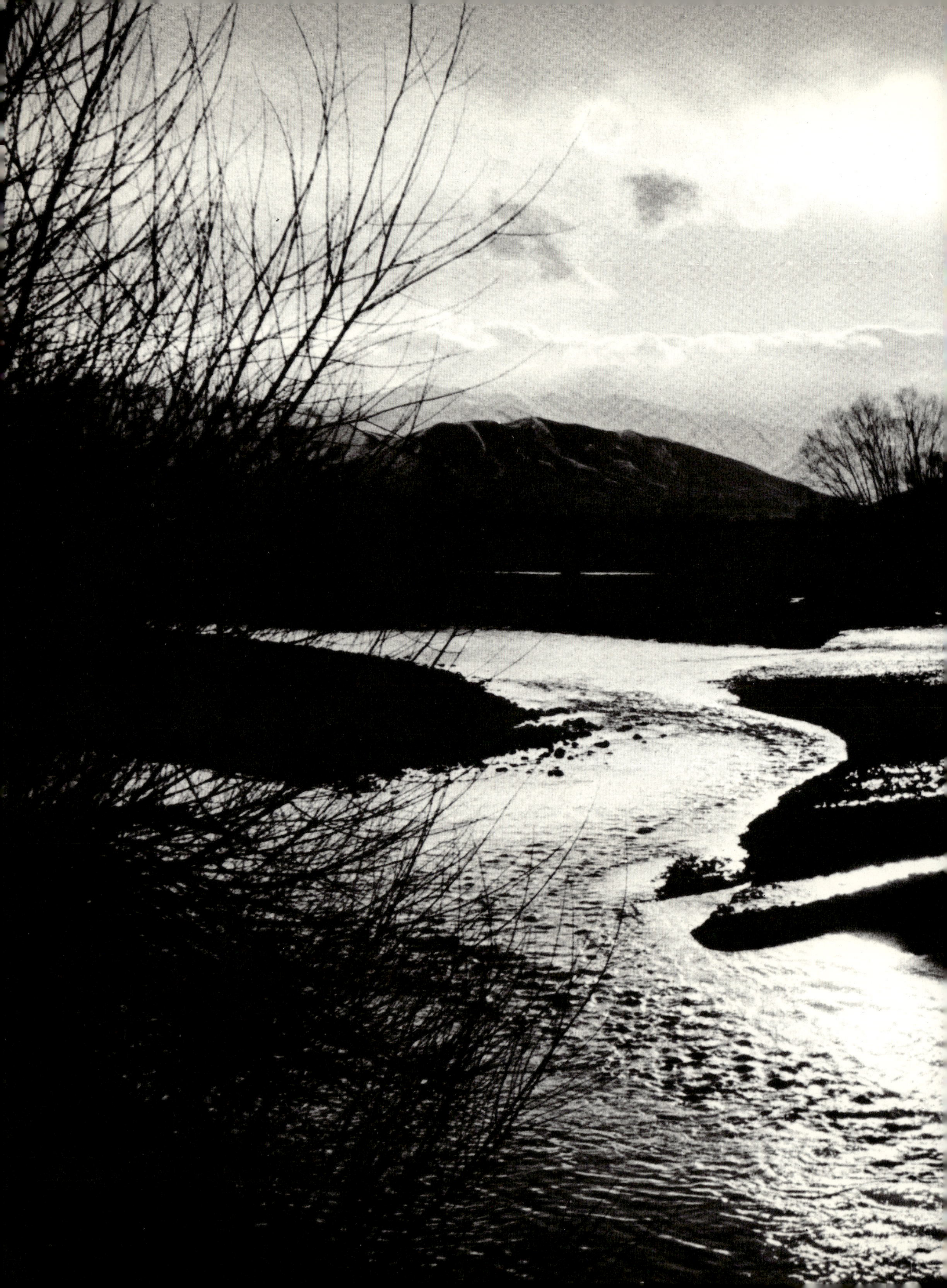

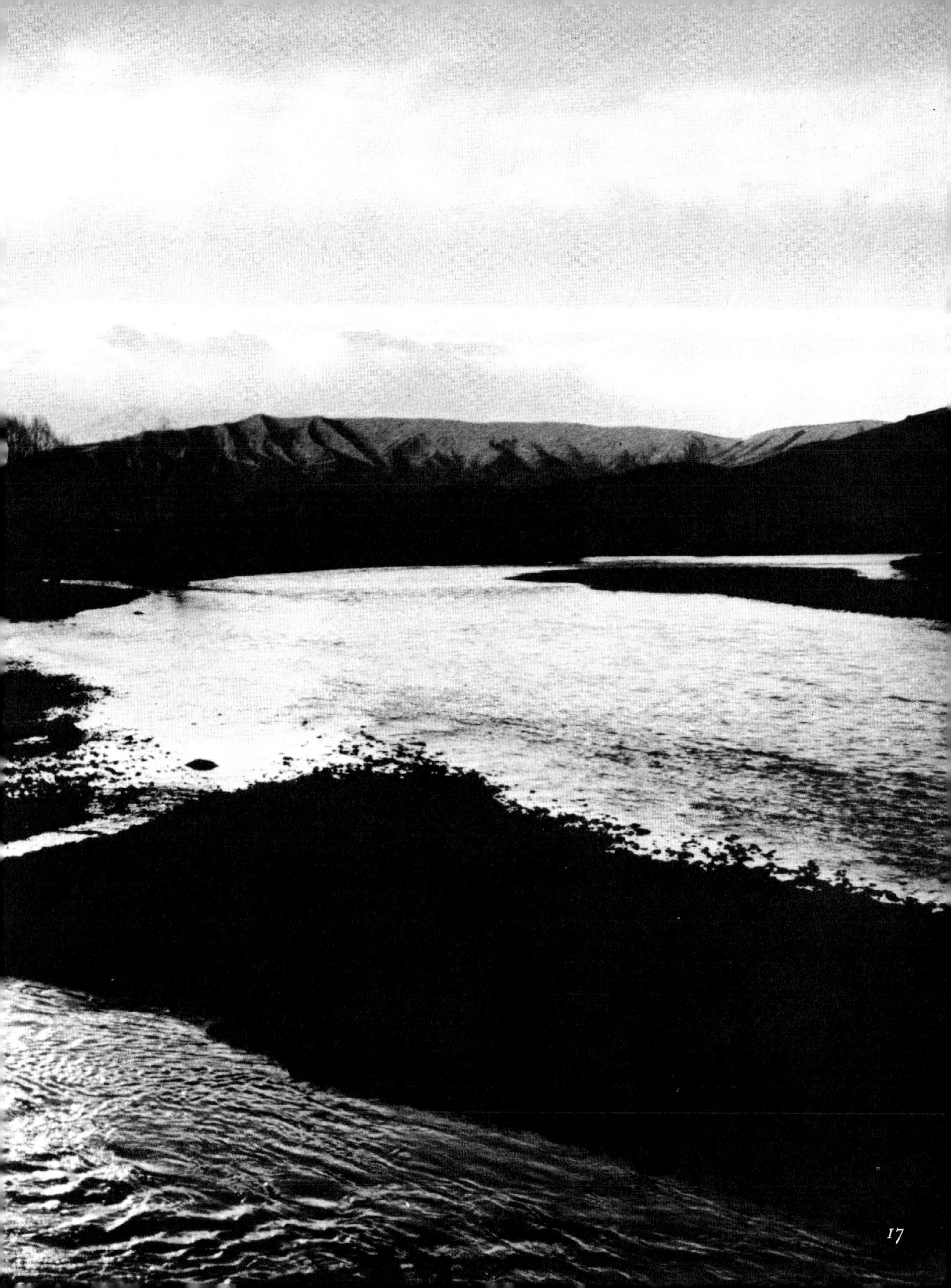

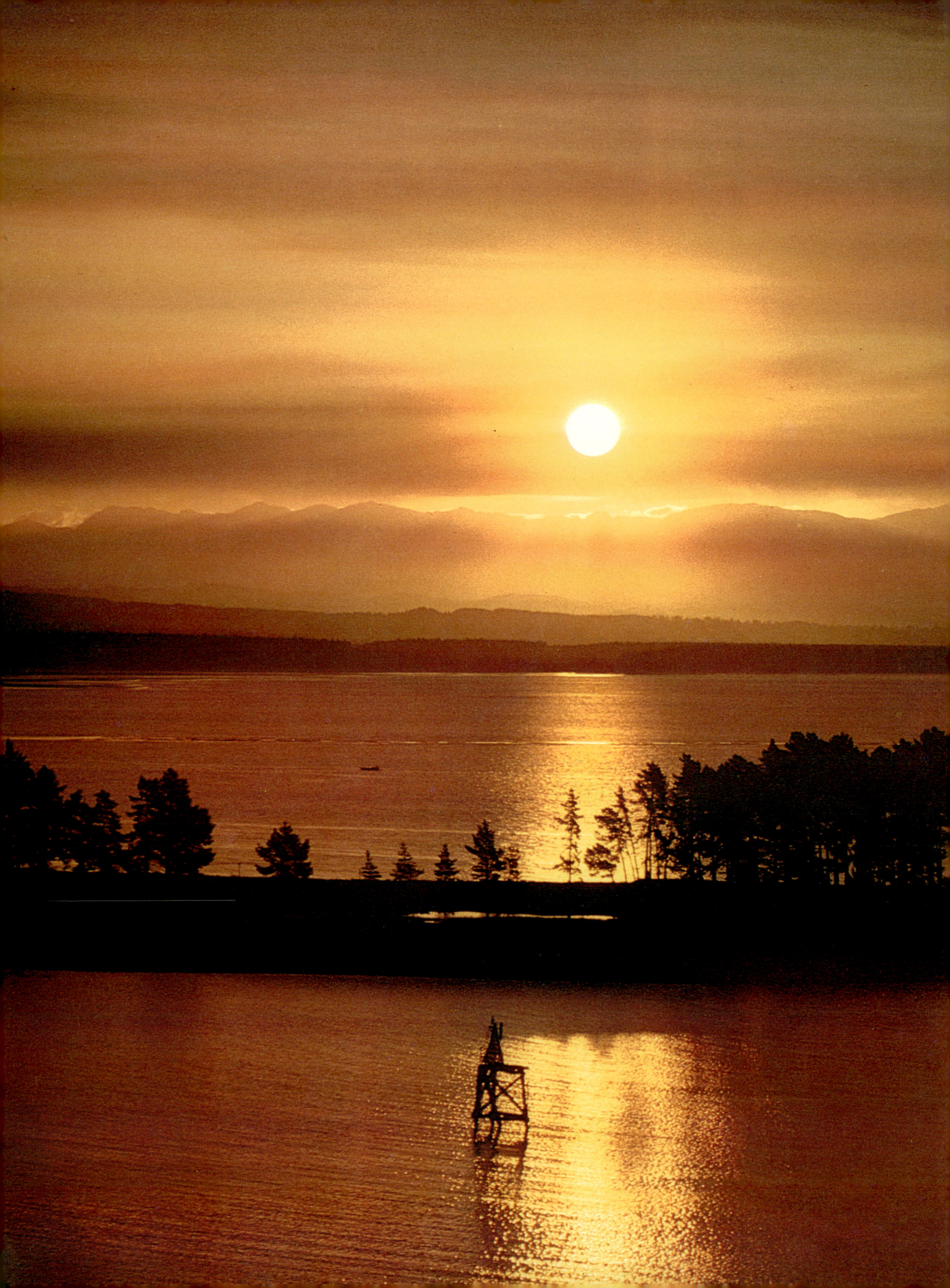

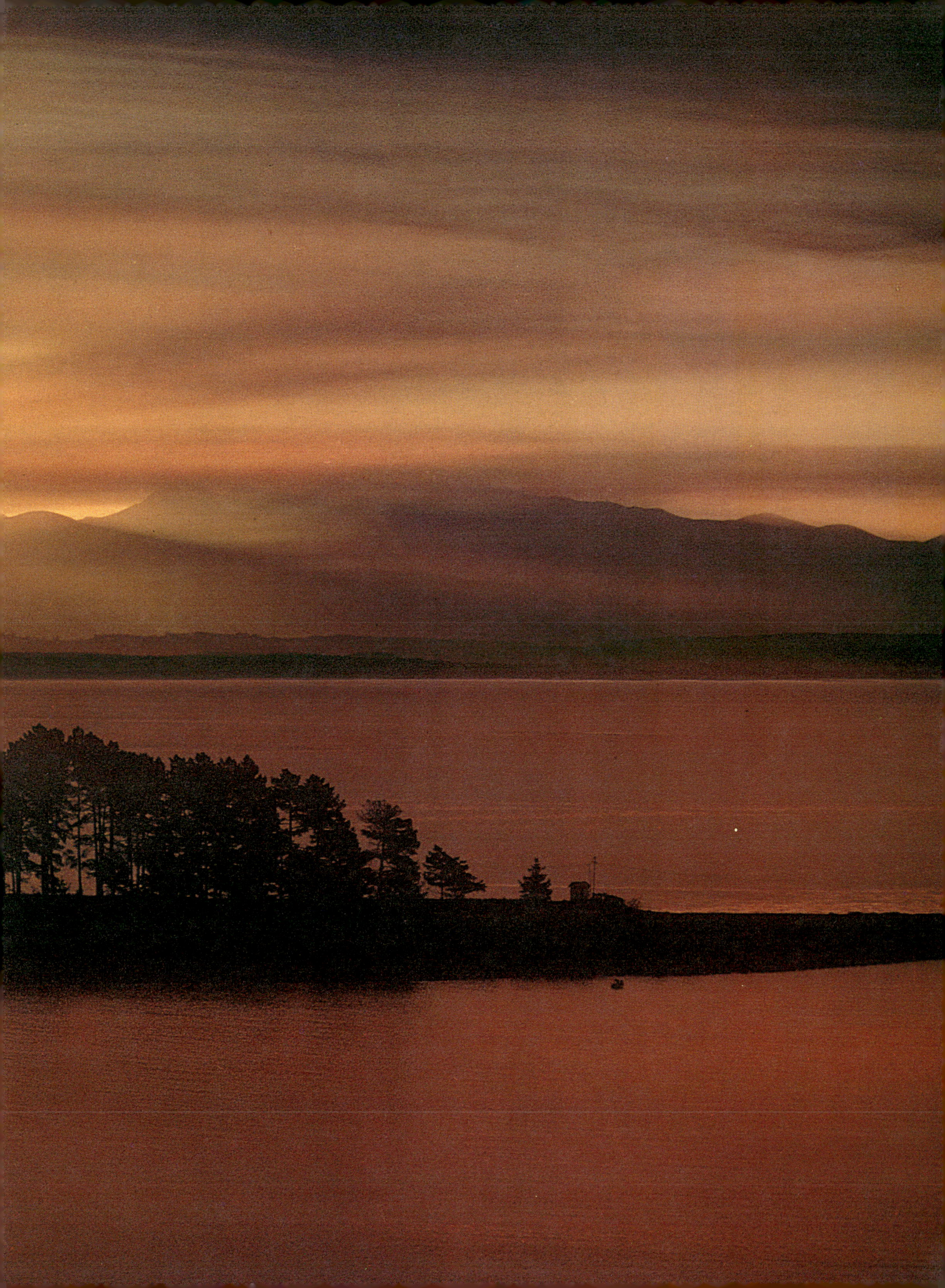

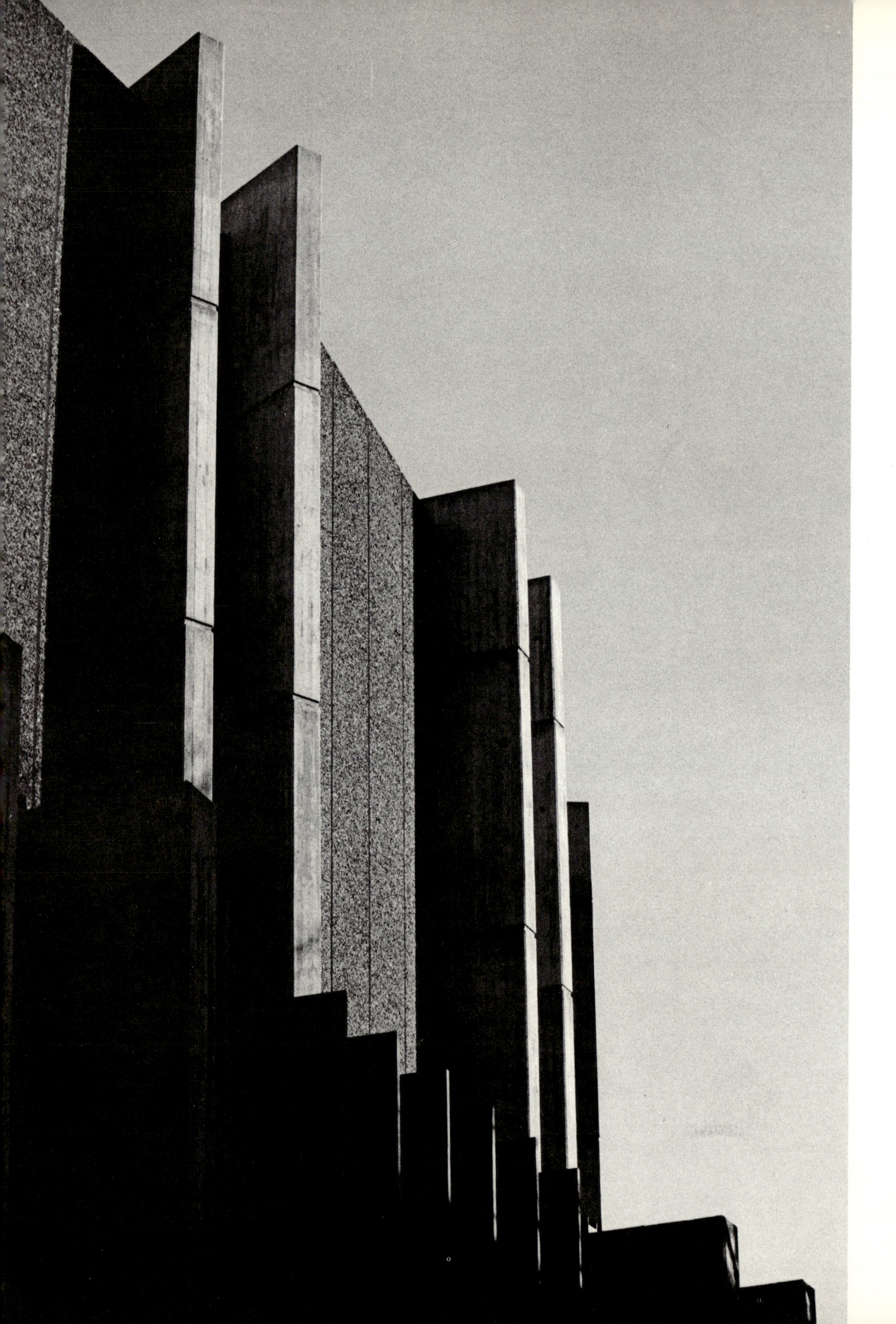

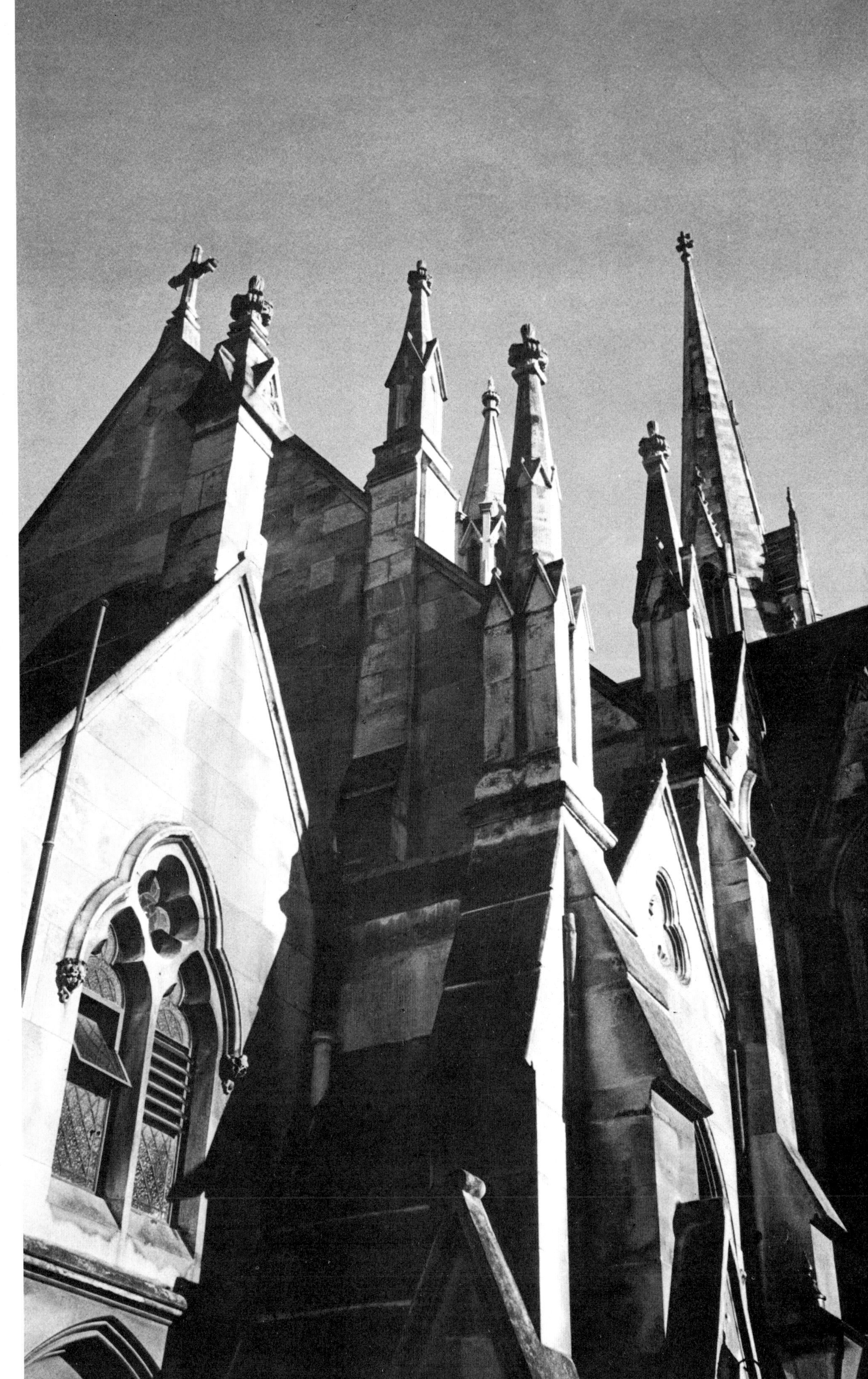

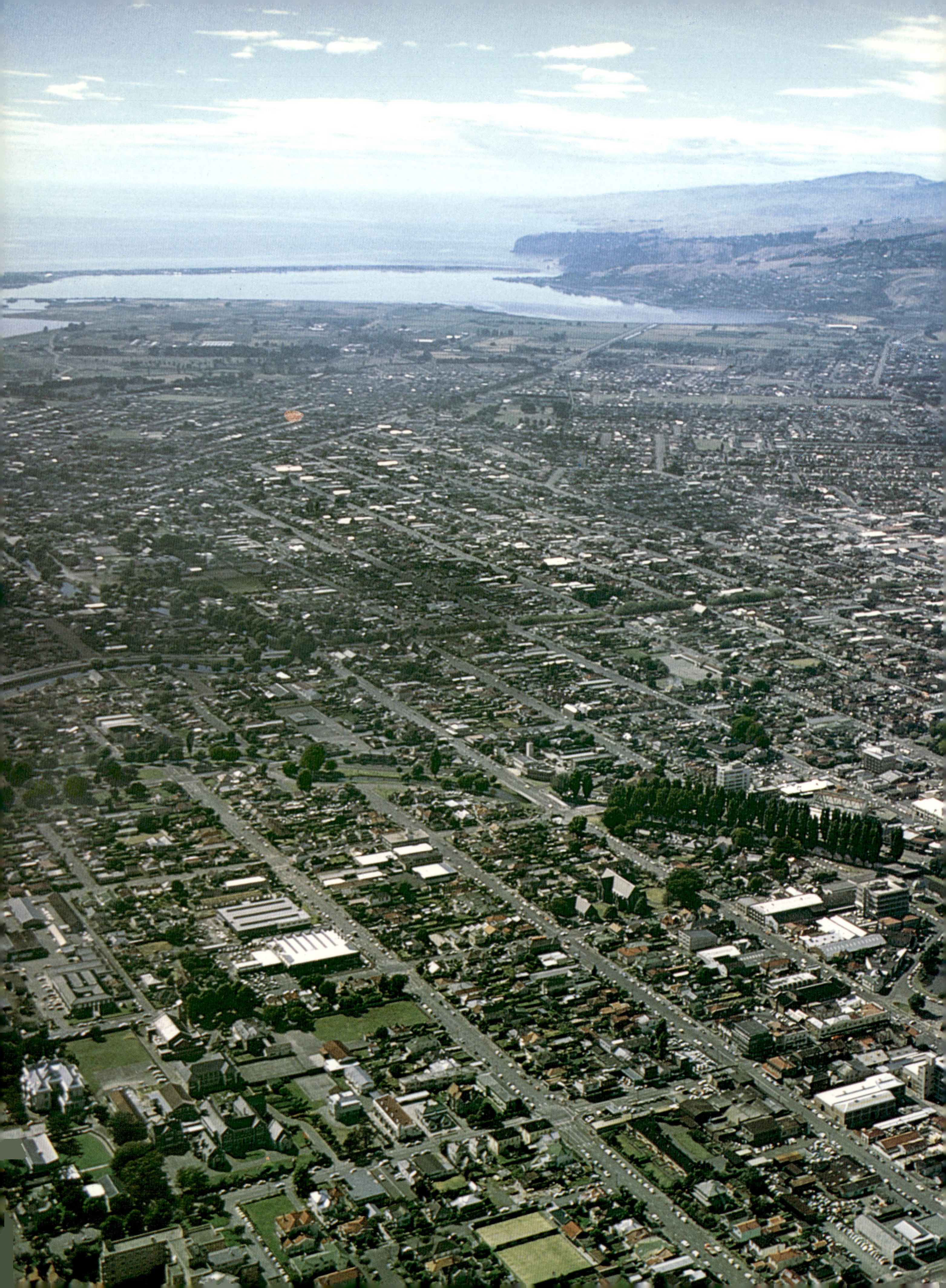

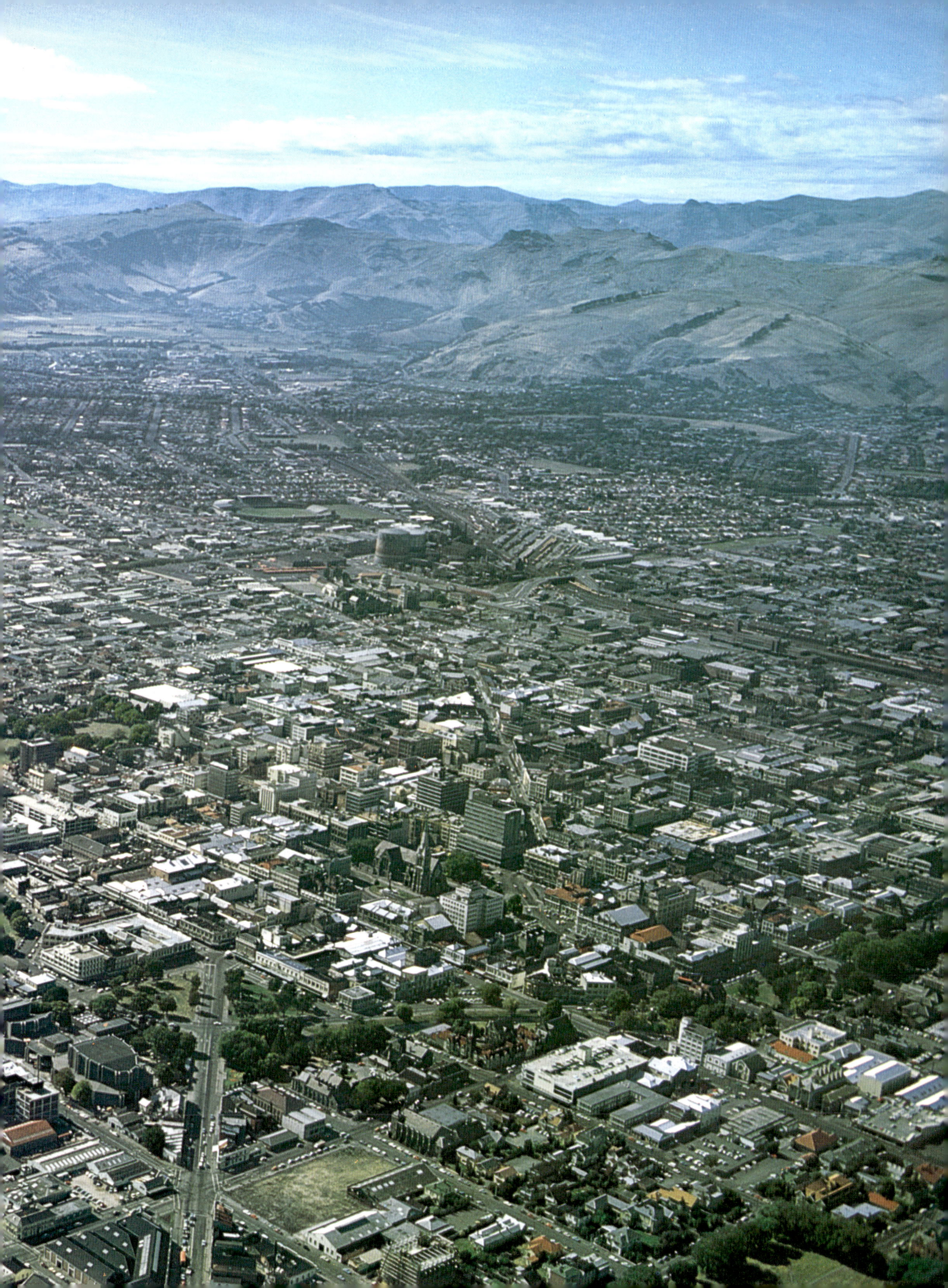

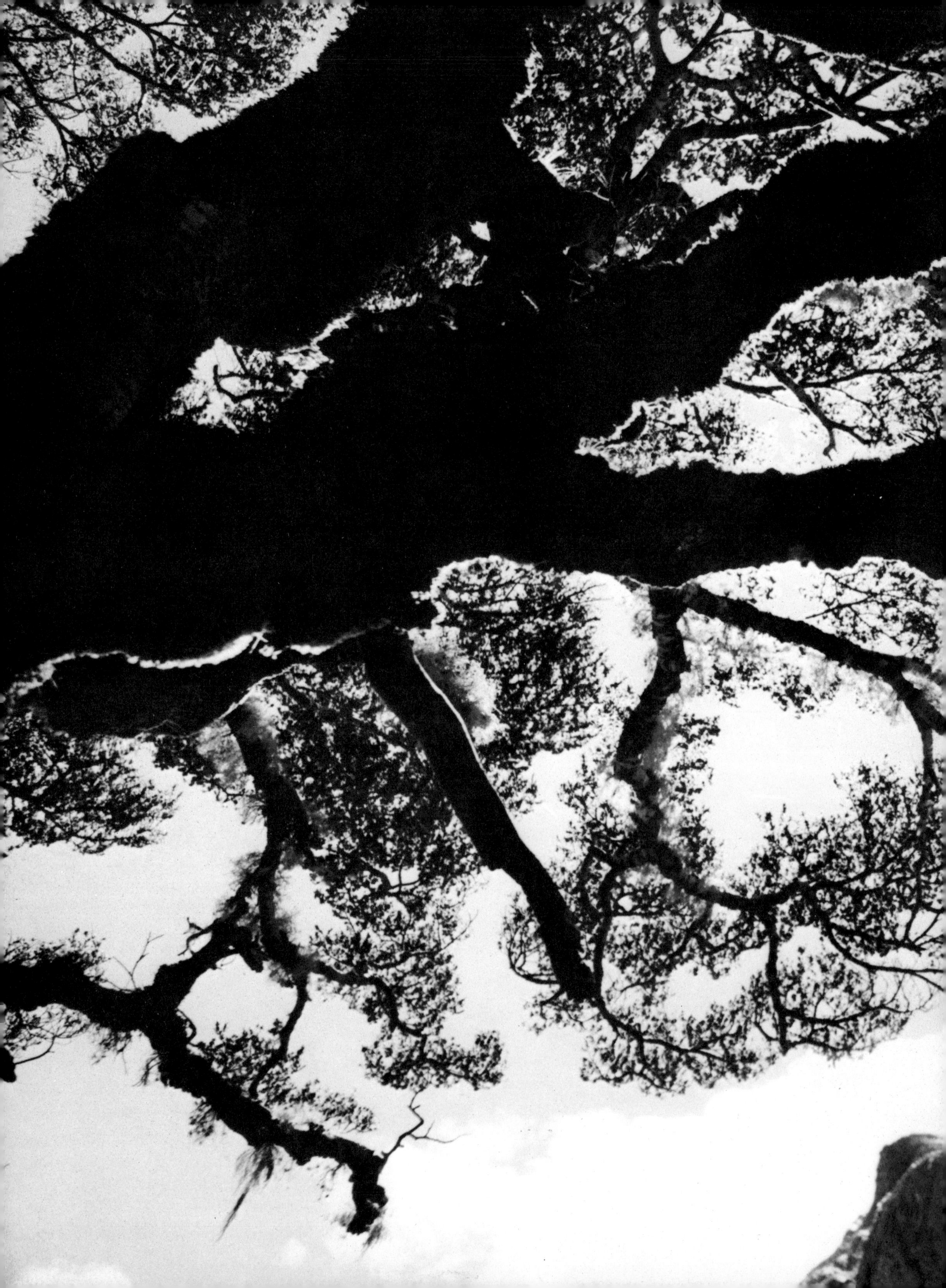

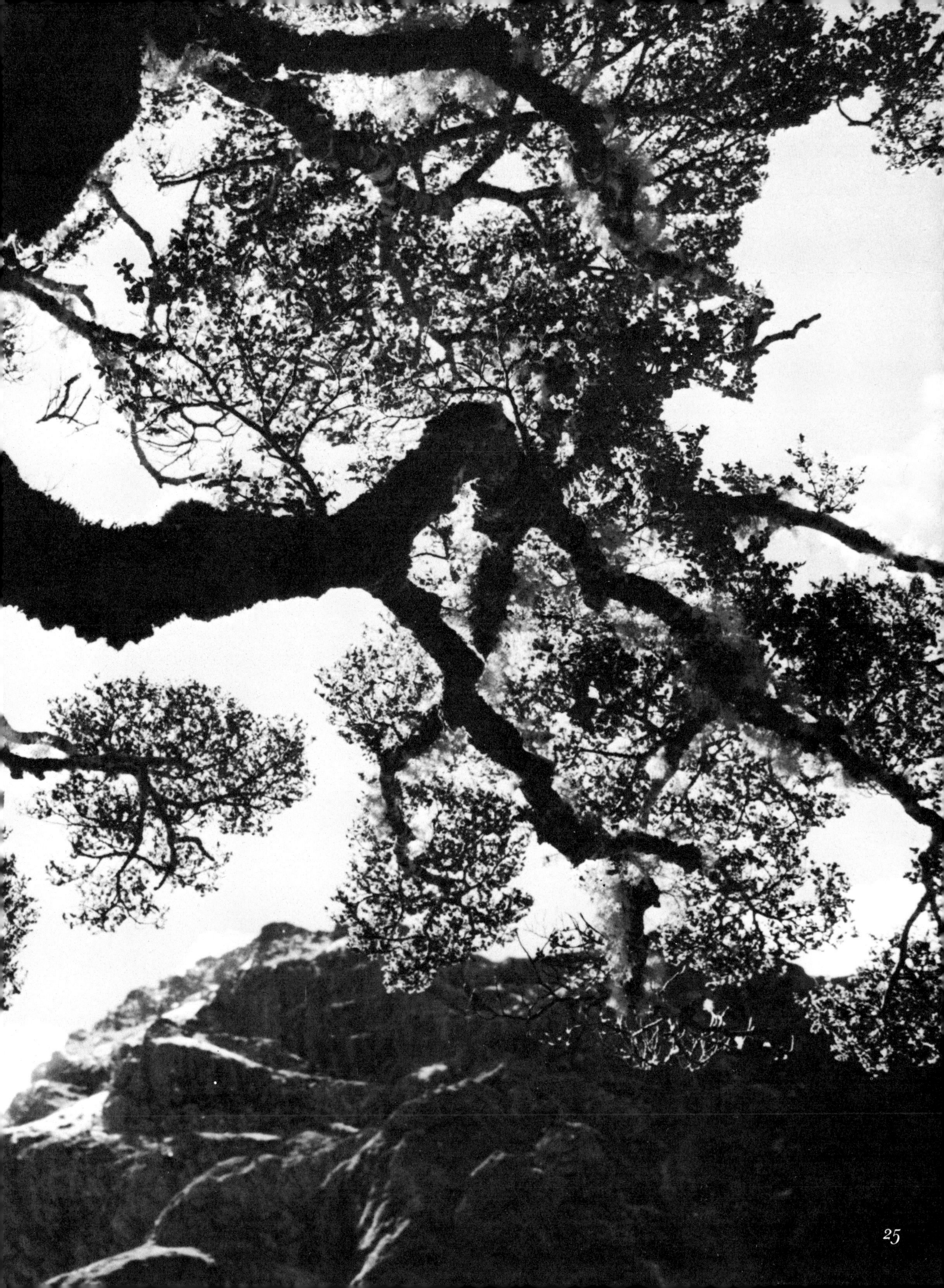

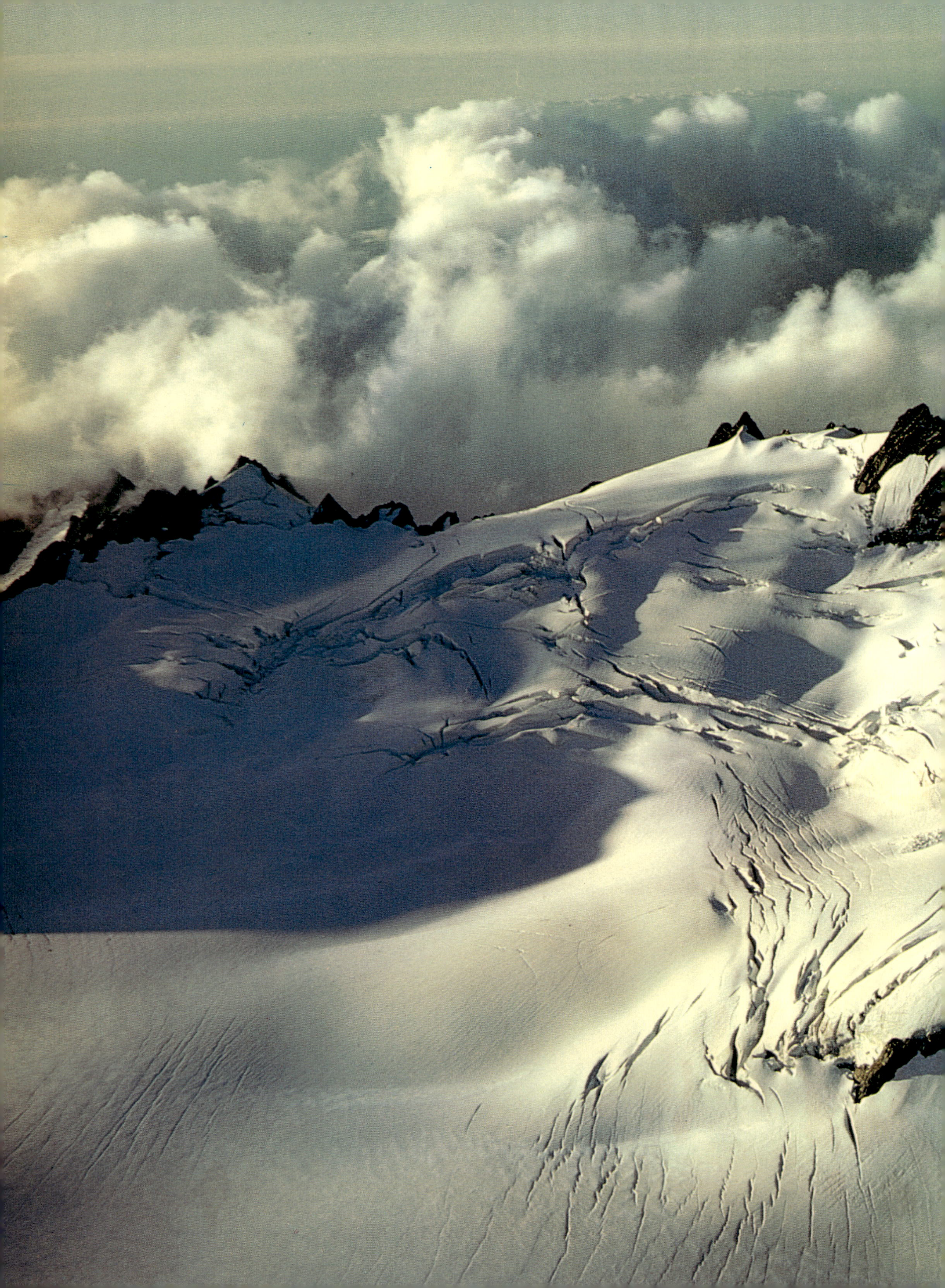

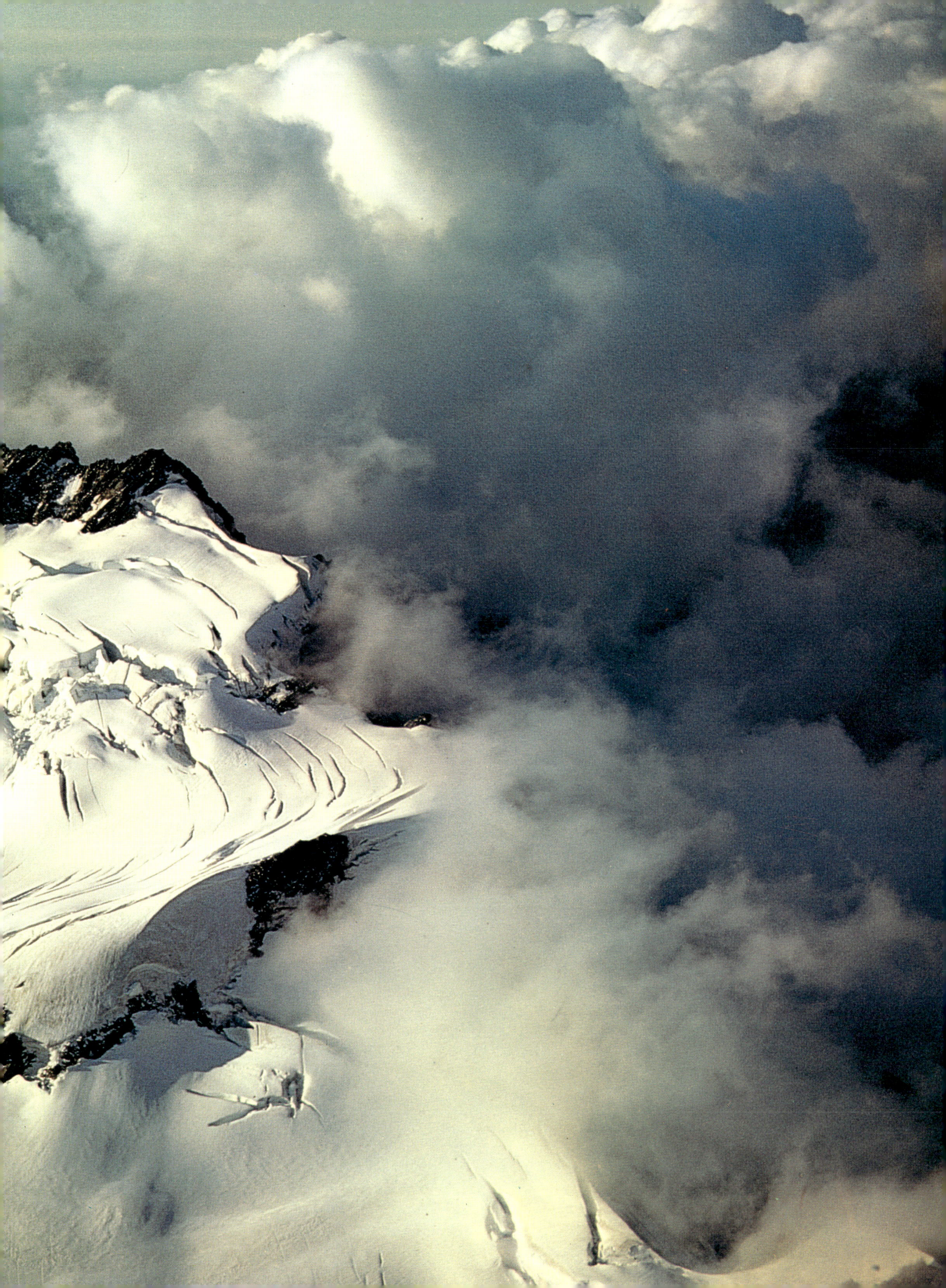

Fʀᴏᴍ the sea it was a big land, 'a large land, uplifted high'.[1] And James Cook, rounding the fiord-cut tail of the South Island in 1770, wrote: 'No country upon Earth can appear with a more ruged and barren Aspect.'[2] No matter how the navigators, the sealers or the whalers came to it, scudding before the bitter winds of the roaring forties, the first landfall was of mountains, white peaks over the breaking wave, stern slopes of rock and tangled forest rising from an ironbound coast. Even beyond the wide plains on the east, the mountains stood in ranks, older, hedging the lowland built from their own dross, scoured down by the braided silver rivers. And there was little refuge for cold wet ships, stinking of plundered animal oil: bays and sounds plucked by the rushing tides and winds of Cook Strait, the bottomless inlets of Fiordland, and the shallow harbours of volcanic peninsulas in Canterbury and Otago. For the rest, it was a shipwreck coast.

To the scattered Maori it was a cold island, only matching the lush warmth of North Island bays in favoured margins of Cook Strait. Further south the kumara would not grow and in winter the snow and frost descended from the mountains to the plains; the few passes from east to west through the complicated ranges were closed. For months there was no way to the wealth of the western rivers; not the gold that white men were to prize, but greenstone, the hard decorative jade, priceless in a world without metal. The Maori named the island for it, Te Wai Pounamu.

Conflict between Maori and Pakeha was sporadic, fired by the habits of sealers and whalers more savage than natives governed by their own law and custom. From a letter, May 1839: 'I fell in with the possessor of the head by merest chance and after a long chase we succeeded in bringing him down by a rifle shot, which fortunately did not injure any of the ornamental tattoos on his face. If you would like his skin, I have it drying, and will send it to you the first opportunity . . . tell me at the same time if you would like the head of a female, as I shall have great pleasure in supplying you'.[3] Little wonder that the Maoris sometimes retaliated in equally savage fashion.

But widespread conflict between land-hungry migrants from Britain and Maori owners of the island never came about. For disease came first in the Pakeha ships; measles and influenza in the 1830s which decimated the Maori on the south and east coasts. Then war and depredations from the north as the great marauding chief Te Rauparaha swept down to settle old tribal scores. By 1840 the populous pas of Canterbury were broken and scattered. Only a few hundred Maoris survived over the great plains and the bays and hills of Banks Peninsula. In the early 1830s there were 2000 Maoris in Otakou, at the entrance to Otago Harbour. When the Scots came to settle in 1848 there were 110.

The island was wide and empty enough so that it would be almost free of the land disputes that led to war in the more populous North Island. It was perfect ground for the practice of planned settlement by zealots in Britain who saw in orderly colonisation a panacea for the economic and social ills of a sordid industrial society. A decent living and dignity might be afforded the poor, a proper usefulness to disgruntled and unemployed gentry. For some a new society offered the chance to preserve the best of British life — embodied in church and class — that was threatened by incipient revolution and democracy. George Rennie, promoter of the Otago scheme, thought that emigration in general might 'save the institutions of England from being swept away in an uncontrollable rebellion of the stomach'. Thriving colonies would be good markets for British traders, too.

The colonising crusade of the New Zealand Company helped push a reluctant British Government into annexation of New Zealand in 1840. The benign influence of Crown law and order might avert 'the process of War and Spoliation, under which uncivilized Tribes have invariably disappeared as often as they have been brought into the immediate vicinity of Emigrants from the Nations of Christendom'. The first Company settlers arrived in Wellington in 1840, coincidentally with Crown representatives in the Bay of Islands, ready to pursue protection of the Maori with the Treaty of Waitangi. Paternal government arrived with capitalist colony, hand in hand, but rarely in step.

Though the first planned settlements were at Wellington in 1840 and New Plymouth in 1841, the greatest impact of the organised schemes was in the South Island where migrants sailed to unbounded if half-understood opportunities in Nelson (1842), Otago (1848) and Canterbury (1850). Already in Canterbury there was a small French colony at Akaroa (1840), but this was soon submerged by the incoming tide of expansion and gain.

The associations which administered these settlements fostered hopes of establishing close and ordered societies, the right balance of landowner, merchant, artisan and labourer. The Canterbury Association's plan was 'to set an example of colonial settlement in which, from the first, all the elements, including the very highest, of a good and right state of society, shall find their proper place, and their active operation'.[4] Otago was to be a Scots Free Church settlement where 'piety, rectitude and industry' would feel at home, and where the inhabitants as a body would form 'a vigilant moral police'.[5]

They would be agricultural settlements and the cankers of speculation and exploitation that had poisoned the social health of colonies in other parts of the world would be avoided by a 'uniform and sufficient price' on the sole source of wealth, the land. A controlled price, low enough for small capitalists to procure land, yet sufficiently high so that speculation would be avoided, so that labourers would be kept in their place but with hope of emulating their betters through industry and obligation to order.

Moral pomposity and economic theories made fine banners. But they offered little material comfort to men and women who stood on empty beaches after four months at sea and, in facing the realities of unknown hills and bush, understood that survival was entirely dependent on their own hard labour. And most of those who came, and stayed, had little faith in the ideal of transplanting an old society that had bred privilege and poverty. They had left nothing behind save hardship and hunger, and though they had little to begin with and new hardships to face, they worked for a new society where the real ideals were freedom, equality and opportunity — the colonial opportunity, where the building of class and institutions was less important than the practical business of living unfettered, breaking the land to support a working dignity and independence, a better material life than they had ever known. Even the young 'leaders' of the settlements were infected by the enthusiasm of the new order: 'Most of them young men of superior education and intellect, they rejoiced in a state of things which allowed of the formation of society as it were anew, with the same complete materials arranged in relations less disheartening to the class who earn their bread by the sweat of their brow.'[6]

William Curling Young, in a letter from Nelson in April 1842, expressed the elation and satisfaction of the settlers: 'You would clap your hands if you could see what great things we are doing here . . . As for coming back to England, I know not what to say. It is something to be here, and to be doing what we are, and to be what we are . . . my life is in Nelson and my place is here.'[6]

The planned settlements gave order and design at the beginning. But the sheer practicalities of colonial life superseded agricultural models and religious ideals. Shortage of labour and distance from markets soon forced reliance on pastoralism — sheep and the export of wool. By 1863 a South Canterbury settler could point to his loaded wool dray and say, 'There goes our breakfast, our lunch and dinner, washing, lodging and everything we need.'[7] And the need for people of all classes to build and secure a lively economy did not permit a religious choice.

By 1854 the last of the colonising associations had ceased to function and the growth and development of the South Island settlements lay in the hands of the settlers themselves and their new provincial governments. Agriculture now was the least stimulus to settlement: sheep, trade and gold dictated the mixture of population. In the early 1860s the population of Otago jumped from less than 13,000 to over 60,000 as the goldfields attracted fortune hunters, mostly from Australia. The discovery of gold on the West Coast in 1864 was the sole reason for its settlement.

In twenty years of settlement the make-up and style of colonial society was complete. There was little for men of taste and fashion in the plain, bustling frontier towns or the primitive scale of life on back-country station or digger's claim. But there was everything for those whose wealth and independence depended solely on their wit and hard work. The character of future society was established early in colonies which Governor Gore Brown in 1859 described as being 'chiefly remarkable for the absence of any order which is an object of respect: a fact racily expressed in a vulgar saying that "every man is not only as good as his neighbour, but a great deal better" '.

Perhaps the satisfaction of most colonists was best expressed in the lines of the Otago poet John Barr. He had left behind a feudal life and in his new home, 'Nae mair the laird comes for his rent.' Instead,

> *At my door cheeks there's bread and cheese.*
> *I work or no', just as I please,*
> *I'm fairly settled at my ease,*
> *And that's the way o't noo, sirs.*

◈

Canterbury, October 1851: 'The feelings of a settler . . . on the morning after his first camp in a new country, are mixed and peculiar. He feels very much as if he had been taken up from this earth, and dropped down promiscuously into another; he is altogether bewildered . . . he hasn't combed his hair, is uncertain about washing arrangements, and idiotically indistinct as to the hitherto regular and distinct fact — the great institution of breakfast. . . . he labours under a sort of momentary hallucination that the thing to do is to do what he has always done . . . viz.: *to ring the bell;* this idea, however, rapidly vanishes as the stern reality of facts force themselves upon his mind . . .'[8]

In February 1842, the first month of settlement in Nelson, the problem was native rats. They 'ran about the house in swarms, walked deliberately over our feet, climbed on the table, and would drop like flies from the thatch. At night we had to keep a stick in hand to thrash them away from the candle, but, worst of all, they ran over us all night, and would come creeping up the blankets to smell our ears and chin, so that we never felt sure they would not want to taste them too.'[6]

No matter how well a settler might be prepared, the uncertainties of life and work and the vagaries of a new climate and terrain created hardships only mitigated by the spirit of common plight and endeavour. Dunedin, April 1848: 'Our first night on shore was one to be remembered. Our blankets were not arrived. Clemie and I dressed as if for going out, and drew a carpet over us to keep the snow off our faces . . . . Our boxes were landed below high water, and the tide flowed and ebbed over them. Then they were piled one above another in front of the house, and it was six months before we could get them unpacked.' Yet they were 'in excellent health . . . and there was something so gladsome in the climate, and novelty in all our surroundings. Everyone alike was roughing, and all were cheery and hopeful.'[9]

A decade after first settlement, Samuel Butler came to 'Christ Church' across country he saw as 'a cross between the plains of Lombardy and the fens of North Cambridgeshire'.[10] He was 'much grieved to find beer sixpence a glass . . . the first intimations which we received that we were in a land where money flies like wild-fire'. He found the men 'shaggy, clear complexioned, brown and healthy-looking' and wearing 'exceedingly rowdy hats'. Conversation centred exclusively on practicalities, 'sheep, horses, dogs, cattle, English grasses, paddocks, bush', and though reduced almost to boredom, he learnt much about the business of setting up a sheep run in new country.

Lady Barker similarly commented on the practical preoccupations that have dominated South Island (and New Zealand) society even to the present day: '. . . people seem gradually to lose the sense of larger and wider interests; they have little time to keep pace with the general questions of the day, and anything like sympathy or intellectual appreciation is very rare. I meet accomplished people, but seldom well-read ones; there is also too much talk about money: "where the treasure is, there will the heart be also" . . . '[11]

The site of Christchurch — on a mixture of swamp and tussock a few feet above sea level — was a constant source of discontent and embarrassment best expressed in this piece of 1860 doggerel, 'Growl in a Sou'wester':

> *Land where men with brains of fog*
> *Built a city in a bog!*
> *Land of rain, and storm, and flood!*
> *Land of water, wind, and mud!*
> *Where six days a week the gale,*
> *Laden thick with rain or hail,*
> *First from sou'west blows a piercer,*
> *Then veers nor'west and blows fiercer!*[12]

Yet in 1865 Lady Barker could describe Christchurch as 'a very pretty little town, still primitive enough to be picturesque, and yet very thriving: capital shops, where everything may be bought; churches, public buildings, a very handsome club-house . . . well-paved streets, gas lamps, and even drinking fountains and pillar post-offices!'[11]

Like Butler, she found no lack of mentors in the practical needs of colonial life. And, in contrast to the scene she had left in England, she was 'struck by the healthy appearance of the people. There are no paupers to be seen; everyone seems well fed and well clothed; the children are really splendid'. The effect of new freedoms and opportunities were clear in the 'great deal of independence in bearing and manner, especially among the servants, and I hear astounding stories concerning them'.

Working class migrants were aware early of the opportunities for equality and independence and the chance for greater social justice than had obtained 'at home'. In January 1849 Captain Cargill, one of the Otago Settlement leaders, spoke of labourers who had come out 'with an exaggerated belief that they were to have large wages and short hours'. Compared to conditions in Scotland he considered that fifty-five hours each week for 18*s* pay 'just and reasonable . . . but many fancy that their hours should be shorter than this even, and their wages proportionably higher'.[13]

Yet the labourer had the last word, for his services were in short supply. 'When you went to hire a labourer, his most favourable reply was that he would think it over and see what he could do for you.'[8]

✦

From the towns and coastal farms the pioneers moved out, first in search of sheep country, later in pursuit of gold. Valleys for grazing and routes to goldfields were discovered and proved more often by sheepmen and prospectors than government surveyors who sometimes arrived barely in time to settle disputes over boundaries and claims.

First the land was fired so that the ashes of native scrub and forest might 'fatten the surrounding grass'.[10] Today we might contemplate with horror Samuel Butler's 'no grander sight than the fire upon a country which has never before been burnt'. But to the sheepman in new country fire was the only tool to clear a way for his flock.

Finding, claiming and firing a run was the beginning; stocking came next. Sheep had to be coaxed through rough, trackless country, cajoled or manhandled through freezing rivers. 'They give immense trouble, for though a few score may be thrust by main force into the water, they obstinately turn round again and again, and re-swim to the bank they have left, exhausting themselves, by hours of resistance, before the struggle really comes in crossing the main stream itself.'[8] Always sheep were lost in the vicious currents, and often their drovers. Death by drowning became so common that a parliamentarian was induced to state that drowning in New Zealand should be classed as a natural death. Lady Barker wrote: 'The common saying in New Zealand is that people only die from drowning and drunkenness. I am afraid that the former is generally the result of the latter.'[11]

First shelter on a new run would be a tent and then, perhaps, a ten by ten sod hut with tussock thatch and an earthen floor. To such a home John Hay took his new wife Barbara in 1858 — 200 kilometres to the wilderness of Lake Tekapo in midwinter in a dray drawn by six bullocks, driving thirty head of cattle and three horses.

Loneliness was the hardest cross to bear for men and women isolated in country which only horse or bullock waggon might traverse, often trapped by snow or confined by wicked rivers. Loneliness generated a code of hospitality that, until the days of highway and aeroplane, was as much a feature of sheep country as the unrelenting scene of tussock and rock.

Hospitality began with lonely runholders who travelled long distances to stay the night with friends for a talk and a game of cards. But soon 'hospitality was extended to all, the humble swagger, even though well known to be a regular sundowner, was very rarely refused. . . . During the time of the rush to the diggings I have seen . . . up to thirty men stopping for the night at a station on the Waitaki. . . . From five to ten sheep were killed weekly to supply food . . . The real seeker after work or the travelling hawker walked in and sat down to meals as if they belonged to the place.'[7]

While a spirit of hospitality was an early antidote to loneliness and hardship, success in physical creation of a home and new life compensated for much that the settlers had left behind. 'While they gained an almost childlike pleasure from the mastery of such practical tasks as building a chimney or making butter, this new knowledge deepened their appreciation of the things of the mind. They rejoiced in all that was new, while not forgetting the old . . . "the first fortnight we went up a ladder to bed, but I have just completed a superb staircase . . . and I have just glazed my last downstairs window . . . day by day something is done by one or both of us to induce us to say, Well this is a great comfort; we shall do bye and bye".'[6]

Even when land was cleared and a home built, the demands and hardships of daily life required unflinching optimism and fortitude. A pioneer wife in South Otago: 'I used to have sixteen hours a day cooking, washing, ironing, sewing and mending. In my spare time I milked three cows night and morning. I fed the fowls and the pigs and the dogs. Making butter was a regular job. Baking bread, salting meat, gathering wood, clarifying fat and tallow, then dipping candles. One time, two of us sat up very late, and we dipped 24 dozen! The dirt floor was an awful nuisance; but how proud I was when I got my first wooden floor.'[14]

For the sheepman there was a perpetual struggle to hold on to the land he had arduously fired and cleared and stocked. Drought, flood, lost sheep, drowned sheep, sheep buried by snow, sheep afflicted by epidemics of parasitic scab. He was to rue his own folly as he battled swarms of introduced rabbits that denuded pastures across the island; and for years there was the man-to-man battle with sheep stealers. 'With a savage snarl and a Gaelic oath, Black Mac dropped the slip rail . . . and sprang back, before the furious figure of his adversary launched the first blow. The two collies quietly drove their unlawful little flock away into the shrouded bush . . . Blow after blow was parried, or sunk home . . . blood darkening some portion of the tattered shirts, and still the fight went on . . . until Black Mac sank into unconsciousness . . . a bruised mass at his opponent's feet. . . . he was given four years in which to contemplate his misdeeds.'[15]

But the greatest trials were caused by those forces which bred a stoicism born of the knowledge that they were beyond control and could be countered only by acceptance and patience and faith. German settlers in 1844 were forced to abandon their holdings in the Upper Moutere district of Nelson after the river took charge with winter flood: '. . . the storm still raged and rain poured down. Now and again there was a lull, but only for a few seconds, and then it started again twice as hard. This night was really the most awful that I have ever encountered — I might say the worst all of us have lived through. It seemed as if both elements were left to go their own way unbridled. I therefore committed ourselves and our neighbours to the gracious protection of God — God who neither slumbers nor sleeps, and whom the wind and sea obey.'[6]

Fire was the other great destroyer of hard-won homes, a constant threat to survival and success on remote farms and stations. Fortitude was common but it is doubtful if many pioneers matched the philosophical calm of this runholder in the Canterbury foothills as his house burned down: 'We . . . could hear the crashing and hissing of the fire, and twisting at full pace sharply round the corner of a low fence, we dashed up to the house. It was in full blaze; only the bones of the building discernible, and a great roaring bonfire flaring far above our heads . . . in front of the whole, on a rude bench, sat the sole inhabitant of the place. Throwing ourselves from our horses, we dashed up to him, called out: "Good heavens! Walker, what on earth can be done?" — to which his whole and sole reply was: "My dear fellow, allow me to offer you a chop!" '[8]

✧

'Jack, I am making my pile fast — £100 per week. This is the richest river in the world. I walk in up to the waist in the water, put down the shovel, and sometimes bring up five or six ounces on the shovel. When the river is down I don't know how much gold I shall get.'[16]

The discovery of payable gold transformed Otago from a confined, bickering coastal colony to the richest province in New Zealand. The rushes opened up the bare hill country and lake basins back to the Main Divide of the island and the wealth that flowed to the coast built Dunedin into the country's commercial and industrial capital.

The city fathers deplored the 'new iniquities' that would assail the town with the burgeoning mob of rough diggers who came from every corner of New Zealand and Australia. But the economic benefits of gold could not be denied and 'Dunedin followed the lead; morning after morning fresh parties left the town, master and man on equal terms, clerks and mechanics, the better class and the shopkeepers . . . and if the ladies hoped to retain the services of even one man with a wooden leg, they must saw that leg off.'[13]

Three years after the Otago rush began in 1861, gold was found on the West Coast, that hitherto useless appendage to Canterbury province beyond the Southern Alps. 'Canterbury, the staid, decorous, deprecatory, respectable Canterbury has suddenly broken out all over. Fever, delirium — marry, a most vulgar disease! An invasion of diggers; an irruption of yellow-breeched Arabs, with immense blanket puddling collars, both unwashed . . . Pack-horses, tents, picks, shovels, billies, Californian pumps, confusion!'[17]

Men appeared on the goldfields as if in flash flood. In July 1862 a census showed that Dunedin had a population of 5850, after fourteen years of settlement; Tuapeka, centre of the first goldfield, could claim 11,472 after one. In 1864 the population of the West Coast was no more than 200; three years later it reached 30,000 as gold was nosed out from the Buller River in the north to the glacier region in the south. Instant canvas towns appeared. Goldsborough, near Hokitika, was created in 1865 by 'an eager mob — lighting fires, pitching tents, drinking, fighting, cursing, and shouting all at once. By eleven o'clock, in the heart of a dense and almost untrodden bush, a street had arisen as if created by the magic wand of an enchanter. Swift as the walls of Aladdin's palace, stores, shanties, public houses, butchers, bakers and doctors' shops were to be found on every side.'[17]

Men with Midas madness picking and digging at the hills, panning and washing in the creeks, crossing mountain passes and climbing river bluffs, finding the fortune that favoured some or meeting the anonymous death that captured many. 'The Maoris, however, plunged boldly into the river and succeeded in reaching the western bank; but their dog was carried downstream and became stranded on a rocky point where it yelped its distress. Dan went to its assistance and seeing some particles of gold in the crevices of the rocks he examined the sandy beach beneath, and calling up his mate, the two of them gathered 25 pounds weight — 300 ounces — before nightfall.'[16]

Such rich finds were rare and to most of the thousands who trekked to the fields the gold seemed to slip through their fingers as easily as the waters in which it was found. The syndicates with equipment made money — and those shrewder heads who supplied the diggers with the essentials of life — food, hardware and liquor. In Dunedin, 1861, 'Prices rose at once: flour to £30 a ton, the loaf to 1s. Cartage to the diggings — 55 miles — was £90 a ton, and flour £150, all to rise still higher within a couple of months.'[13] On the West Coast in 1865 bread cost 5s a loaf, milk 4s a quart and eggs 10d each.

By the end of 1861, after six months of the Otago rush, 187,695 ounces of gold had been exported, worth three-quarters of a million pounds. Between them, the Otago and West Coast fields were to yield more than 12 million ounces of gold by the turn of the century, a good half of this in the first ten years of mining.

With so much wealth finding its haphazard way from river and hillside to the ultimate safety of banks and overseas markets, the risks of violence and robbery were great. 'They surrounded him, and had him off his horse in a twinkling. First of all they took away his revolver, then possessed themselves of his treasure (824 oz of gold). Walmsley turned round to have a look at them . . . so that he could recognise them again, but two of the number produced revolvers, which they placed at his head, and swore that if he moved an inch they would blow his brains out.'[17] The gold and the robbers were never found.

By the 1870s the rushes and the big gold yields were over. The company men moved in with sluices and dredges to maintain a steady production of the precious metal that contributed much to the economic development of the South Island and New Zealand as a whole.

More than money, commerce and industry came from the goldfields. The search for gold — together with the search for sheep country by pioneer runholders — brought about the exploration of the most inaccessible regions of the South Island; new communities were established, new lines of communication across the mountainous hinterland. Though 'old identities' in the early settlements saw 'new iniquities' in the diggers and the speculative crowds that followed them, the character and strength of the colonies were inevitably broadened and diversified.

After thirty years of settlement, exploration and endeavour, the sheepman and the prospector together had established the economic base for the future. And in their character and style they fashioned much of the social fabric of South Island heritage. Simply stated, in historian Keith Sinclair's words: 'The history of the North Island is one of racial relations; the South Island story is of Europeans, their sheep, and their gold.'[5]

REFERENCES

[1] Abel Janszoon Tasman, Journal, 13 December 1642.

[2] Lt James Cook, *Journals* (ed. J. C. Beaglehole), Vol. 1, Cambridge 1955.

[3] Hon. Fred Waite, *Port Molyneux: The Story of Maori and Pakeha in South Otago,* 1940.

[4] Plan of the Association for Forming the Settlement of Canterbury in New Zealand, London 1848.

[5] Keith Sinclair, *A History of New Zealand,* London 1959.

[6] Ruth M. Allan, *Nelson. A History of Early Settlement,* Wellington 1965.

[7] E. Holdgate, *Canterbury Old and New,* Christchurch 1900.

[8] Laurence J. Kennaway, *Crusts,* London 1874.

[9] A. and L. R. Drummond, *At Home in New Zealand,* Auckland 1967.

[10] Samuel Butler, *A First Year in Canterbury Settlement,* London 1863.

[11] Lady Barker, *Station Life in New Zealand,* London 1883.

[12] J. C. Andersen, *Old Christchurch,* Christchurch 1949.

[13] T. M. Hocken, *Contributions to the Early History of New Zealand* (Settlement of Otago), London 1898.

[14] Hon. Fred Waite, *Pioneering in South Otago,* Dunedin 1948.

[15] J. T. Scrymgeour, *Memories of Maoriland,* Ilfracombe 1960.

[16] F. W. G. Miller, *Golden Days of Lake County,* Dunedin 1949.

[17] Philip Ross May, *The West Coast Gold Rushes,* Christchurch 1962.

THE CITIES...

grown from the wealth of the land,
looking both to the sea and the hills,
places to live and learn and work and play...

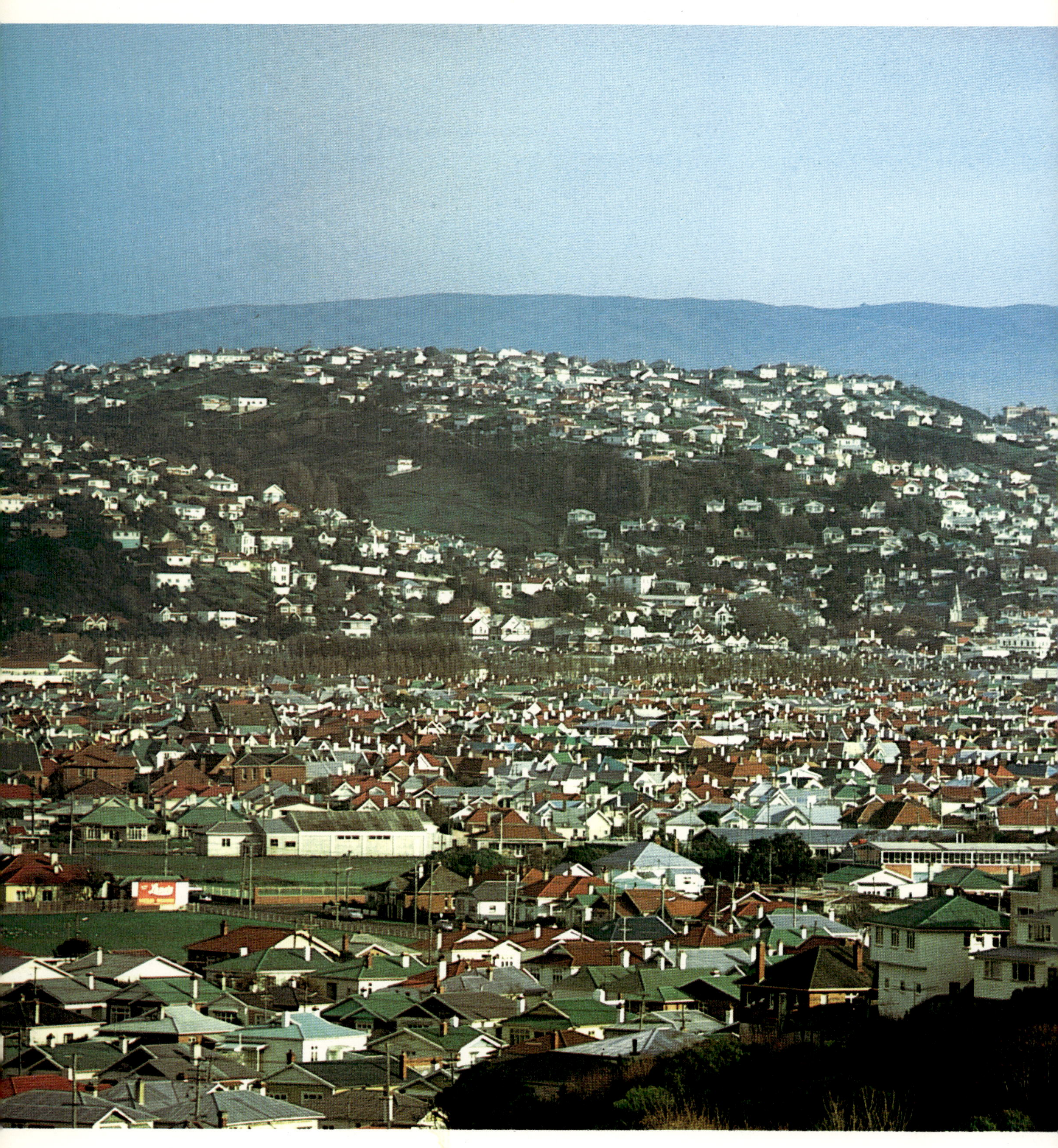

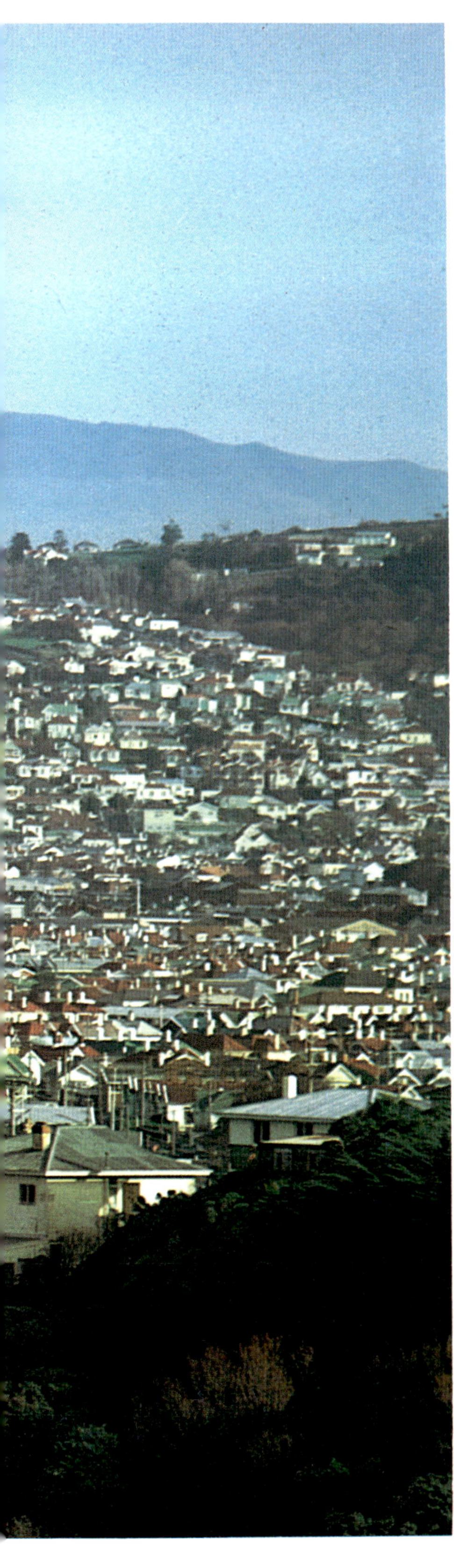

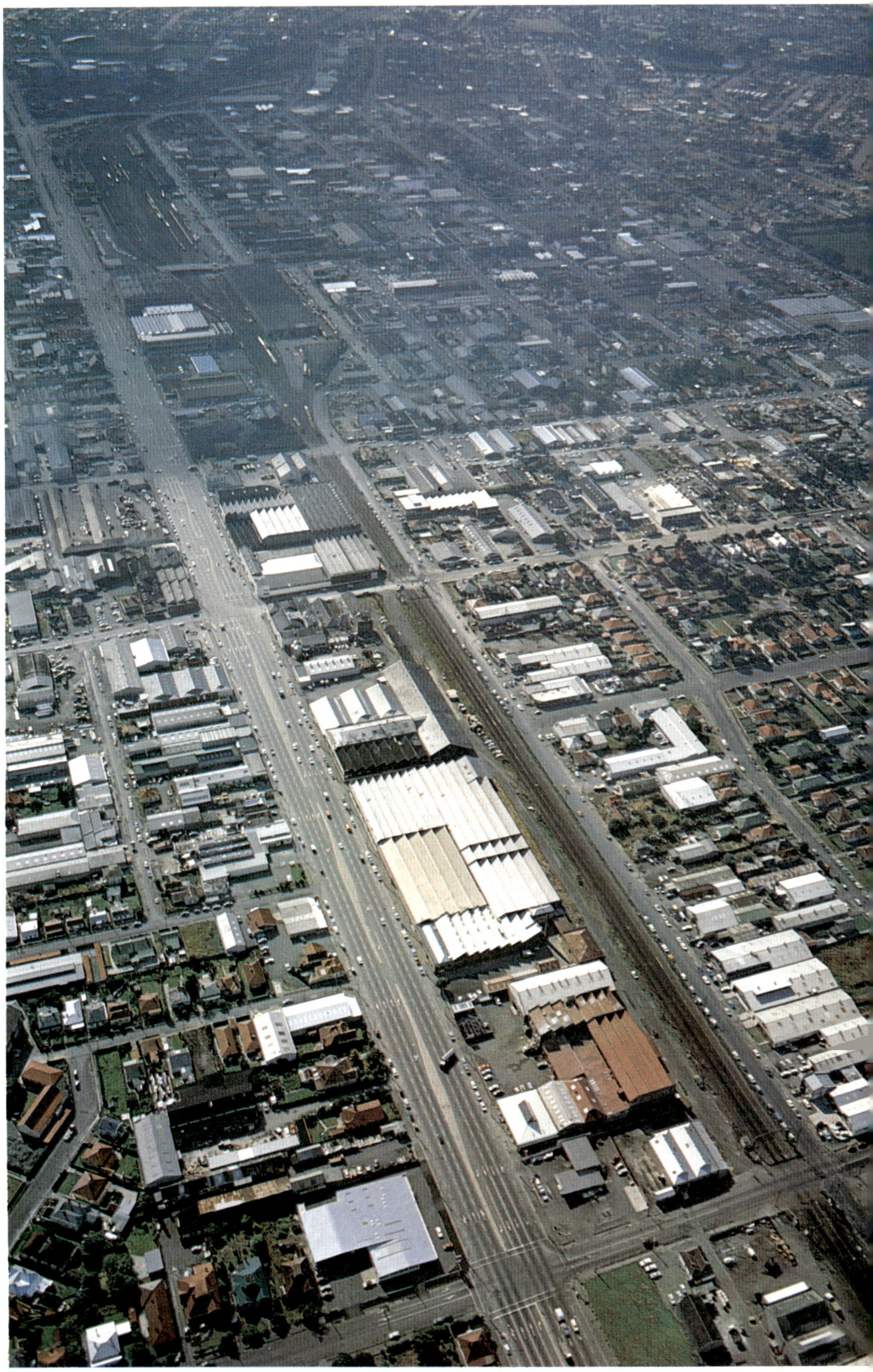

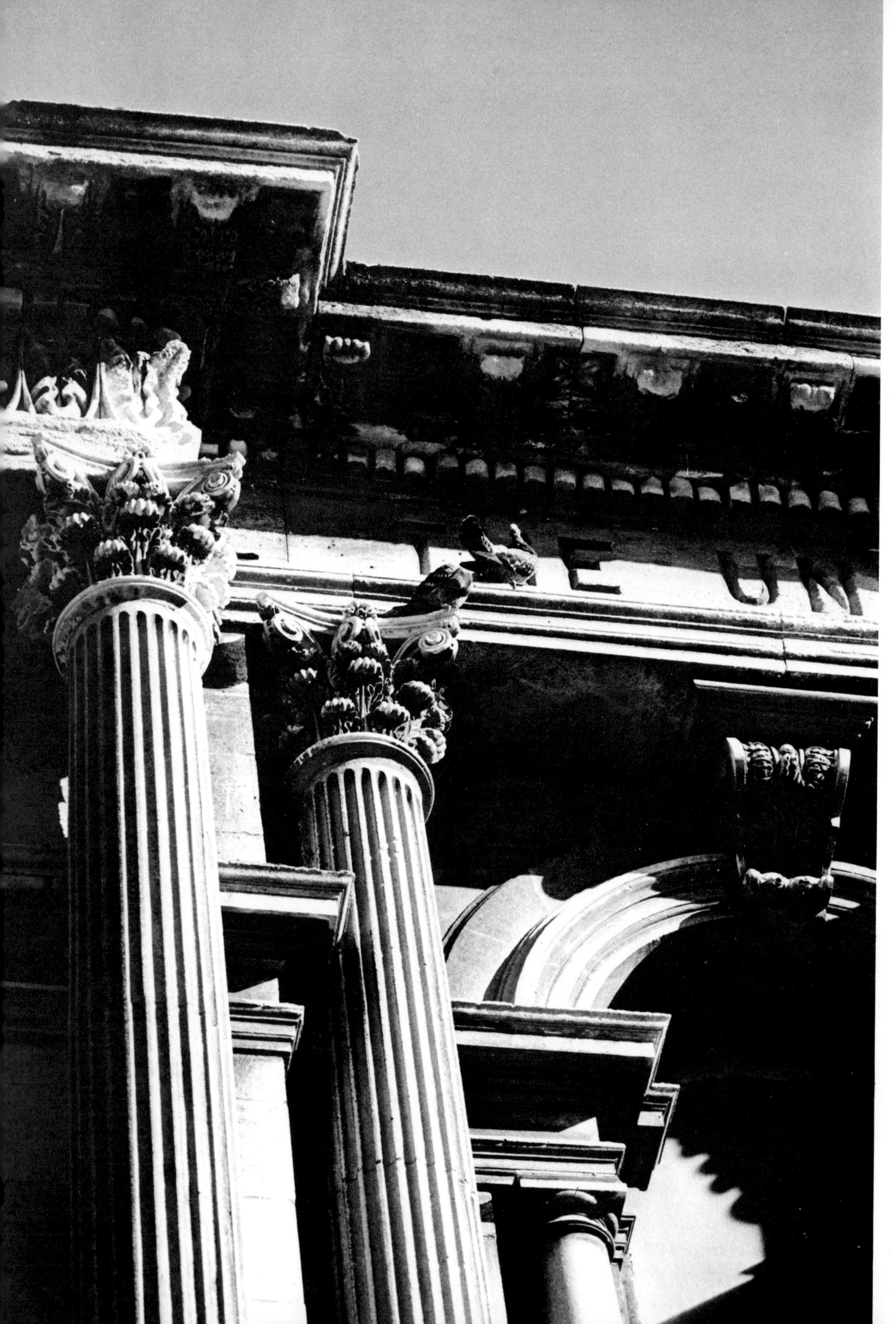

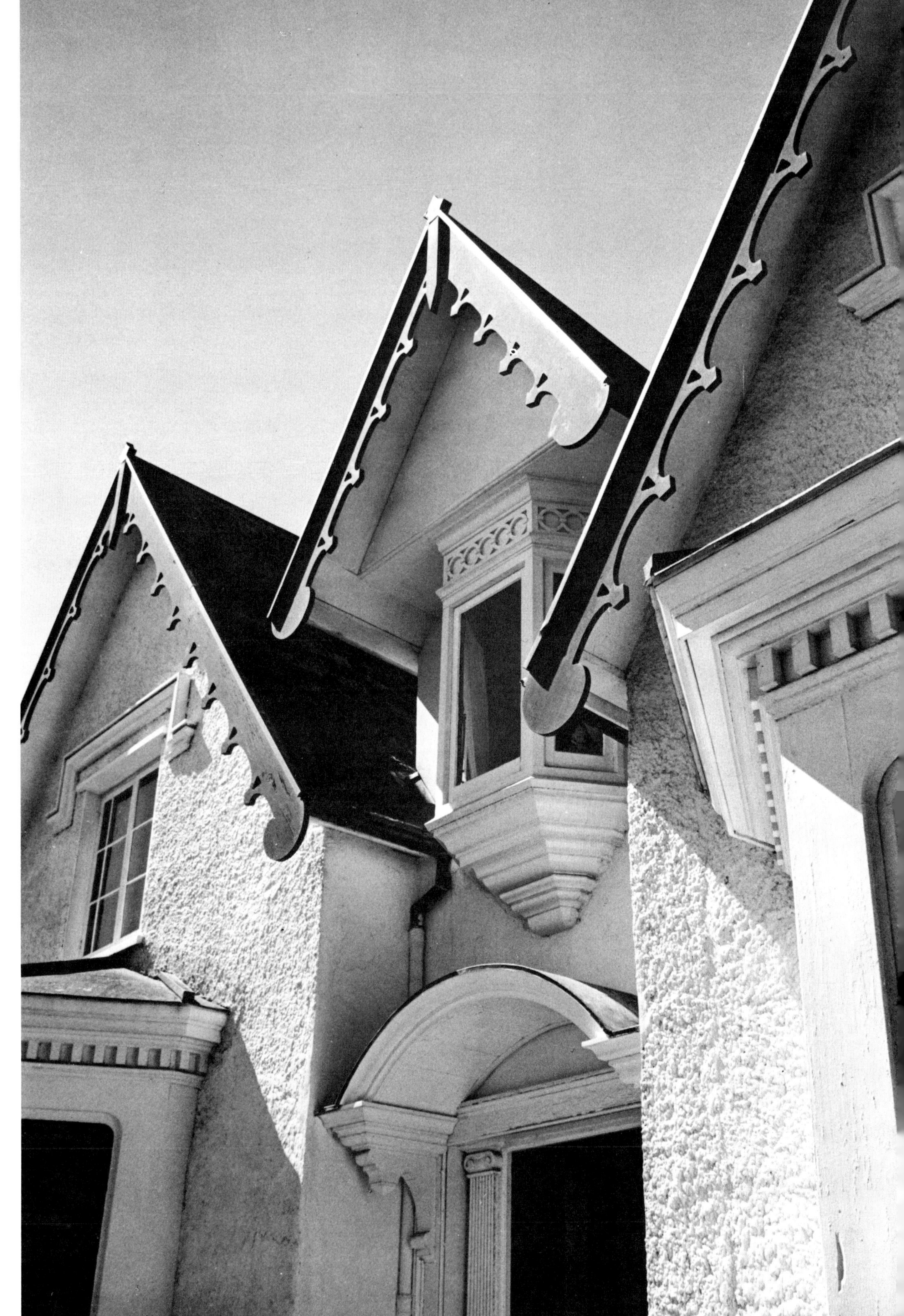

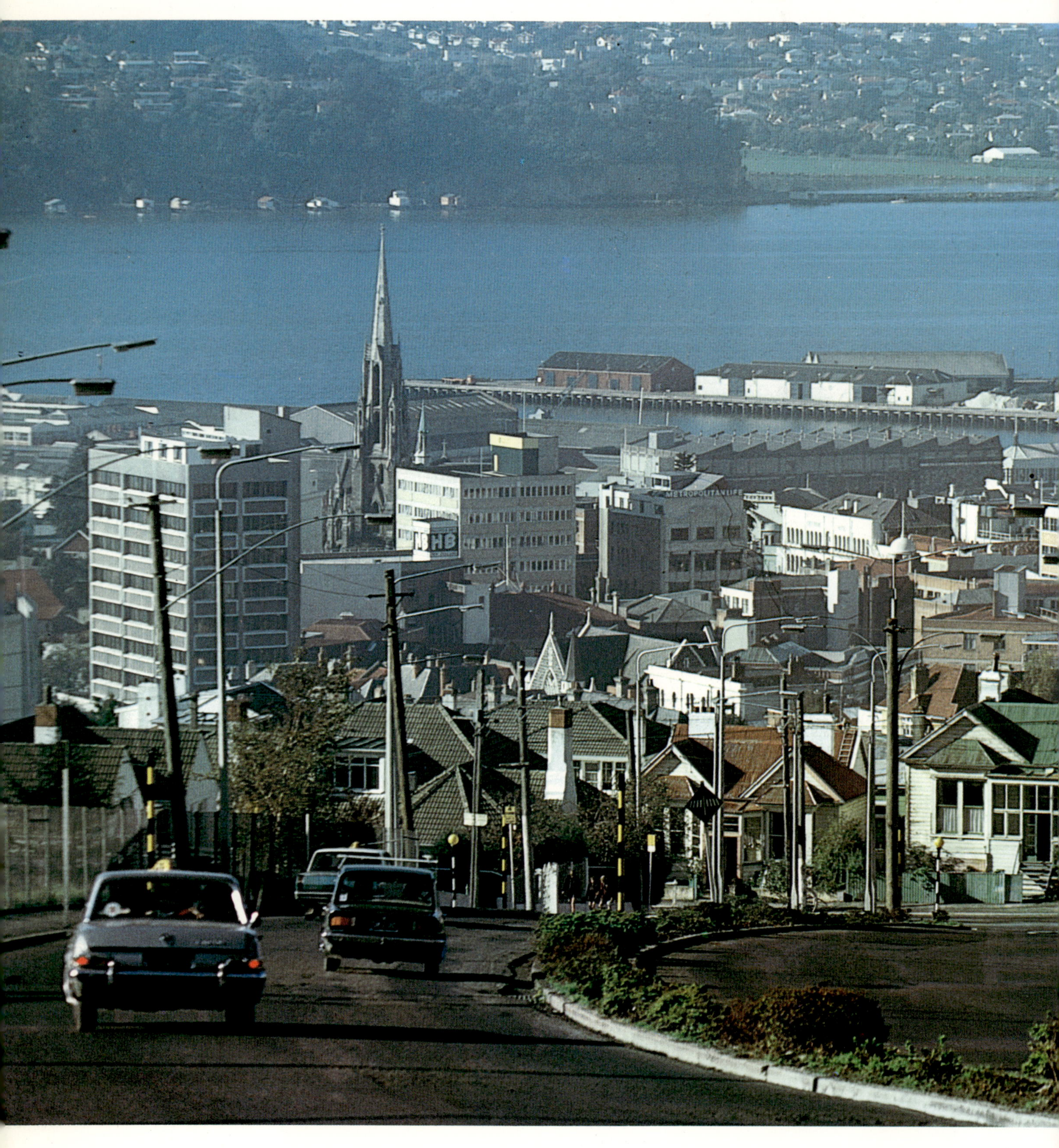

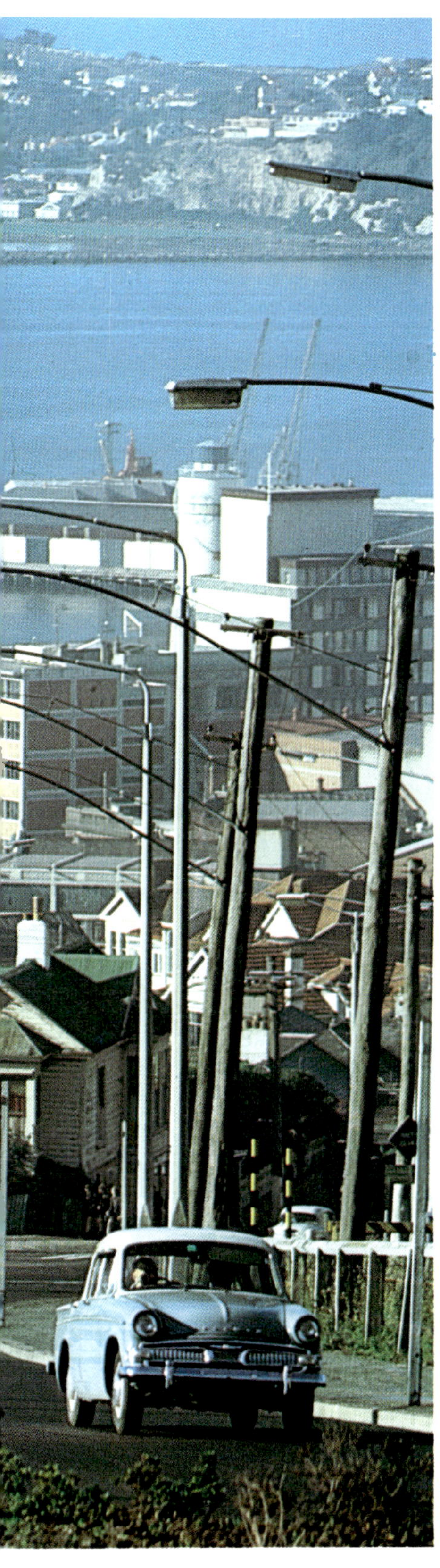

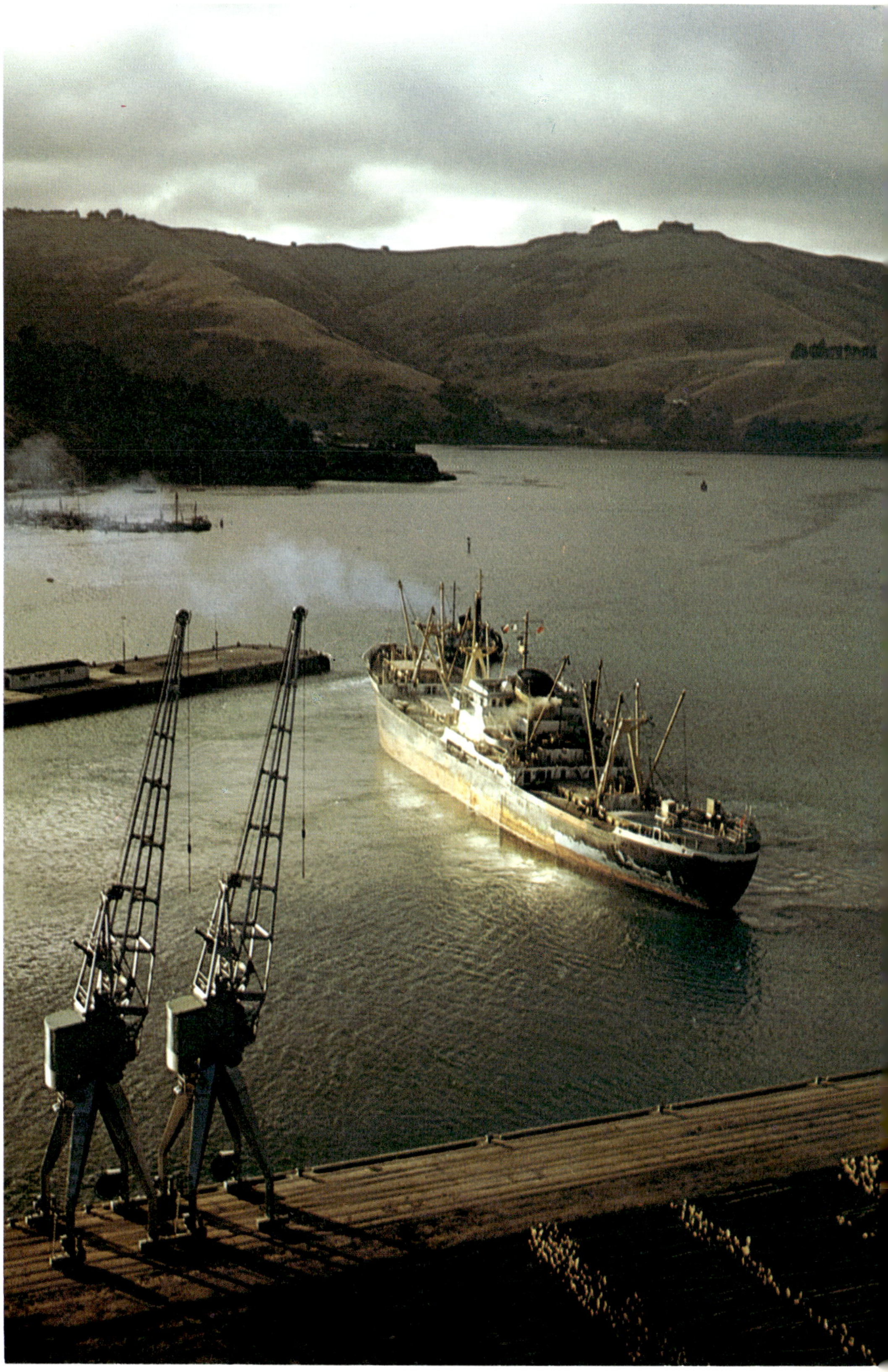

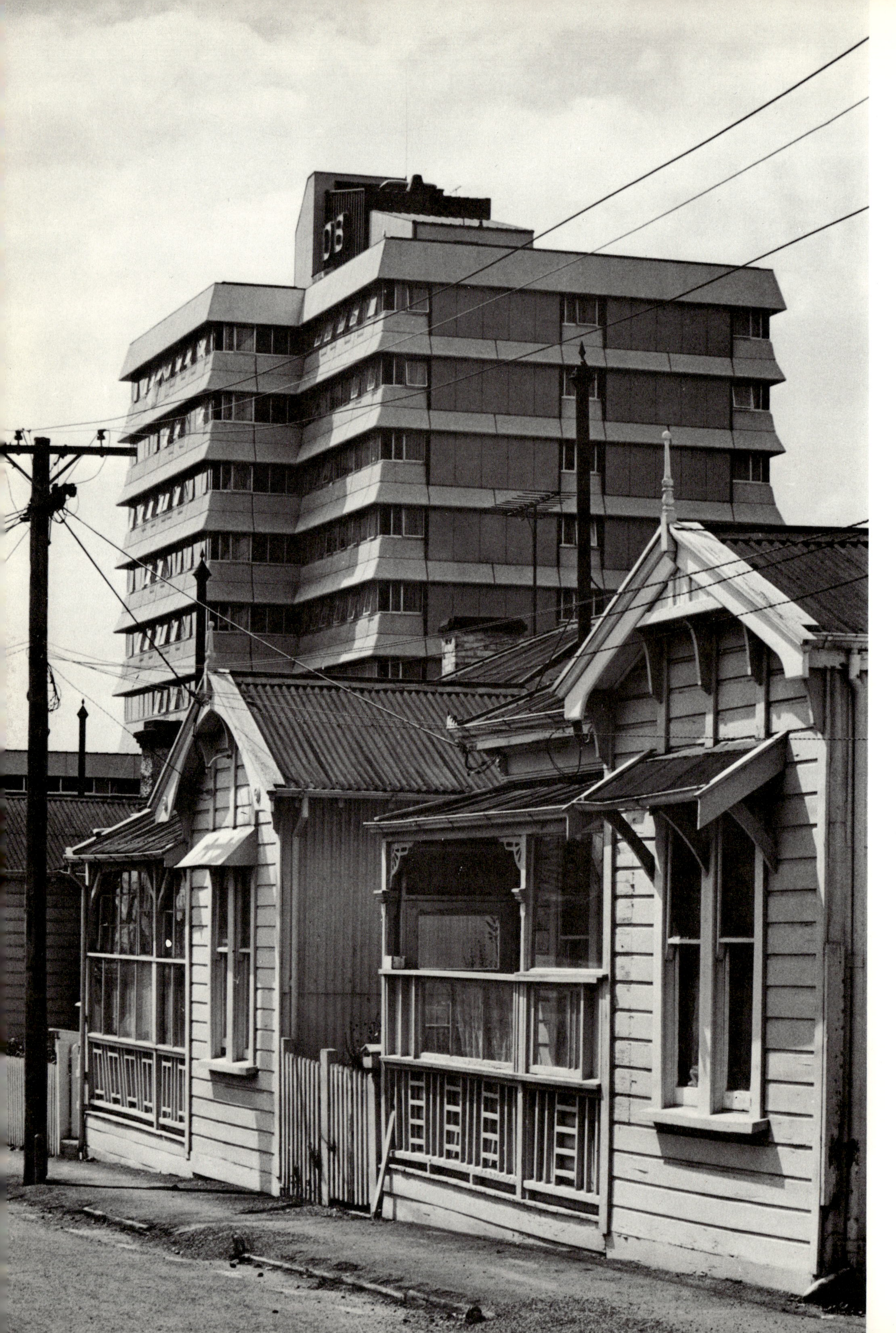

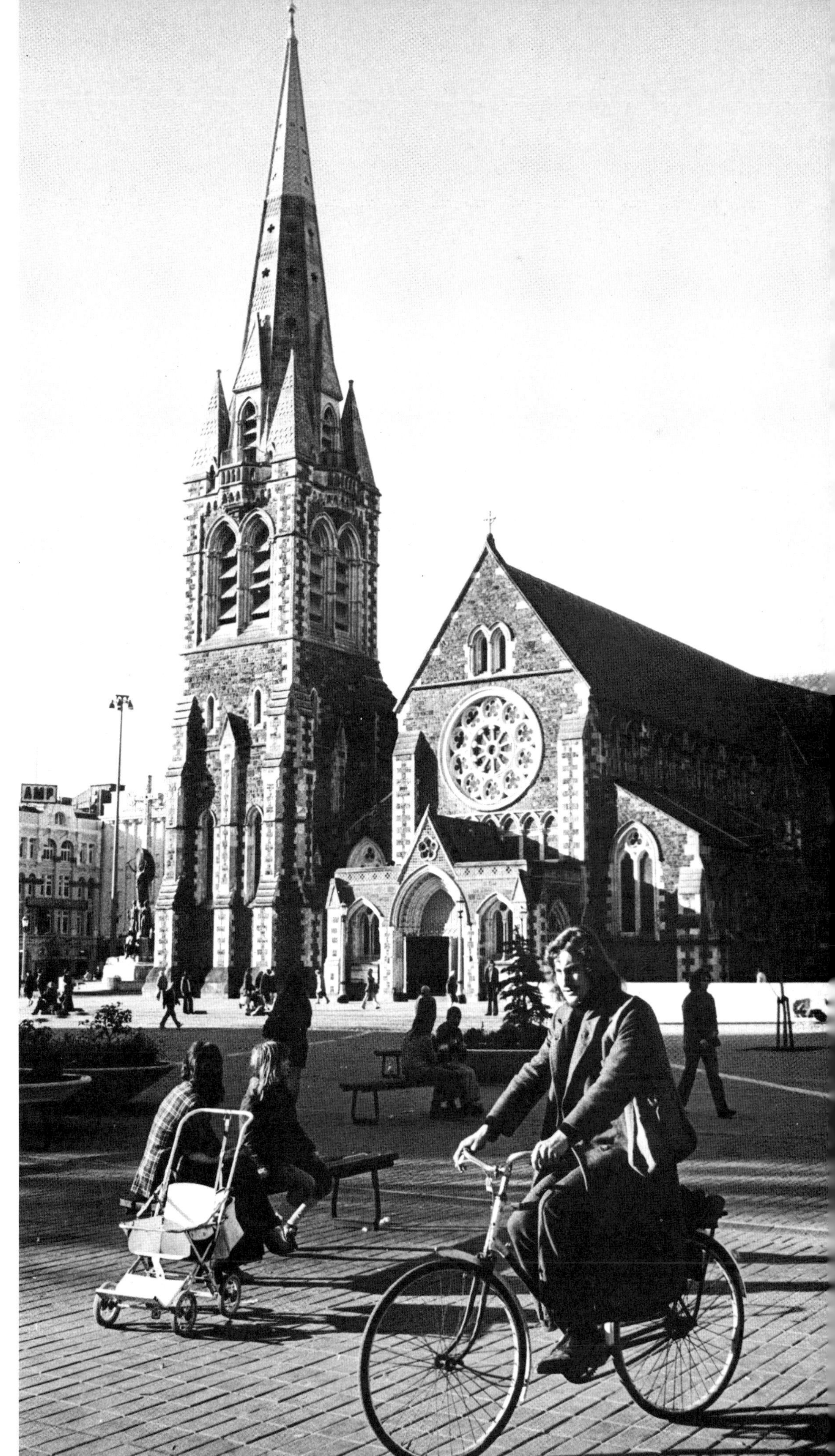

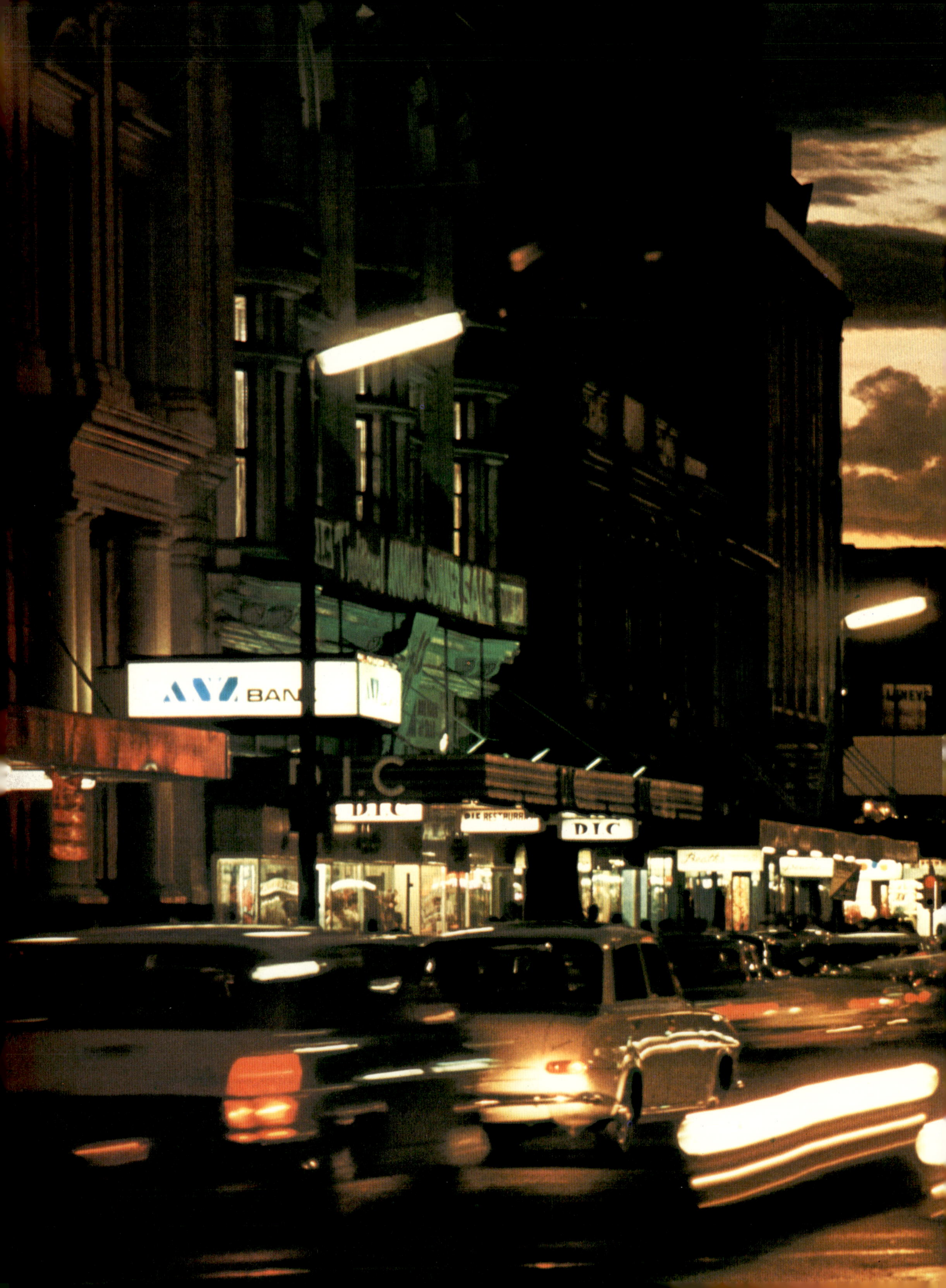

ANZ BANK
D.I.C
DIC
DIC
ANNUAL SUMMER SALE

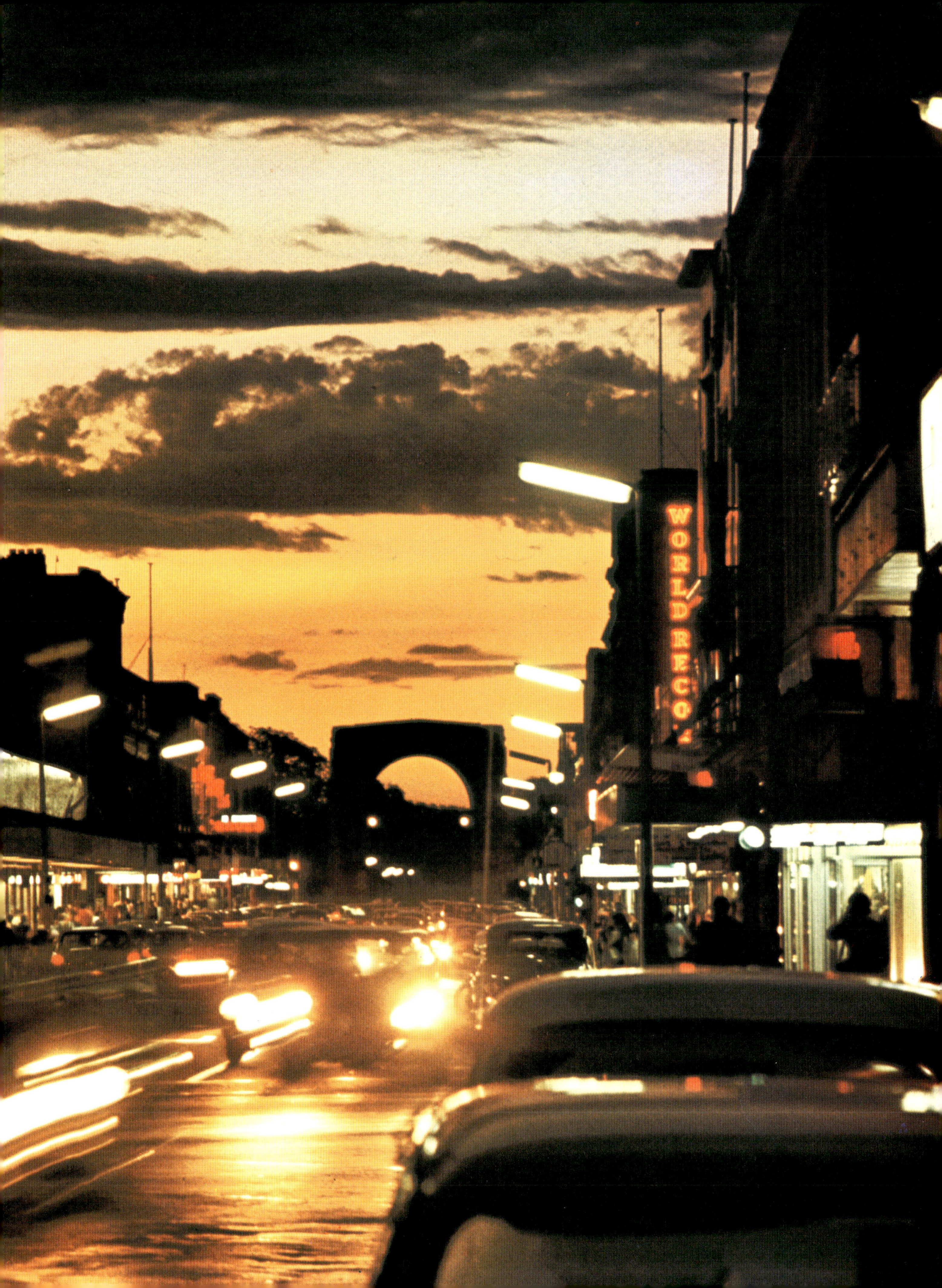

WORLD RECO

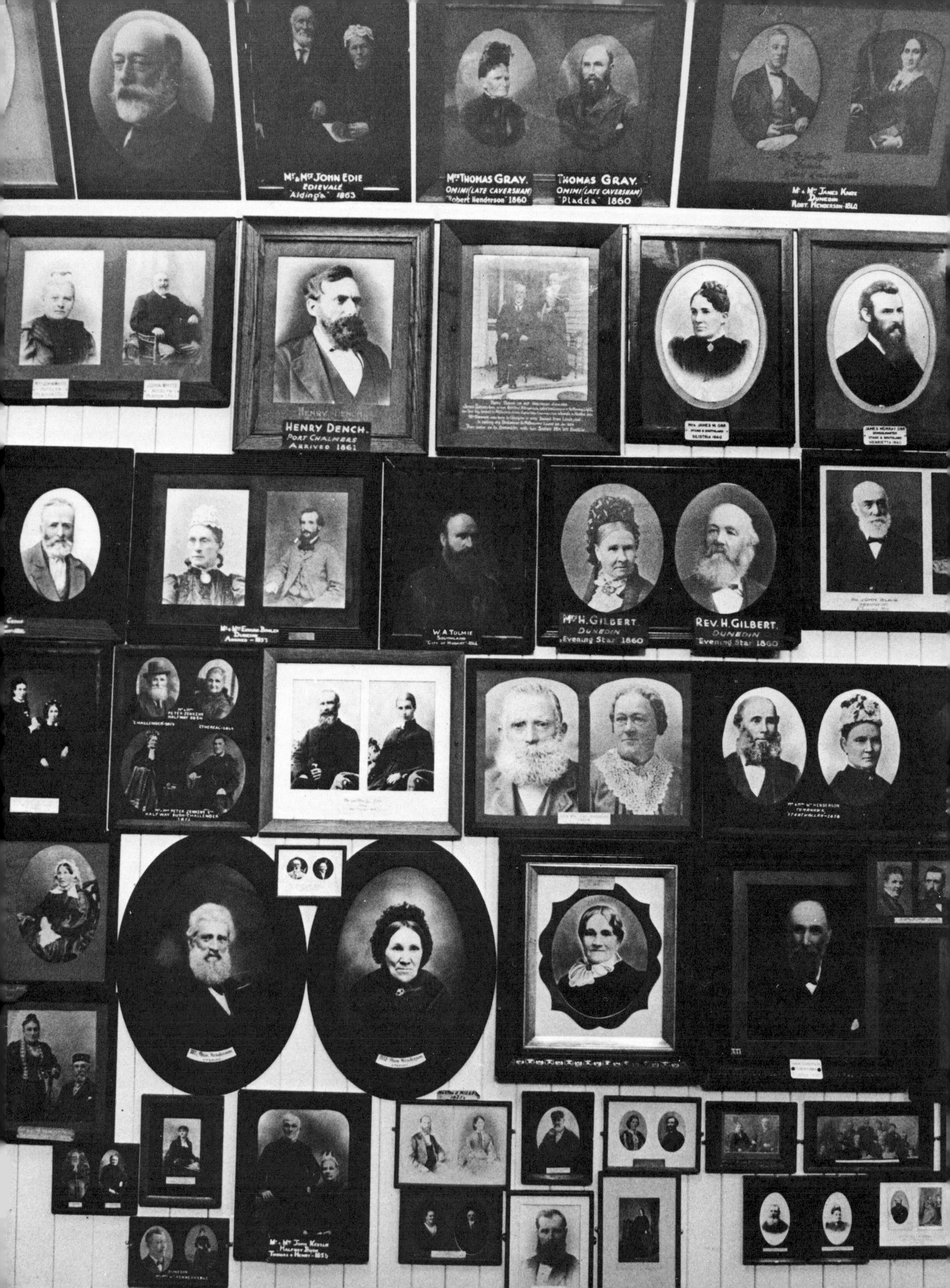

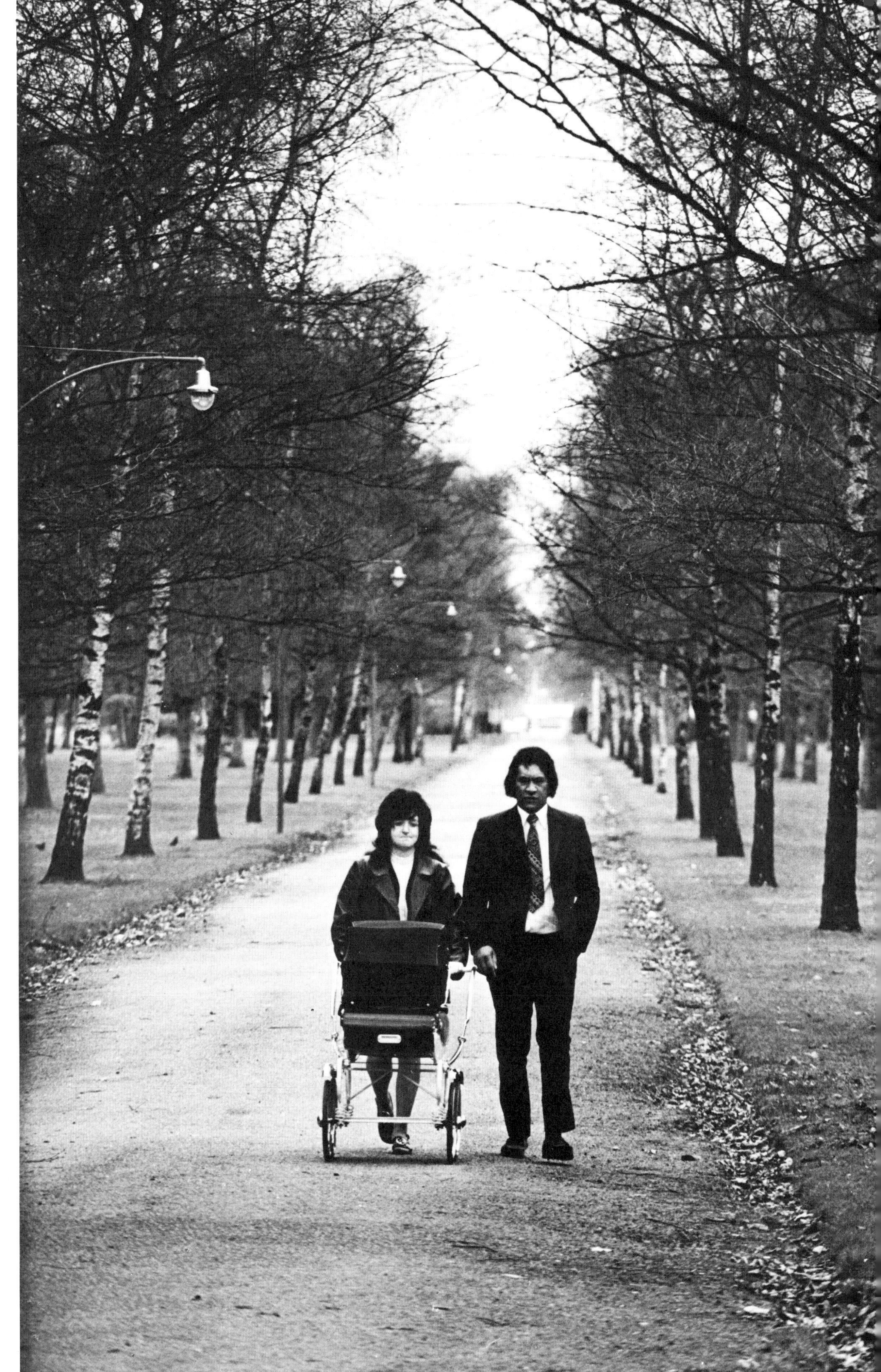

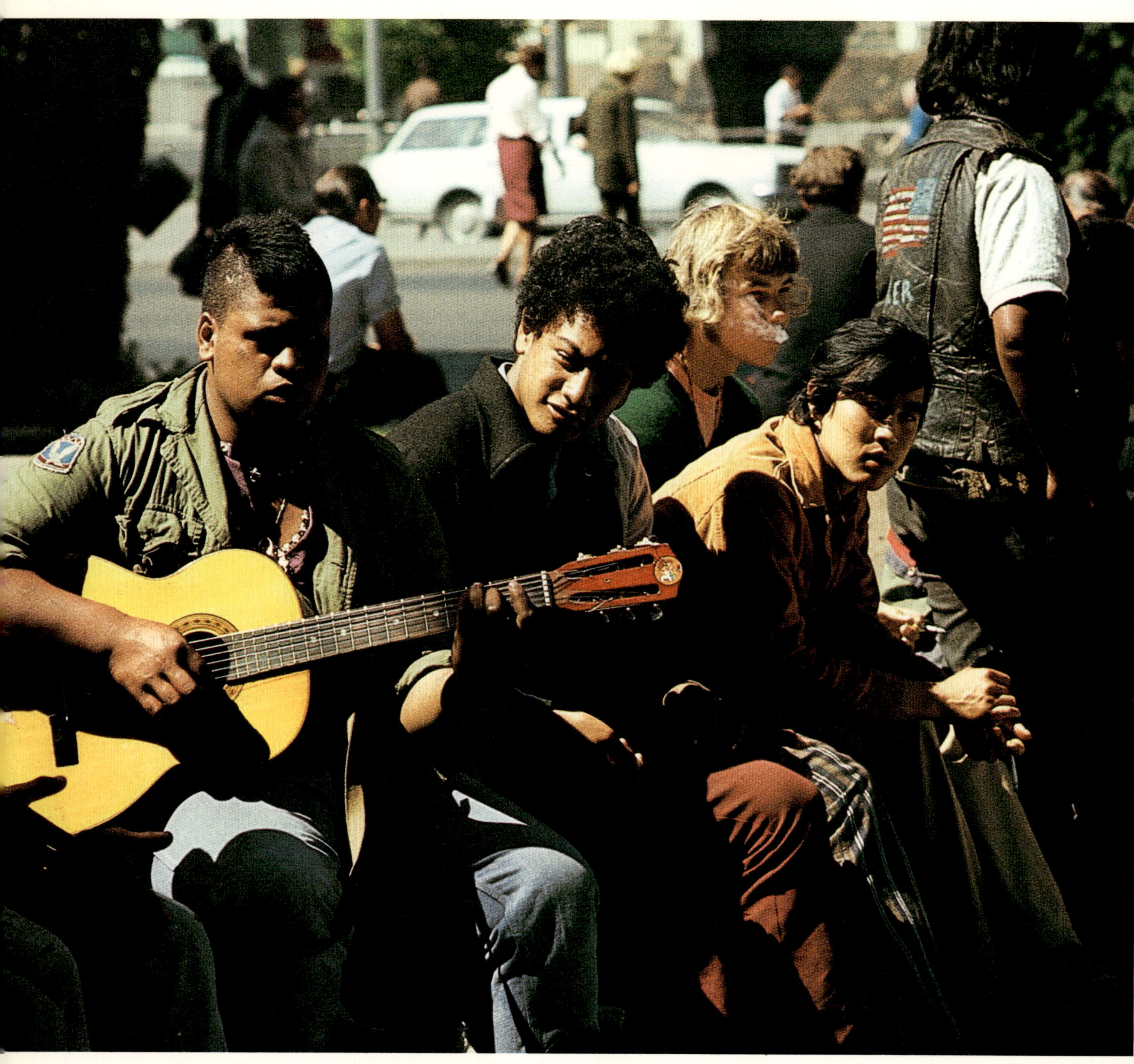

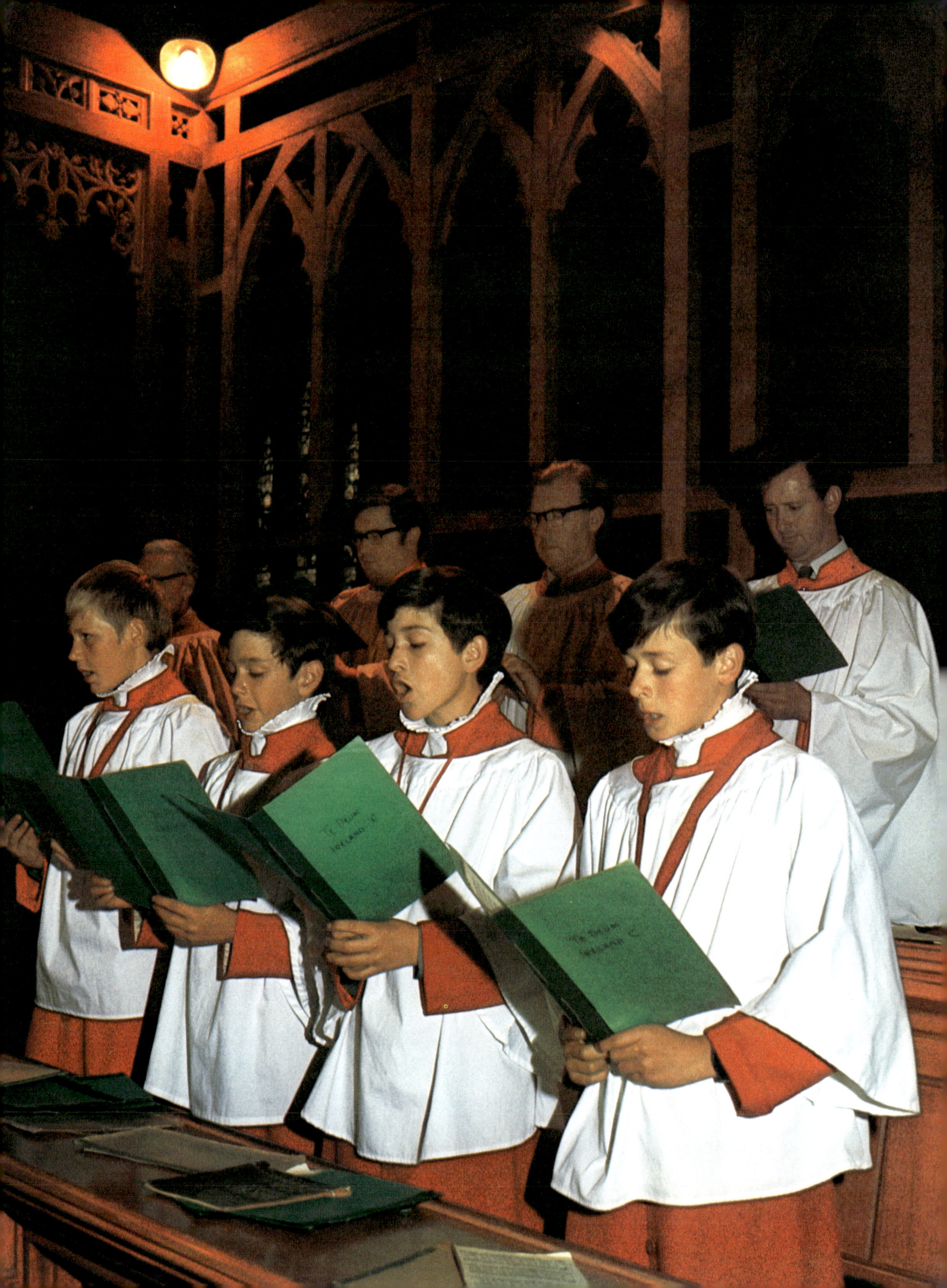

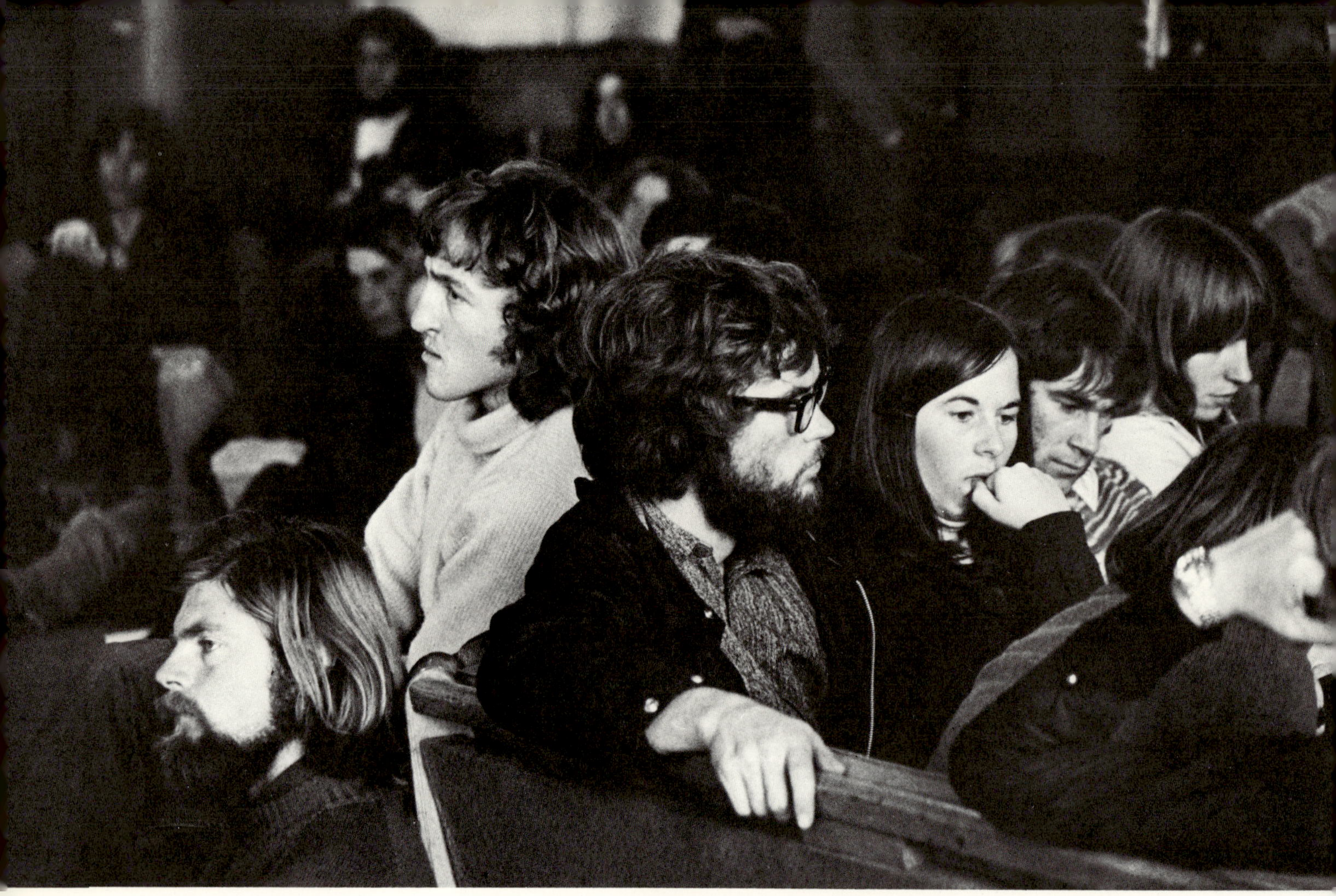

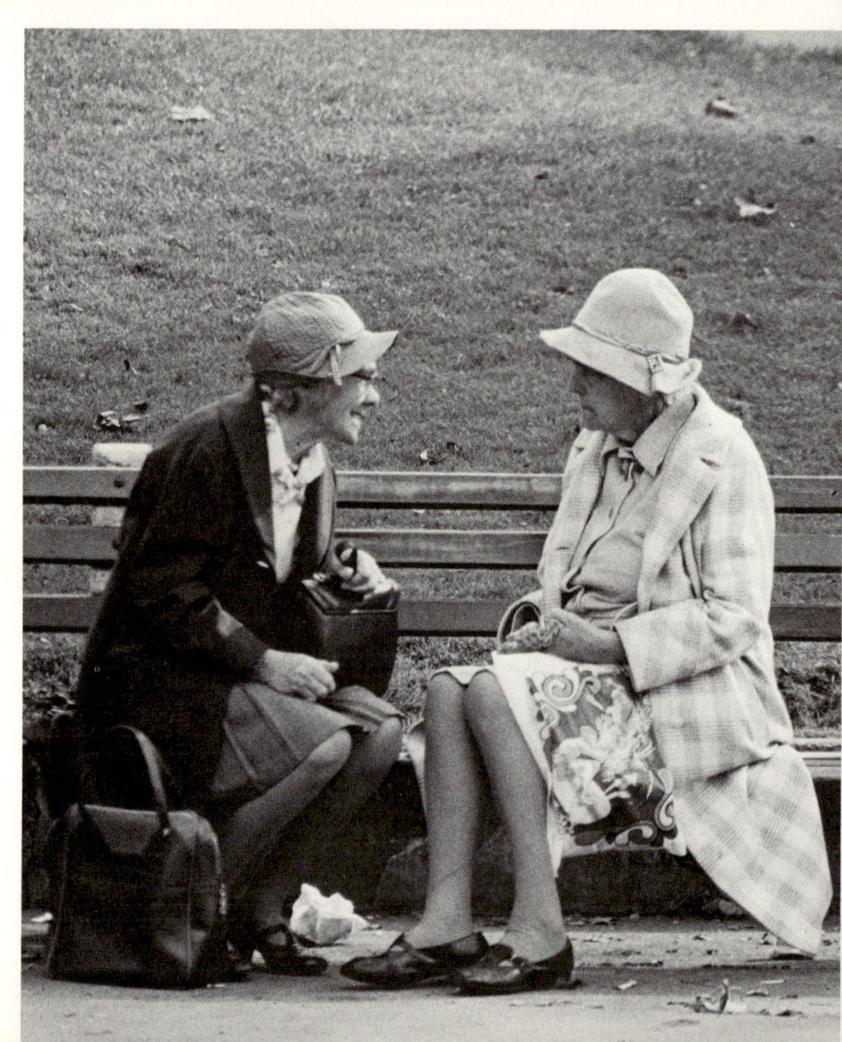

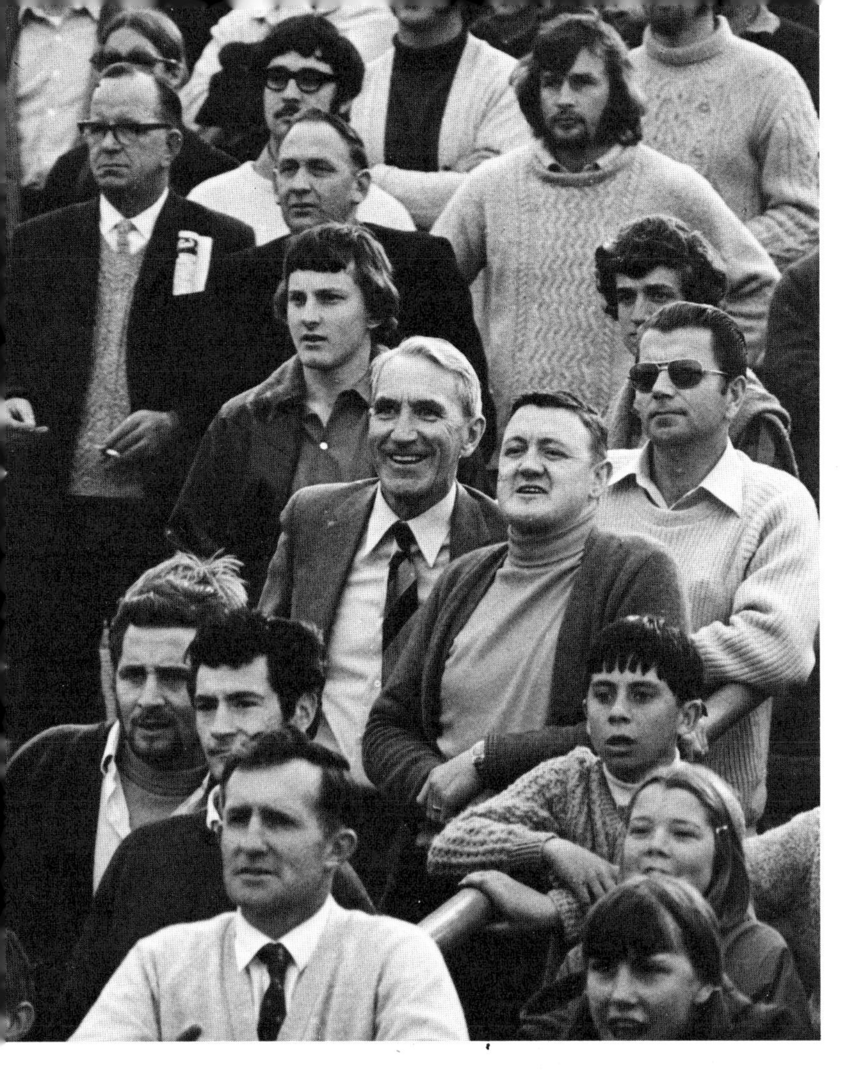

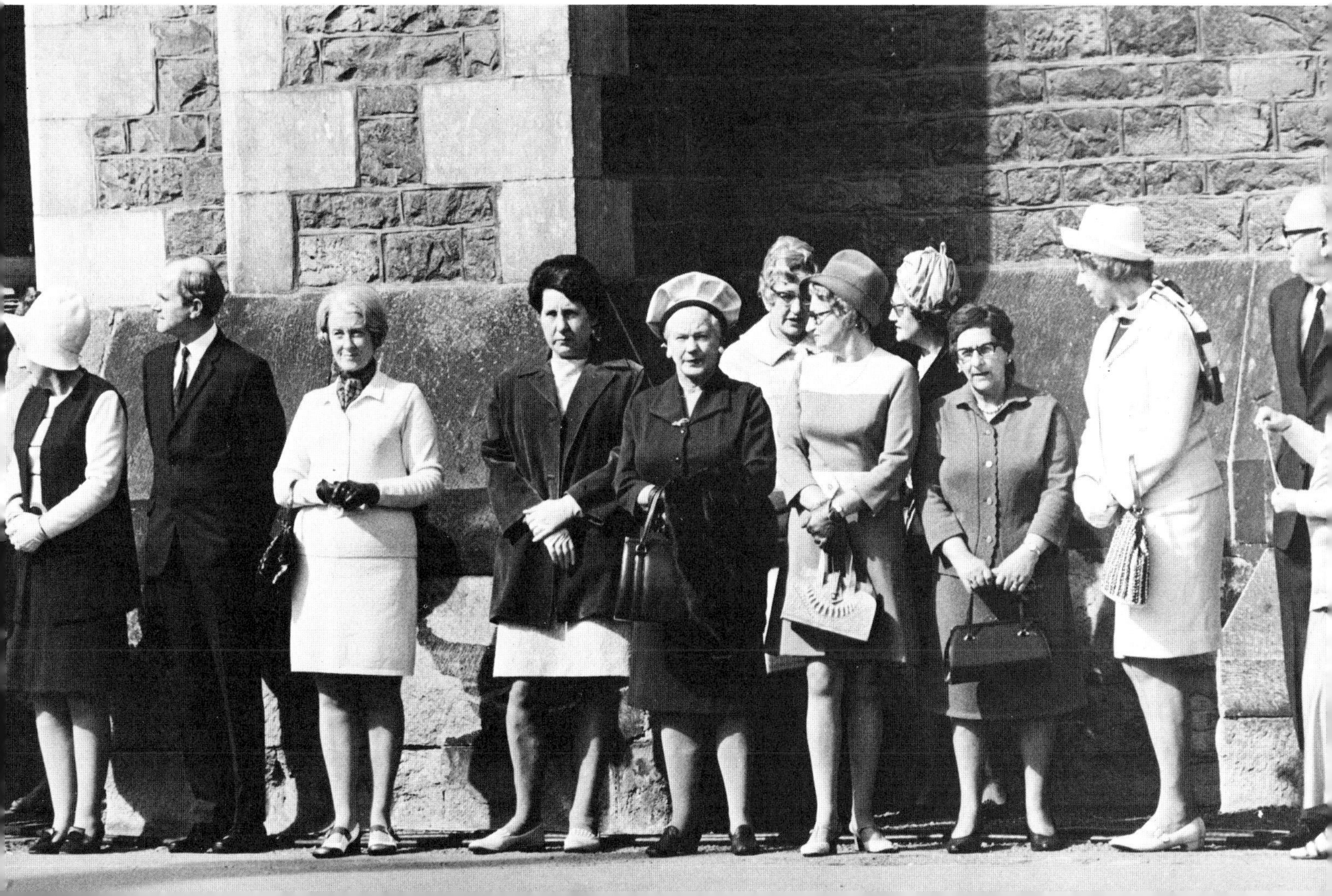

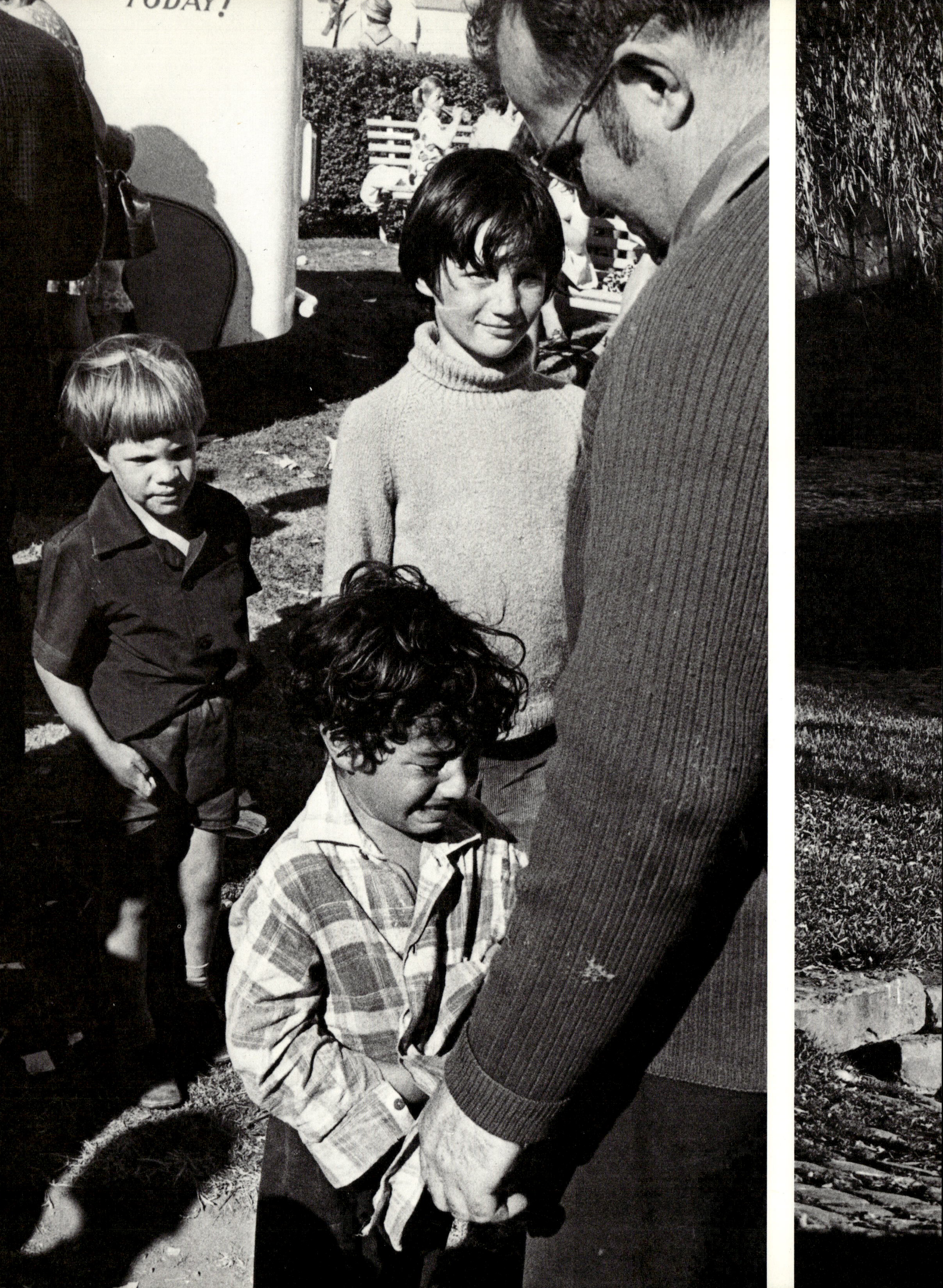

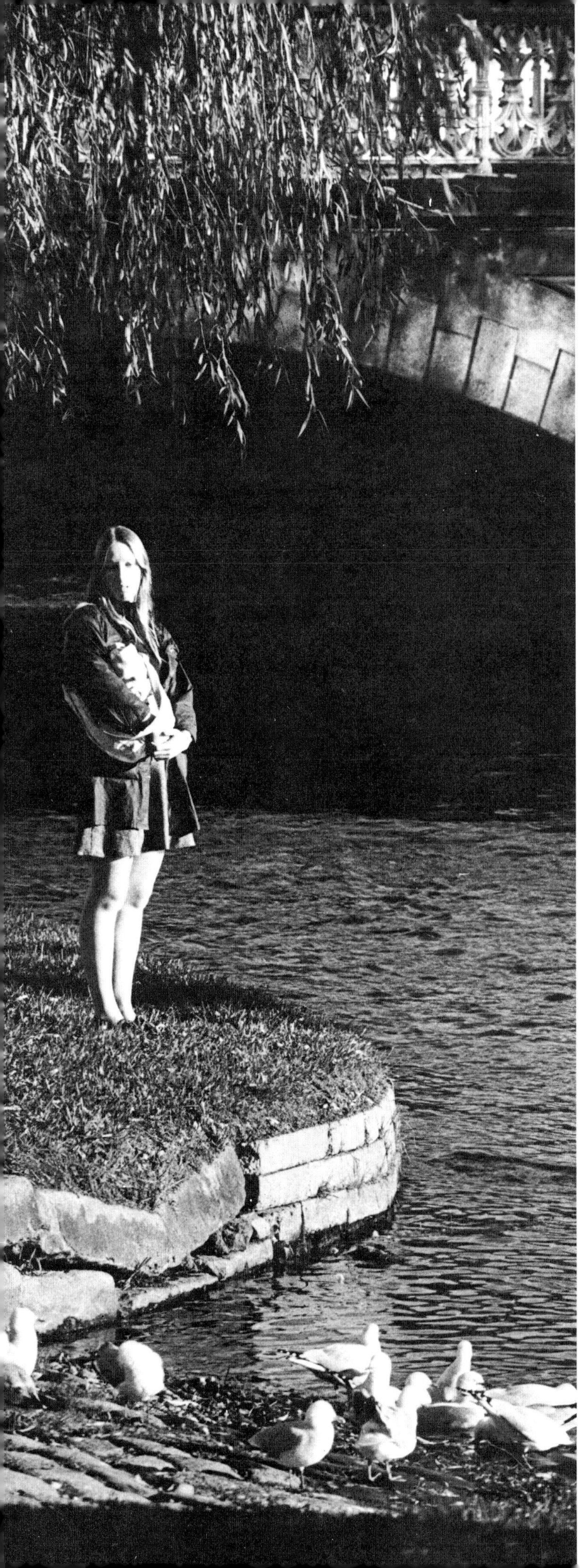

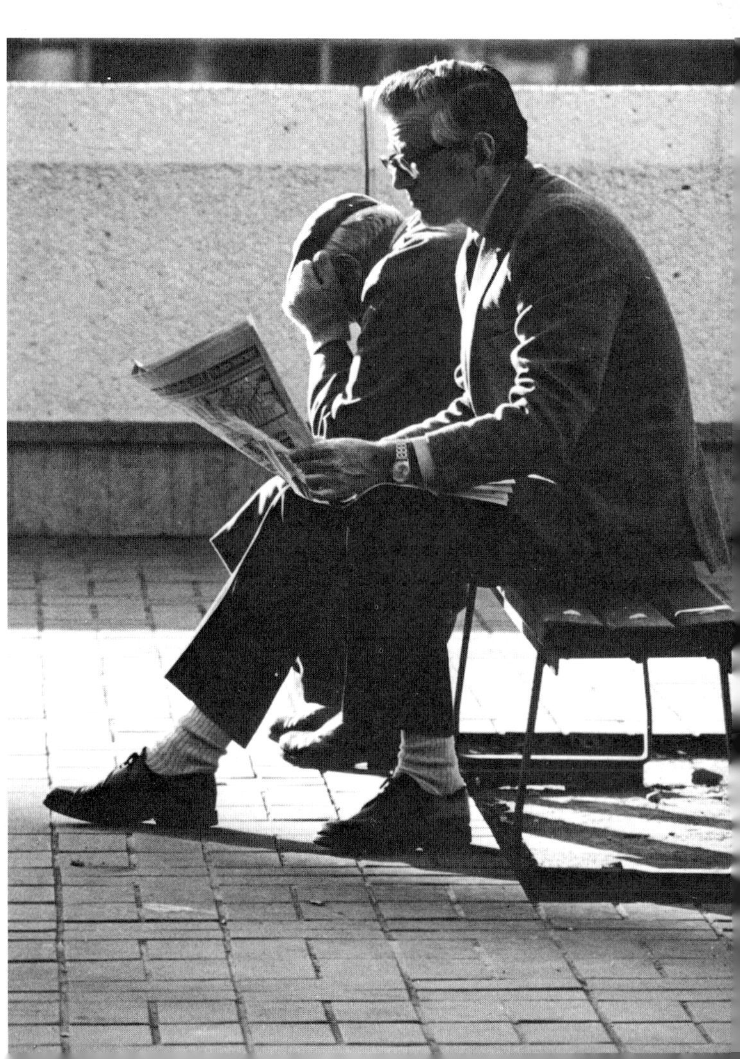

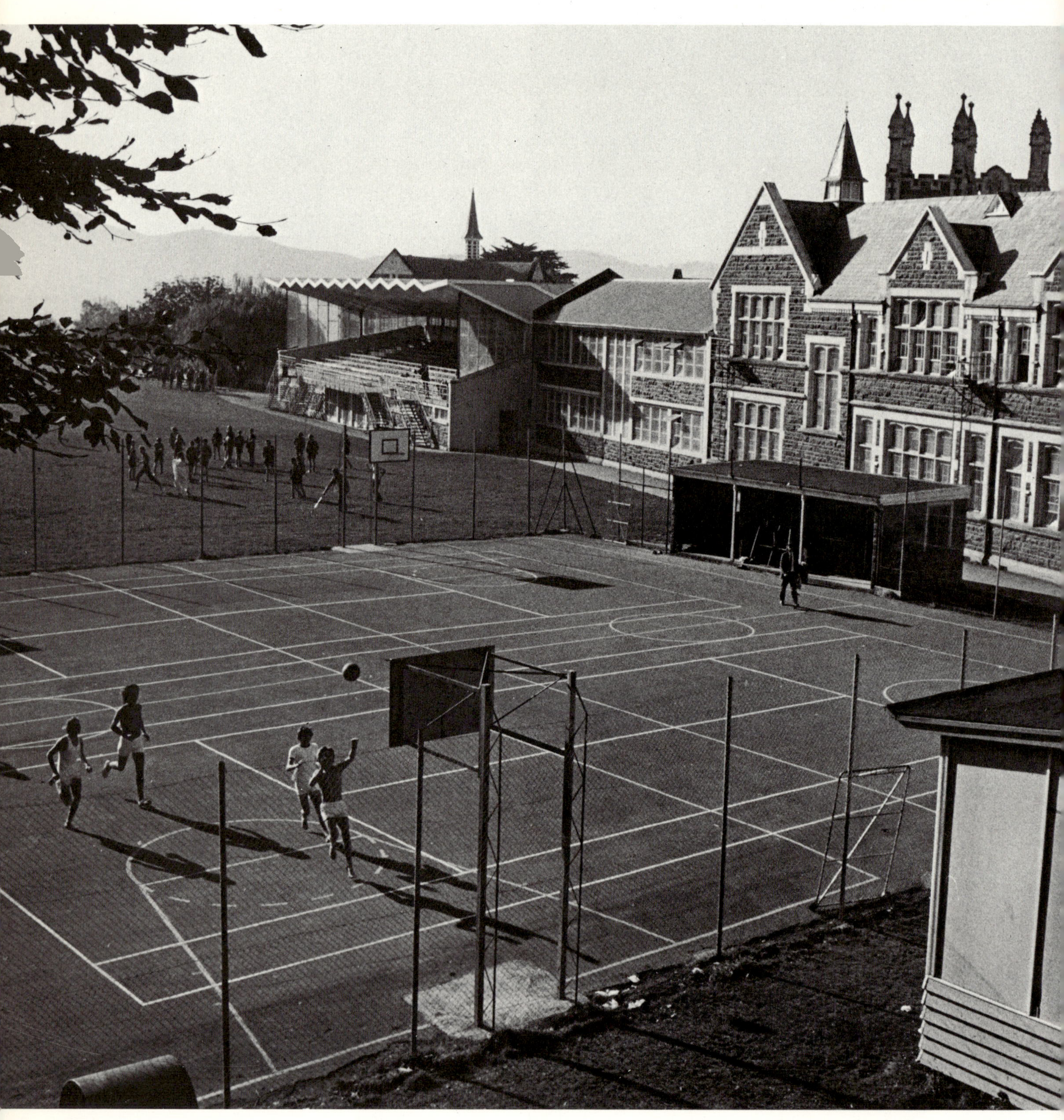

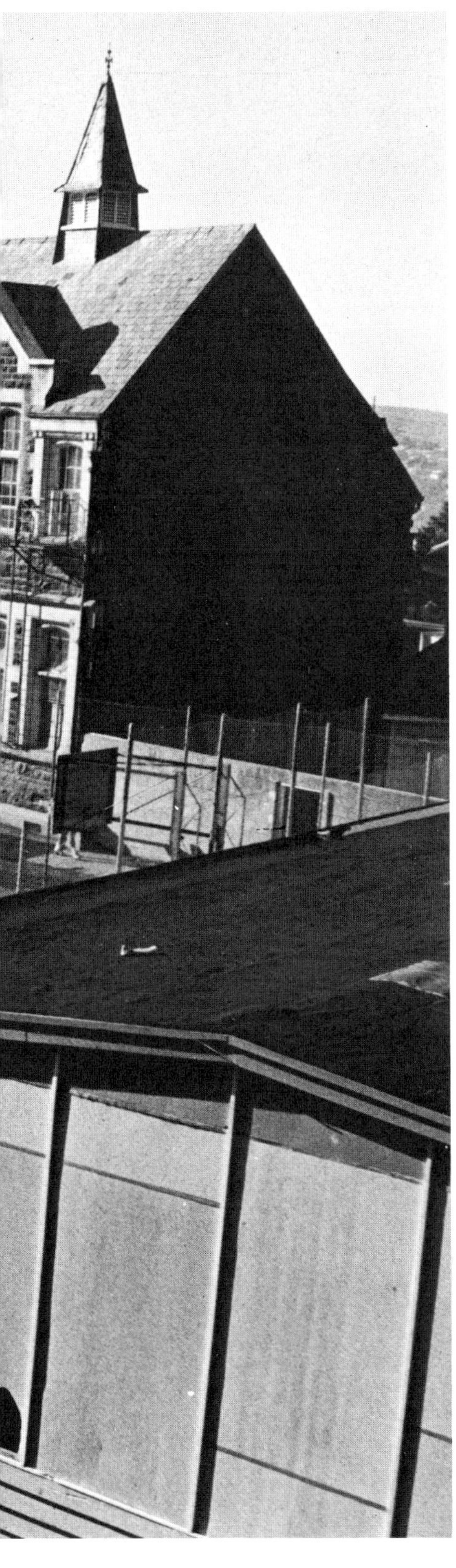

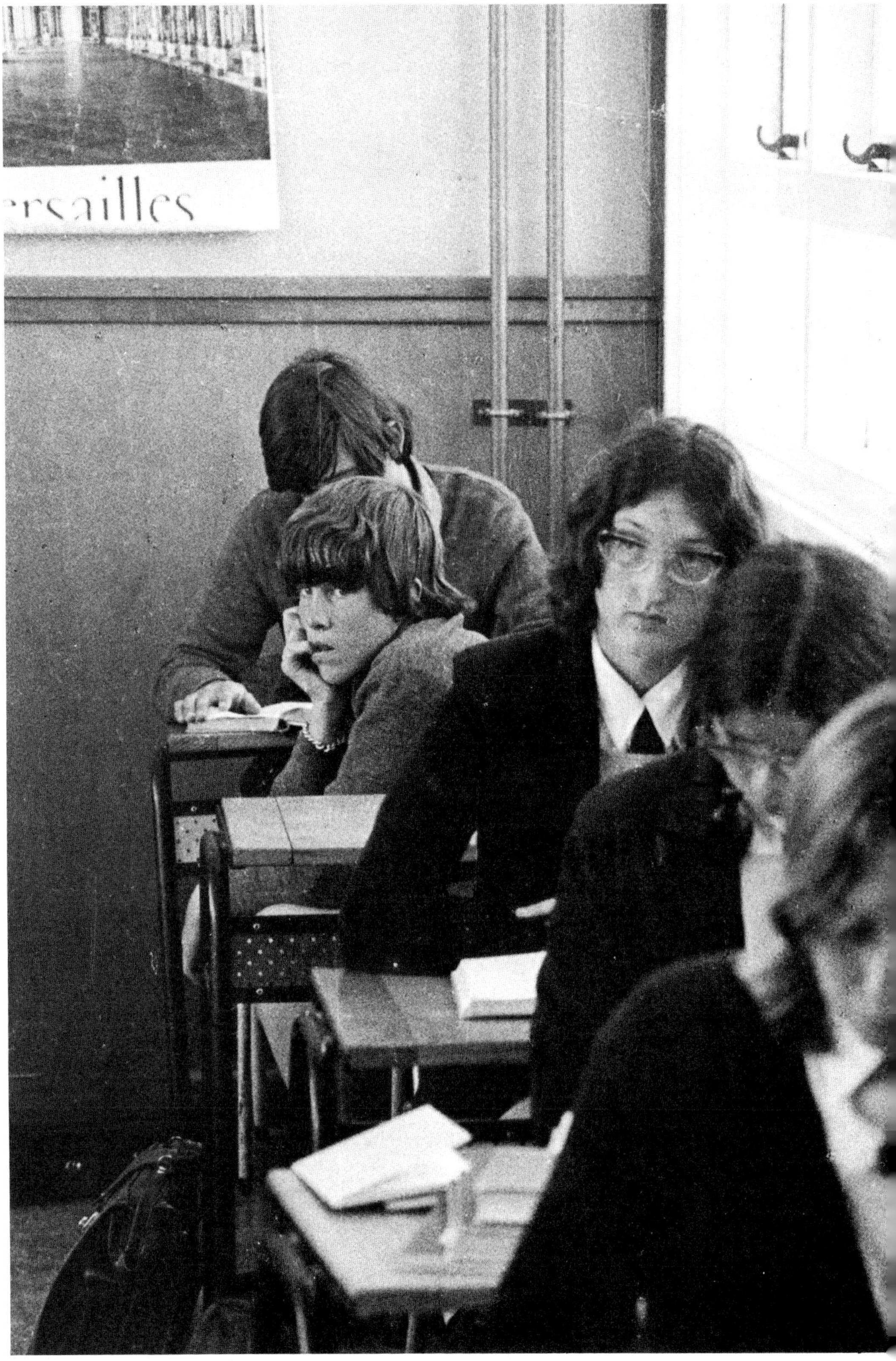

rsailles

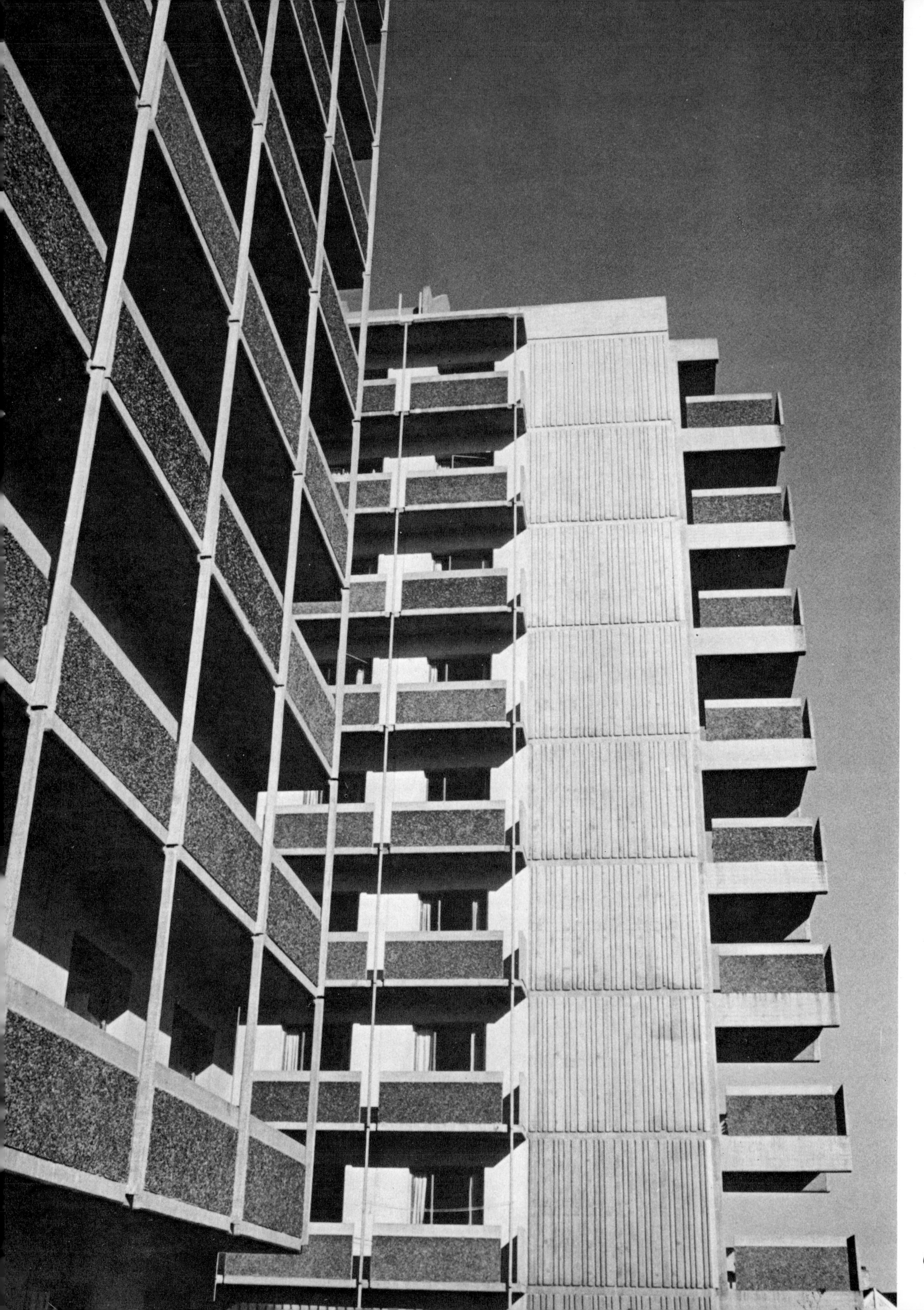

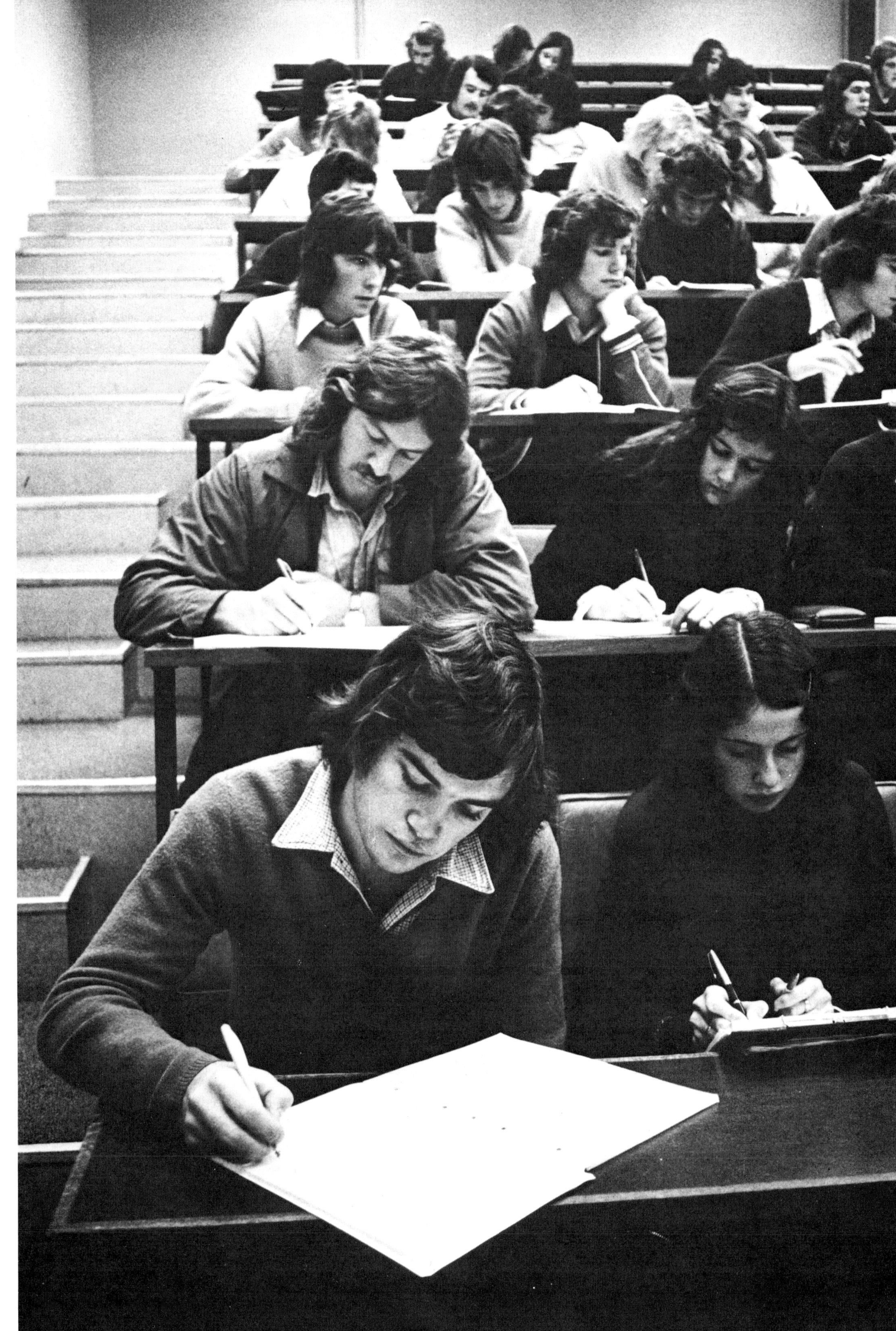

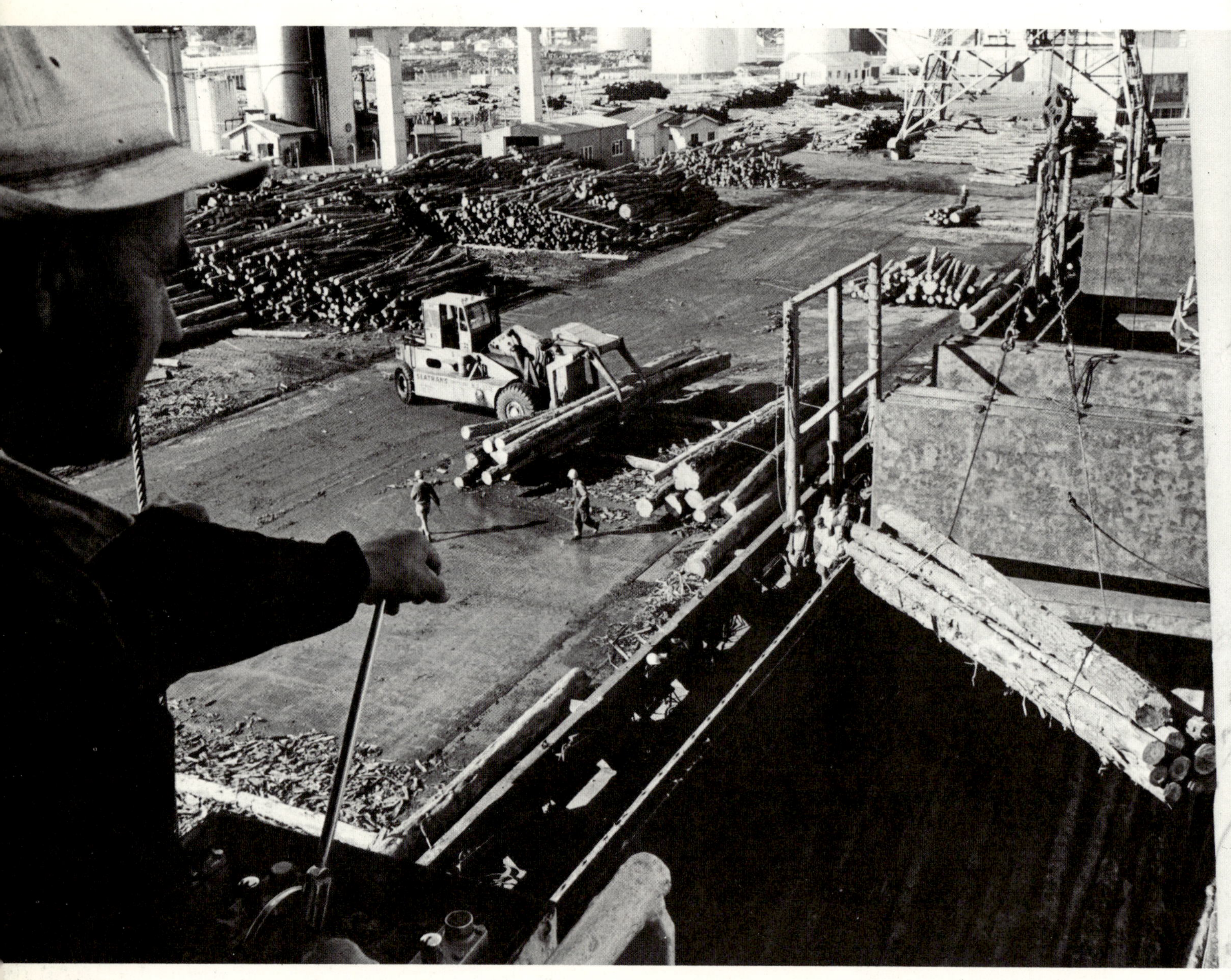

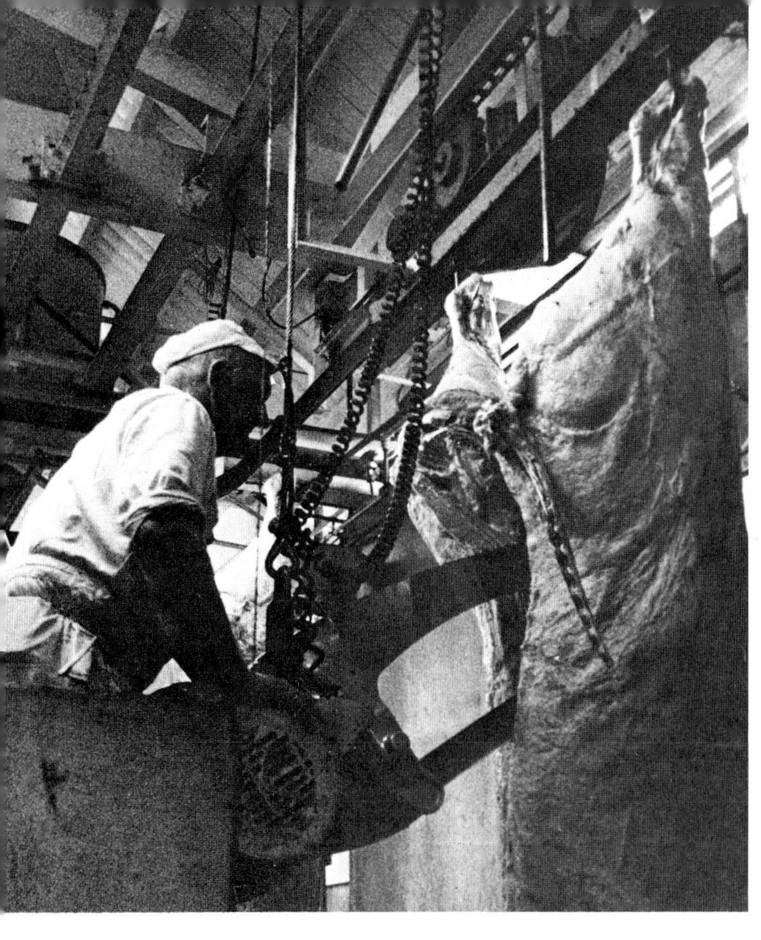

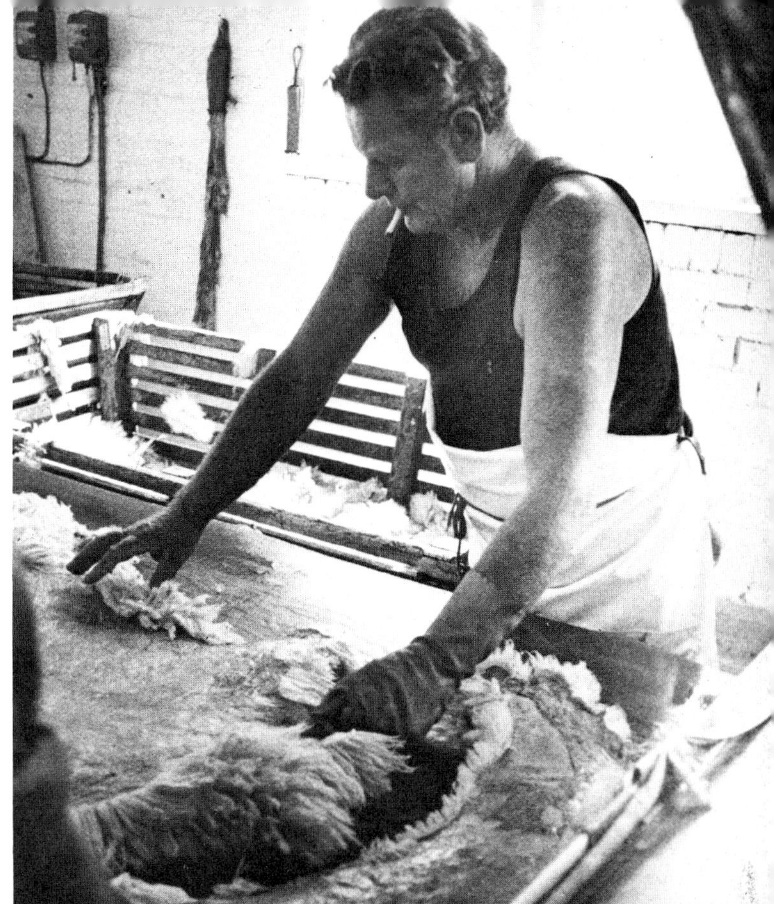

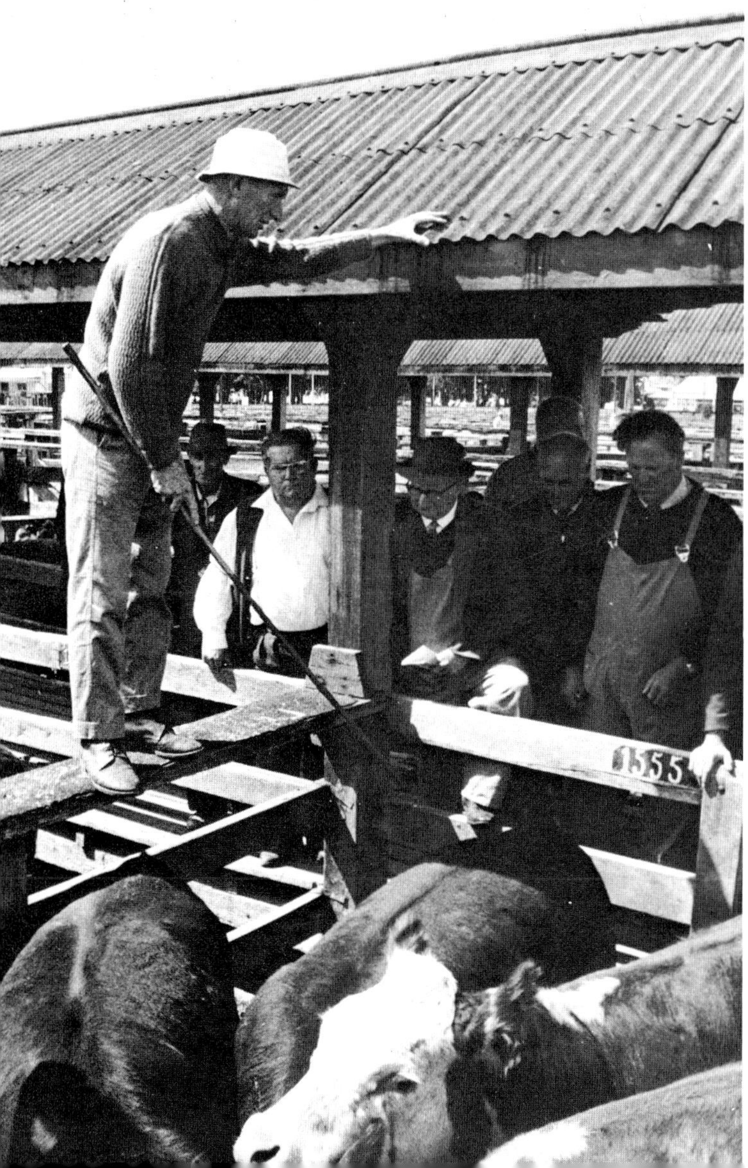

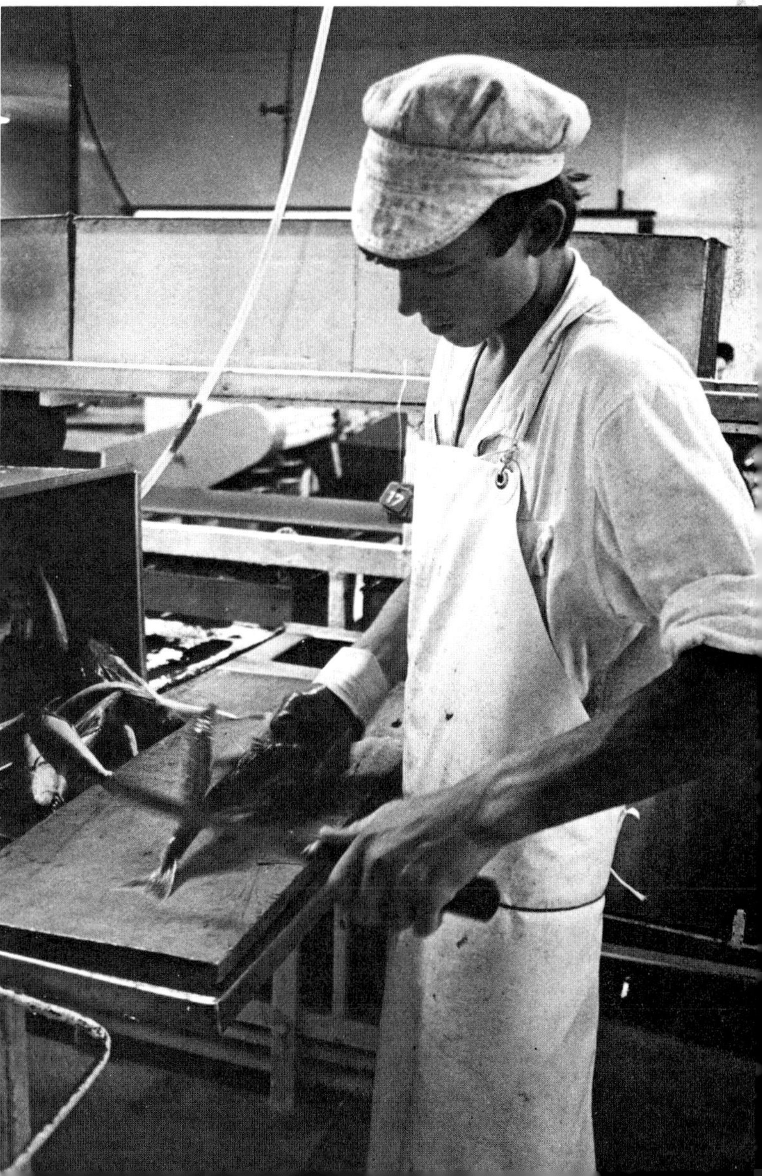

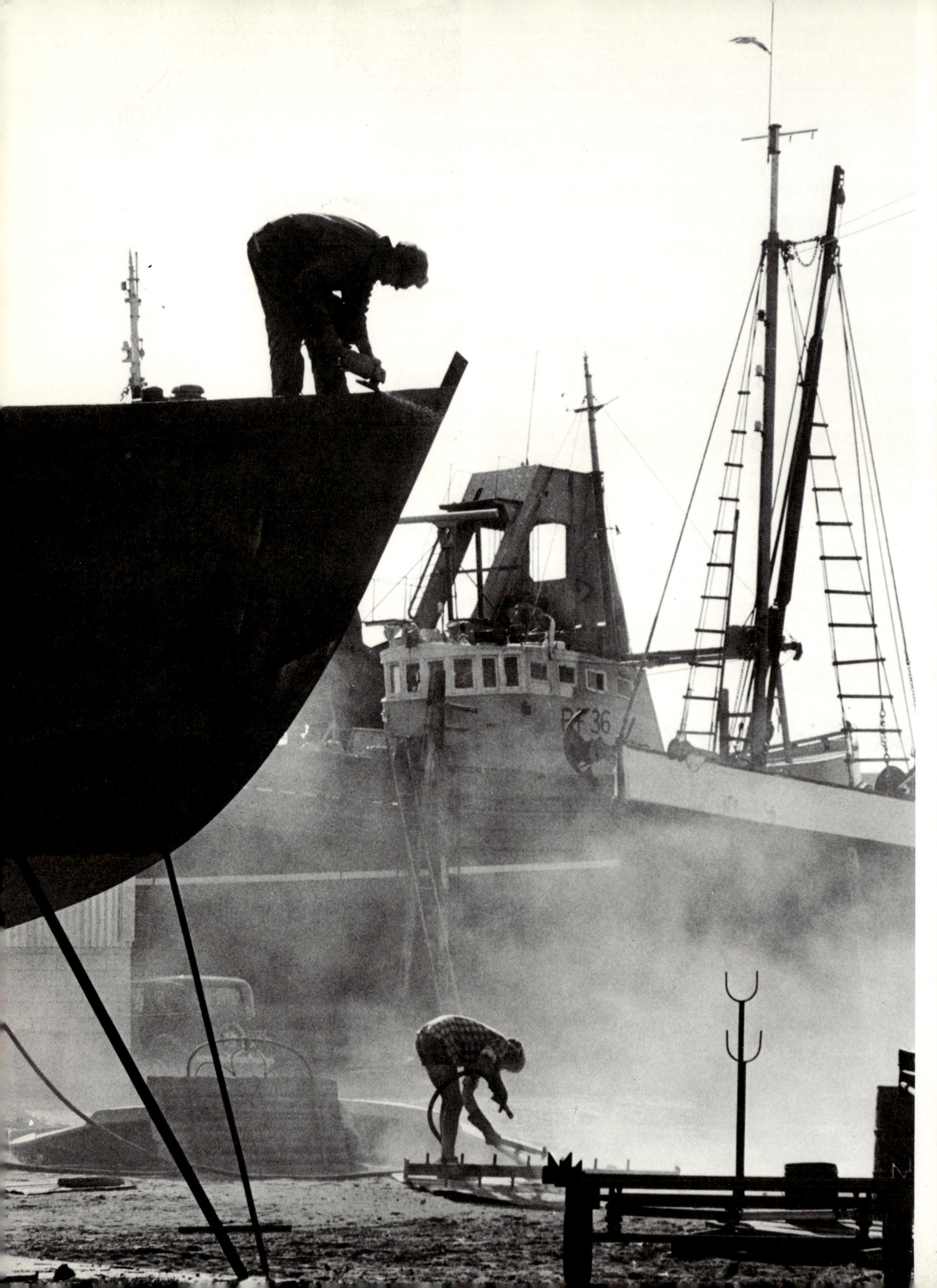

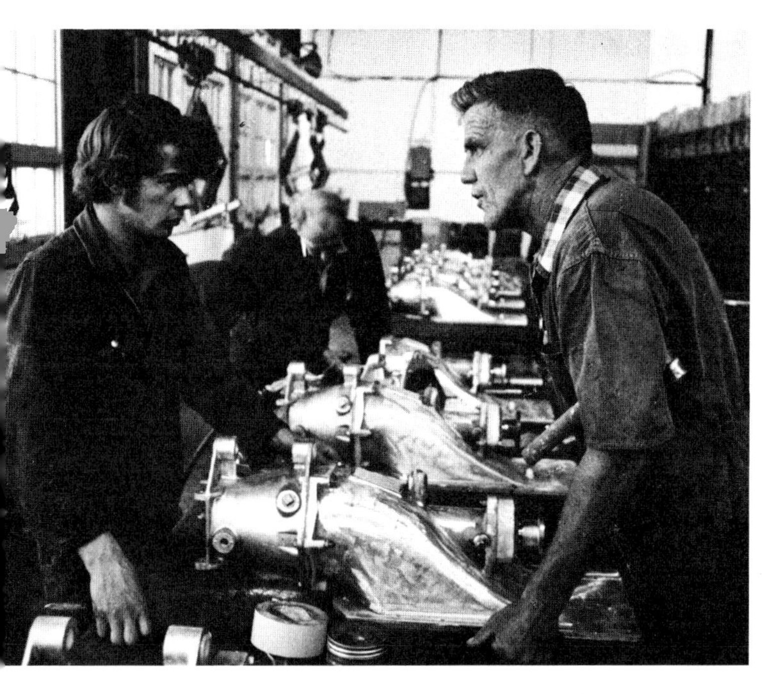
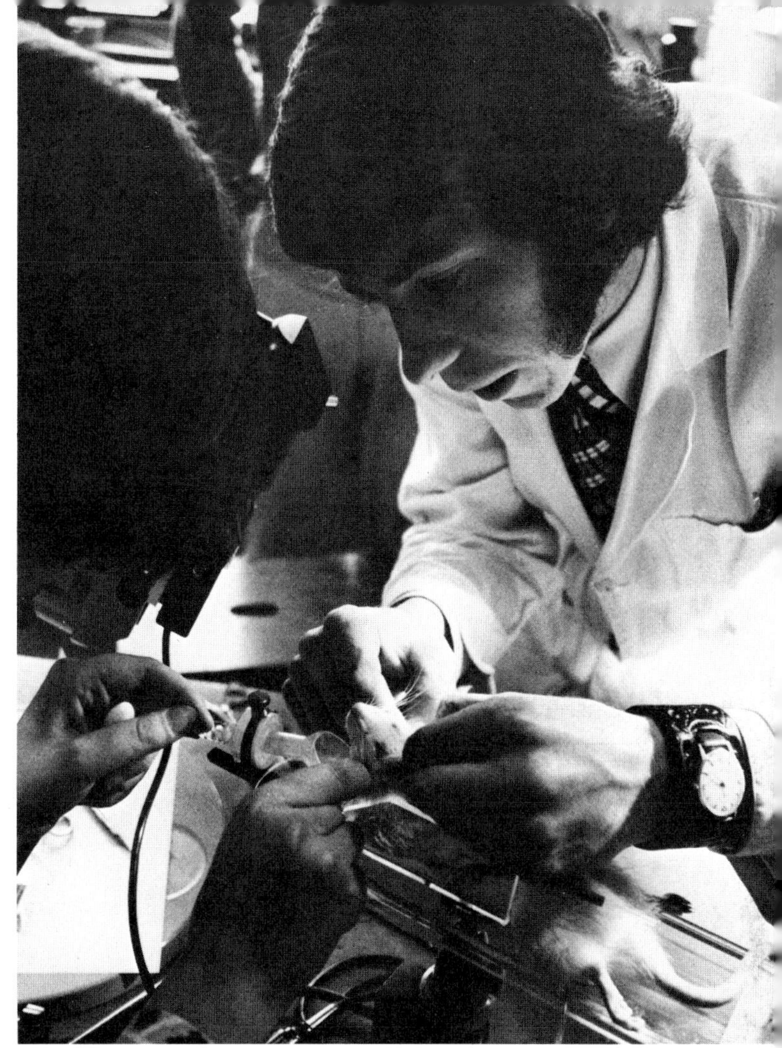
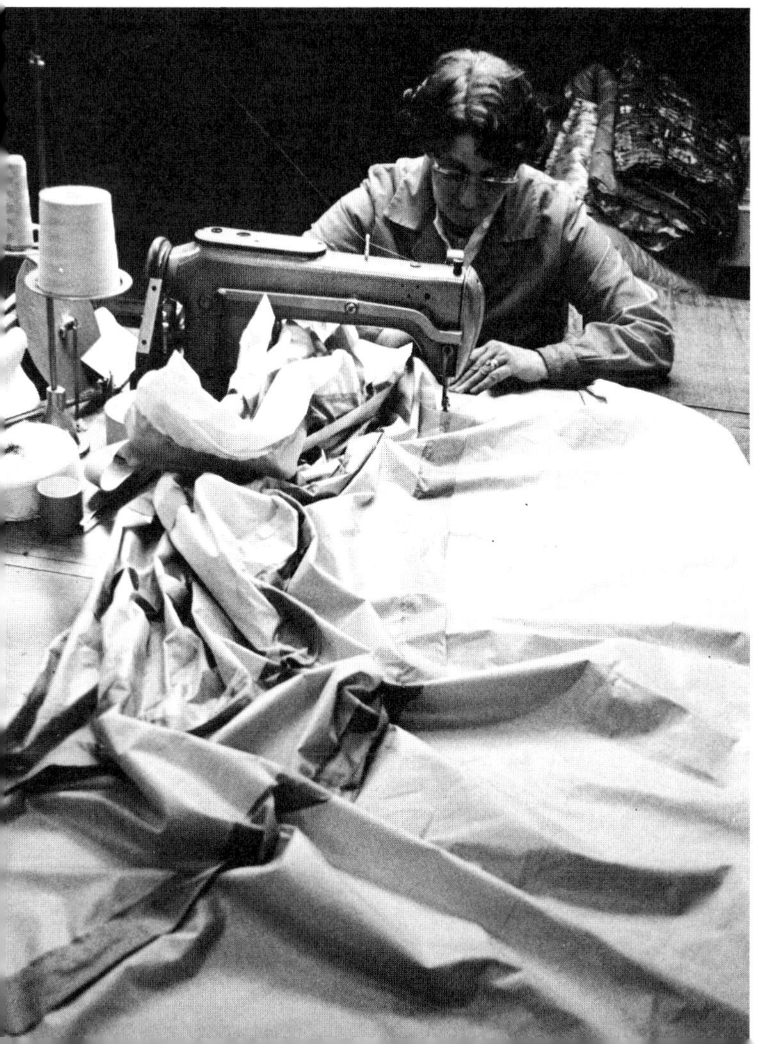
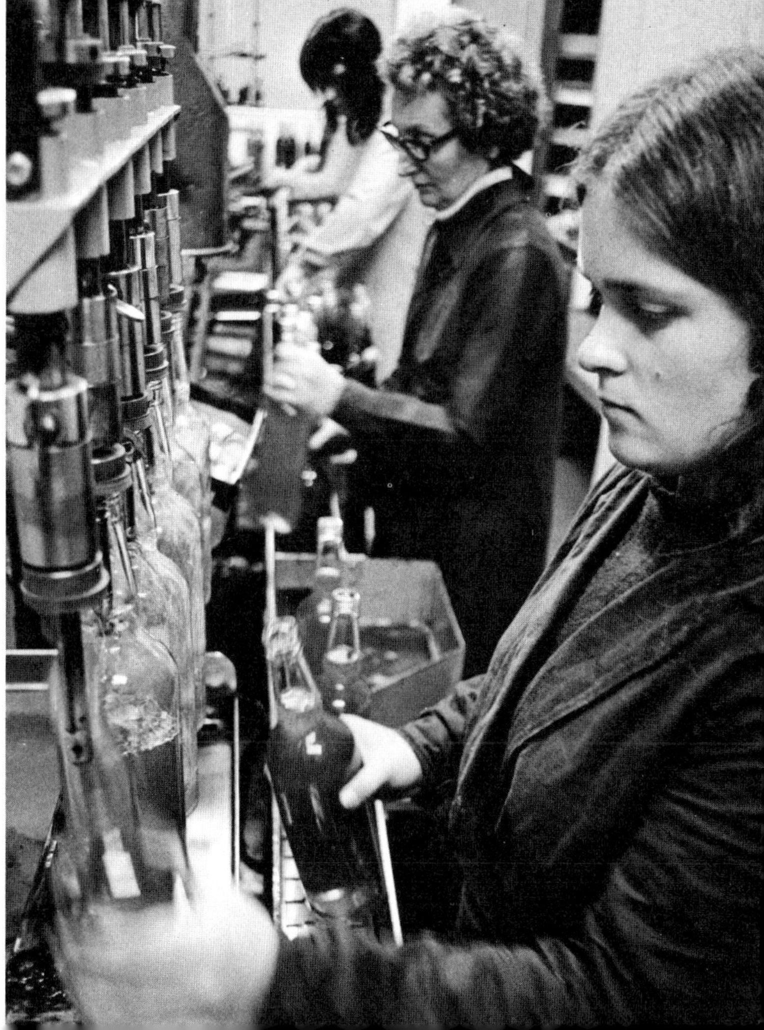

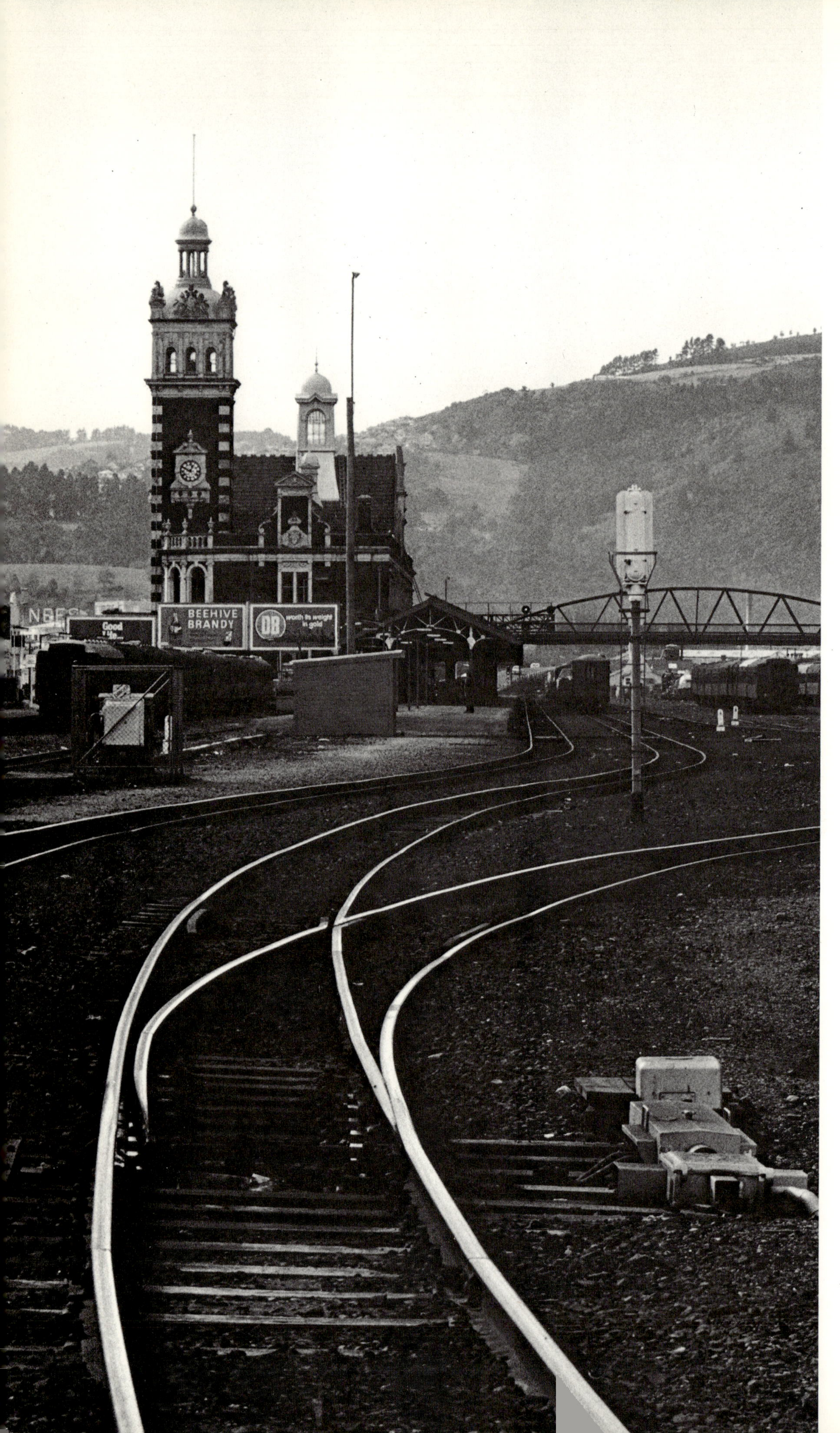

NBS
Good
BEEHIVE BRANDY
DB worth its weight in gold

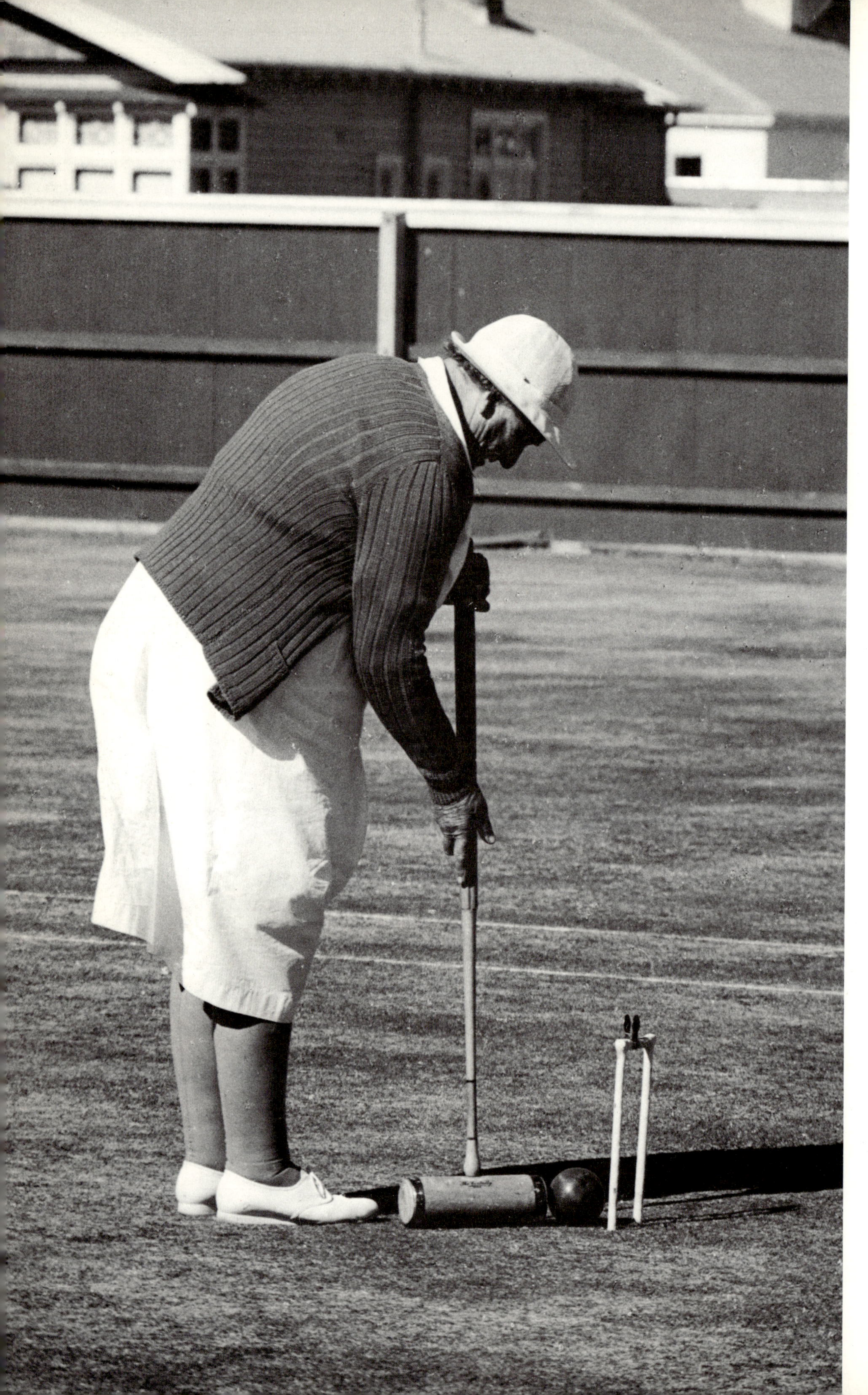

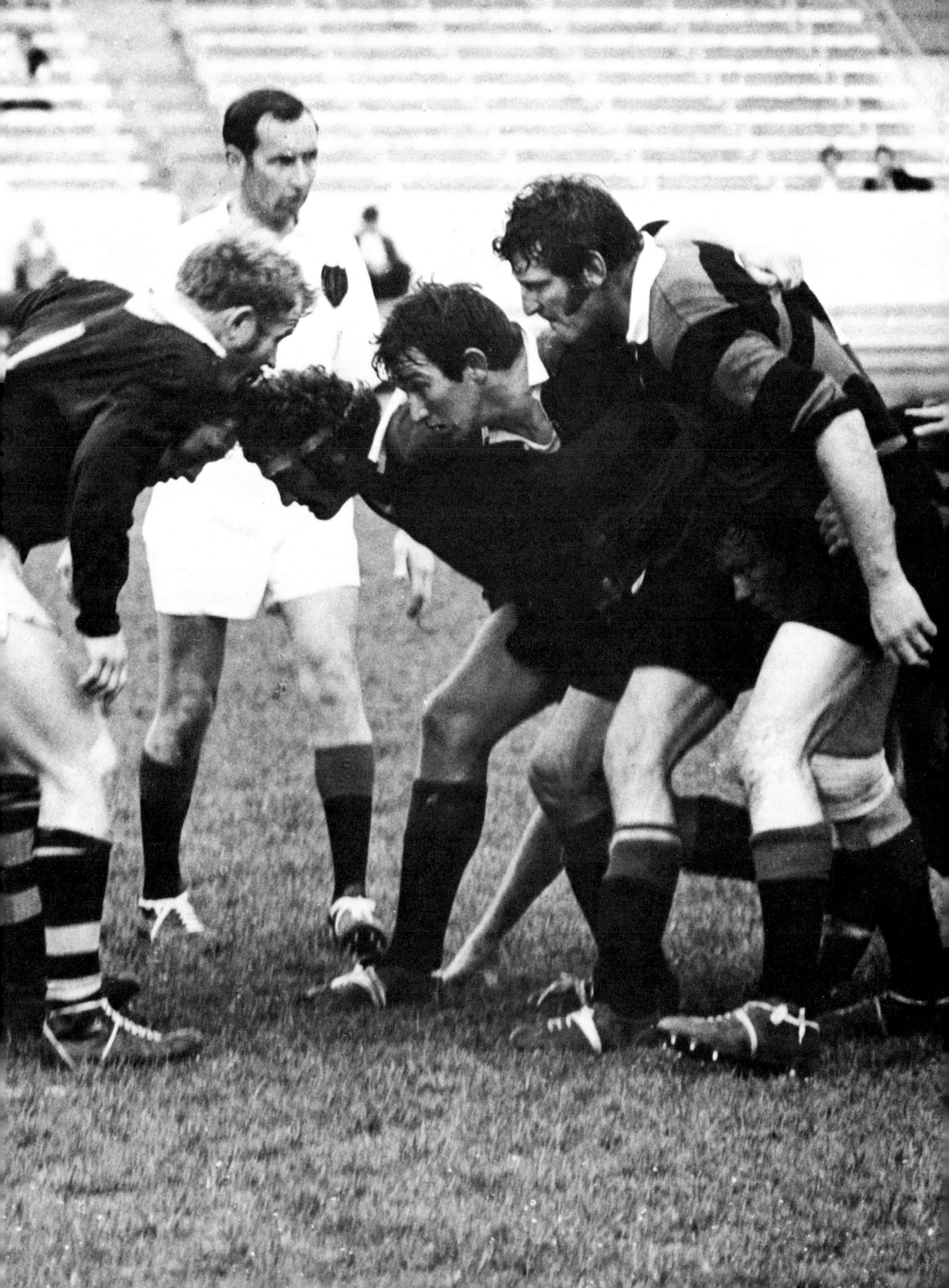

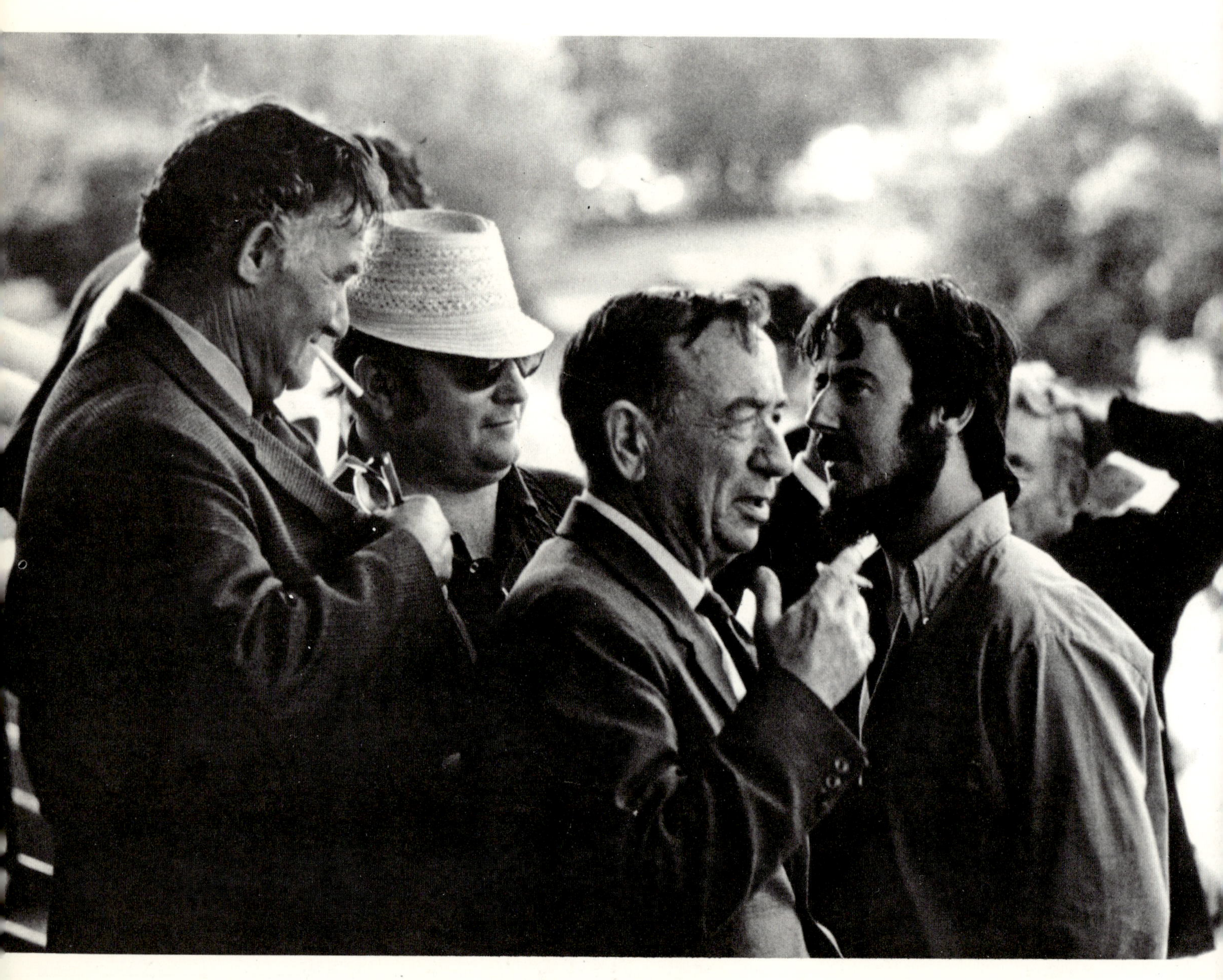

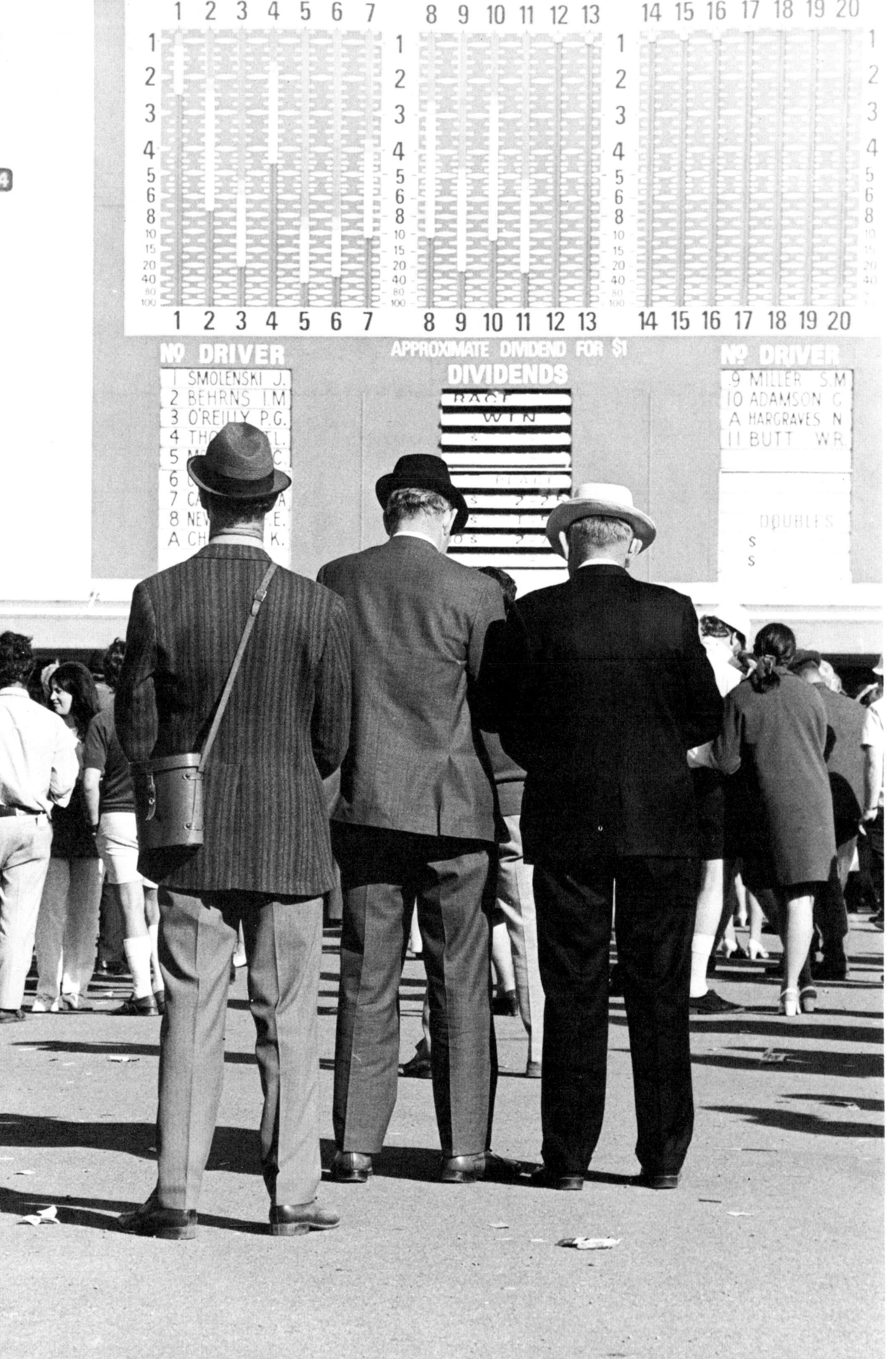
1 2 3 4 5 6 7 8 9 10 11 12 13 14 15 16 17 18 19 20
Nº DRIVER
APPROXIMATE DIVIDEND FOR $1
DIVIDENDS
Nº DRIVER
1 SMOLENSKI J.
2 BEHRNS I.M
3 O'REILLY P.G.
9 MILLER S.M
10 ADAMSON G
A HARGRAVES N
11 BUTT W.R.
RACE
WIN
DOUBLES

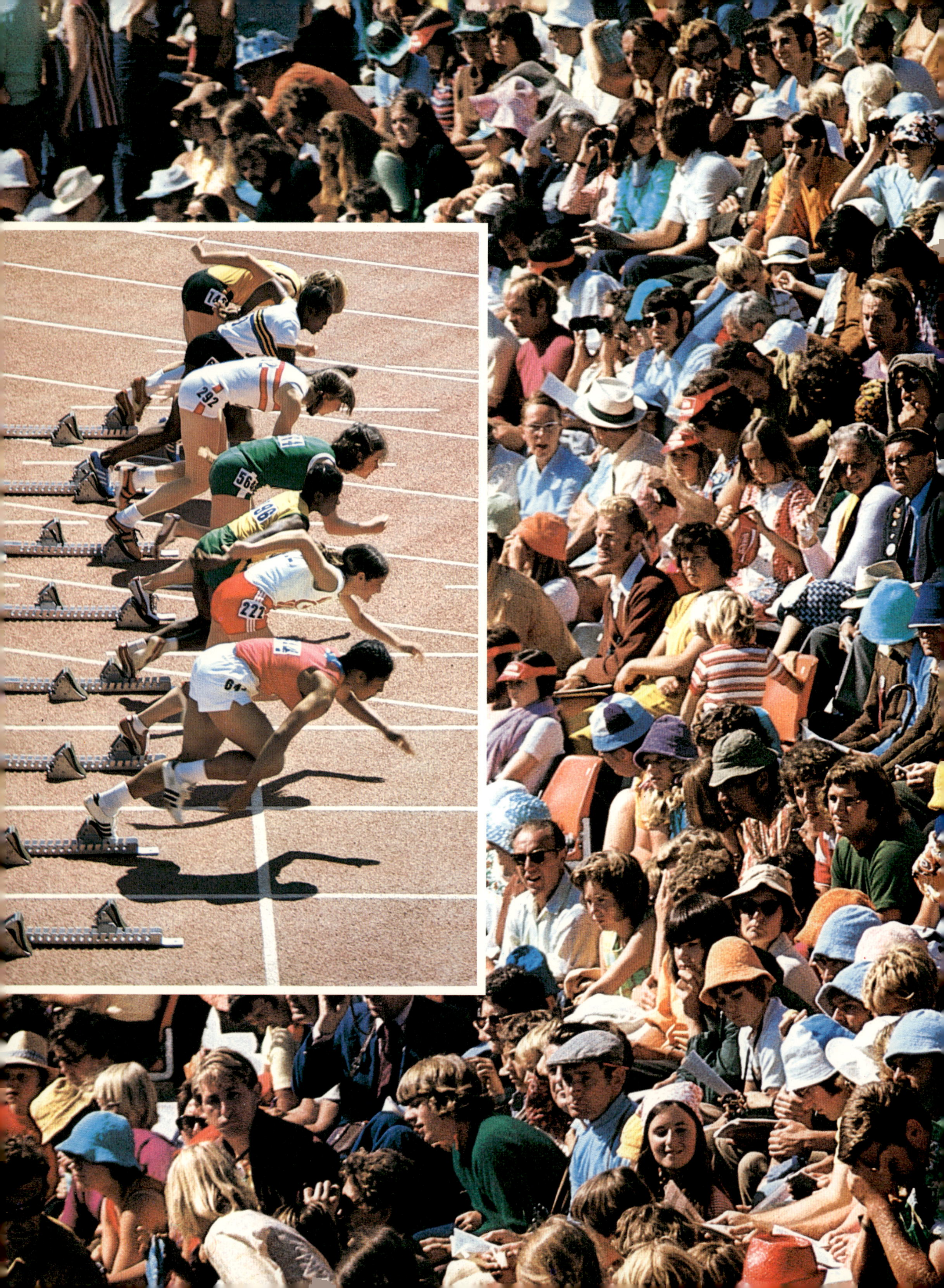

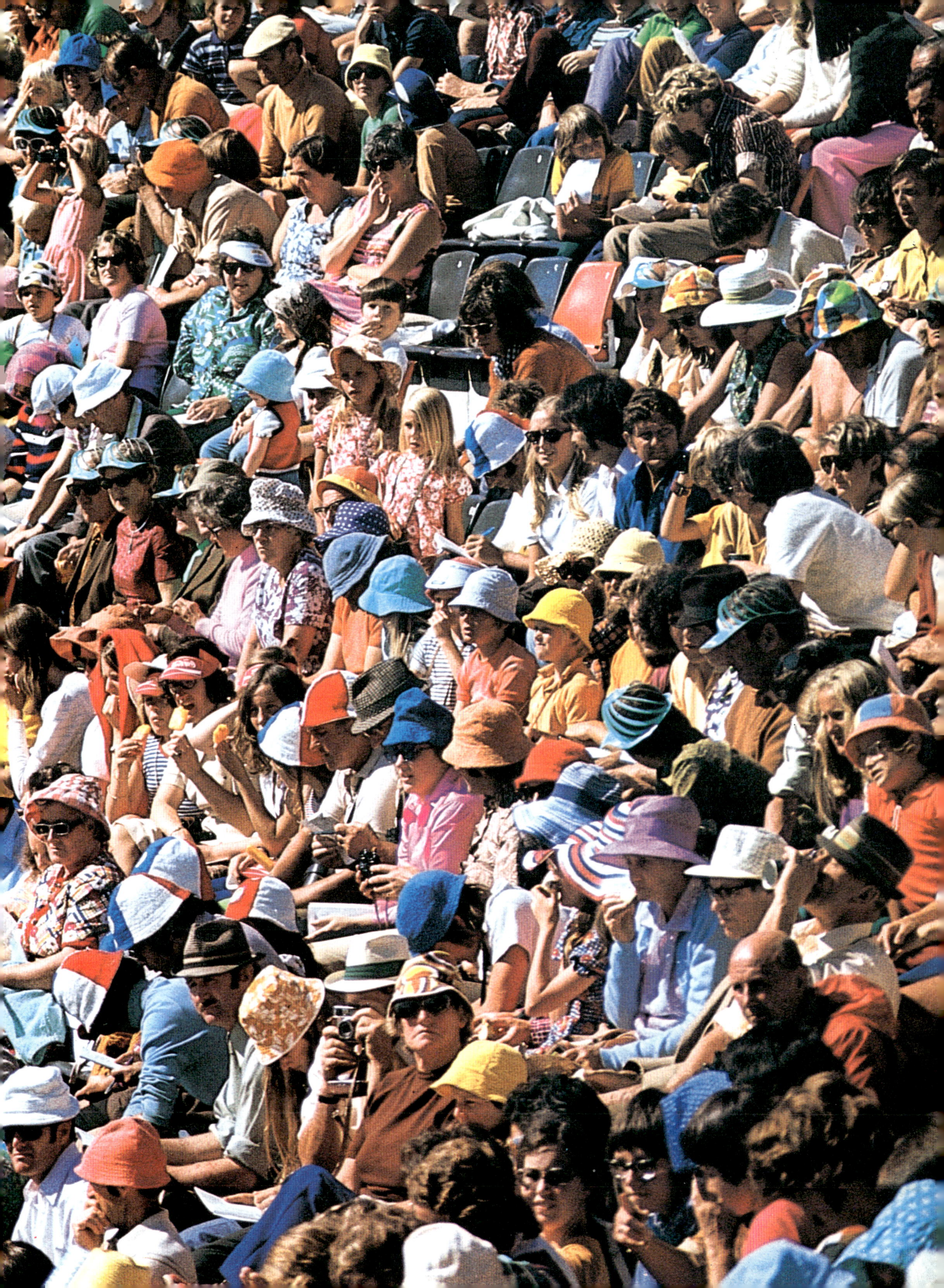

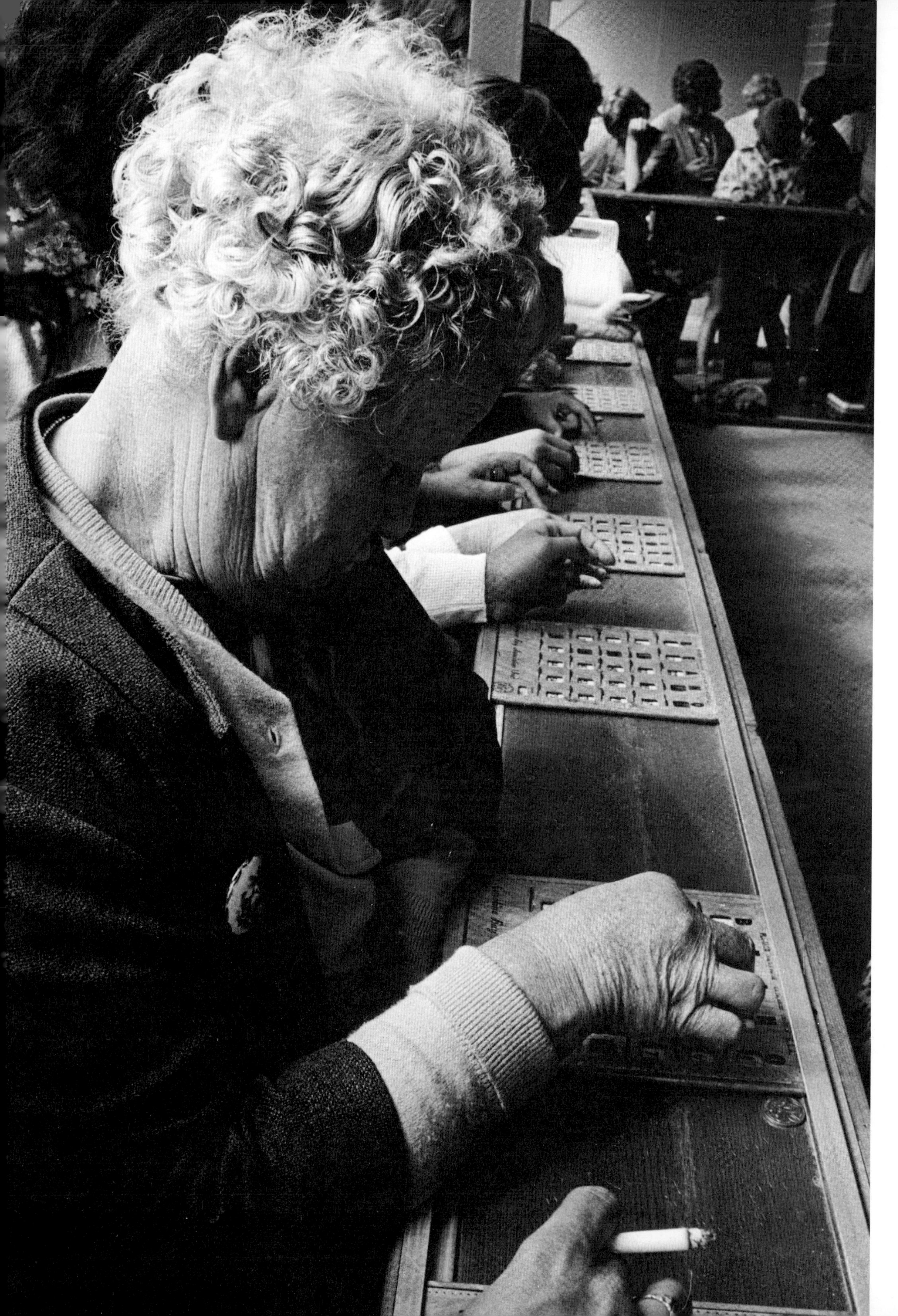

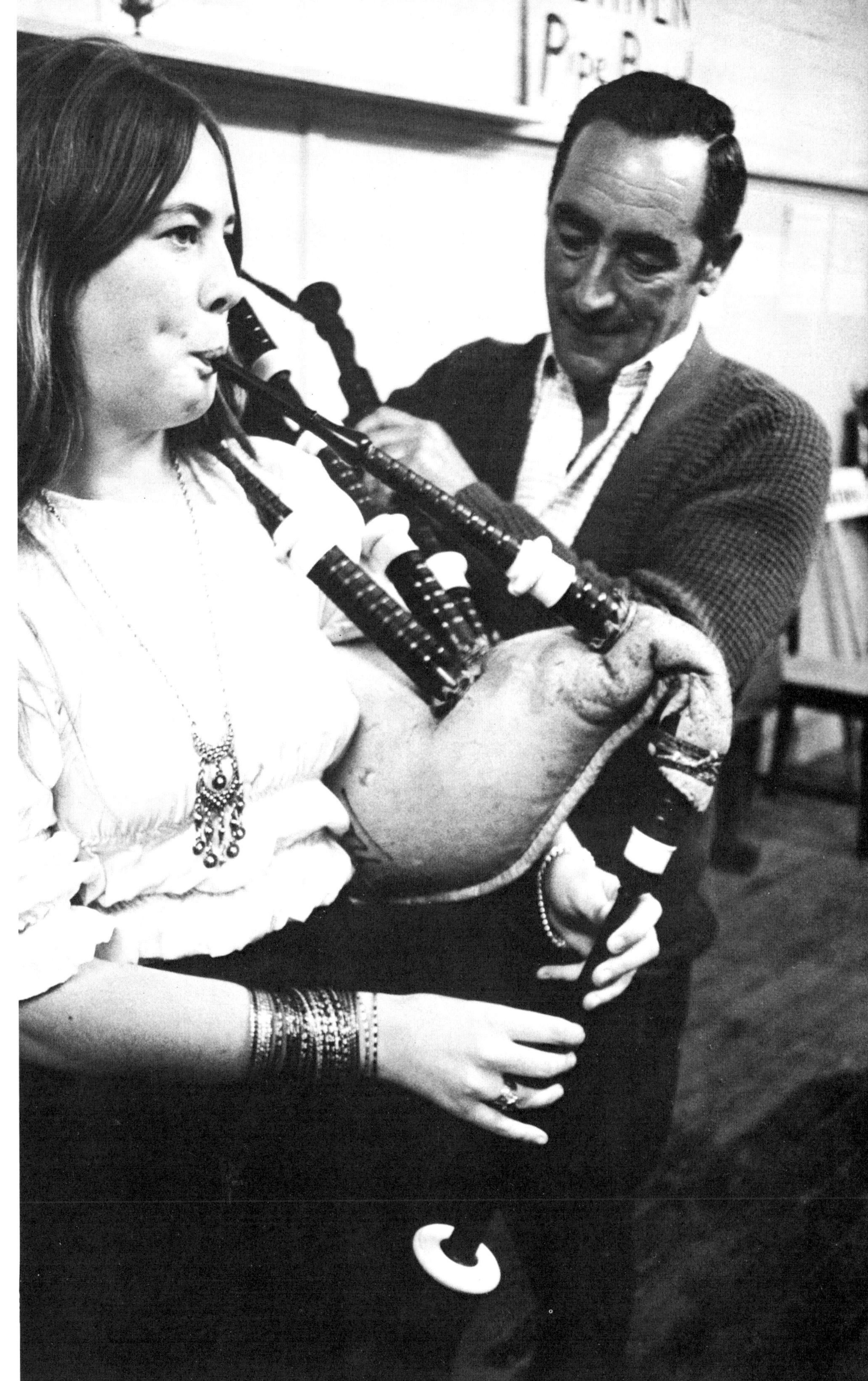

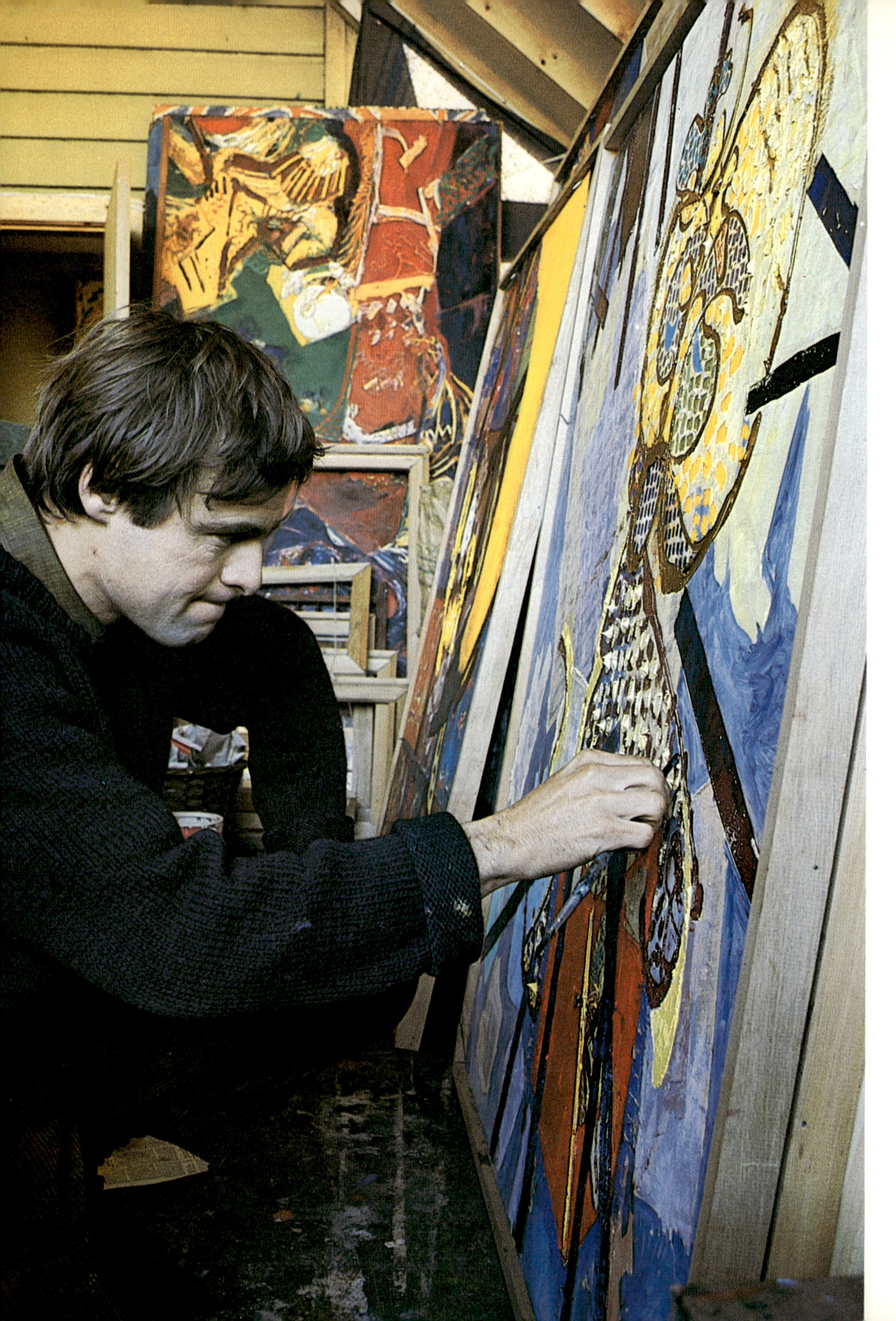

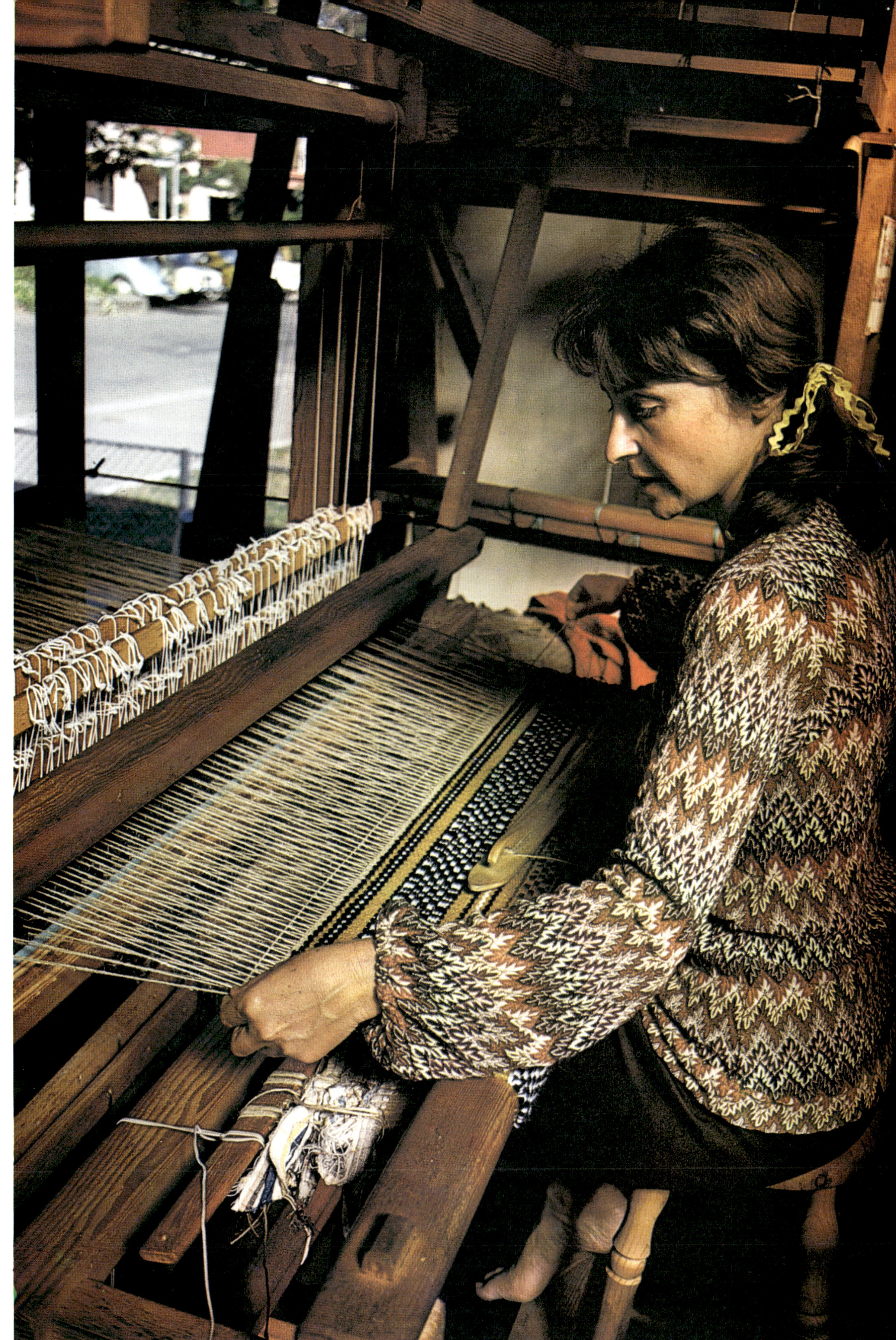

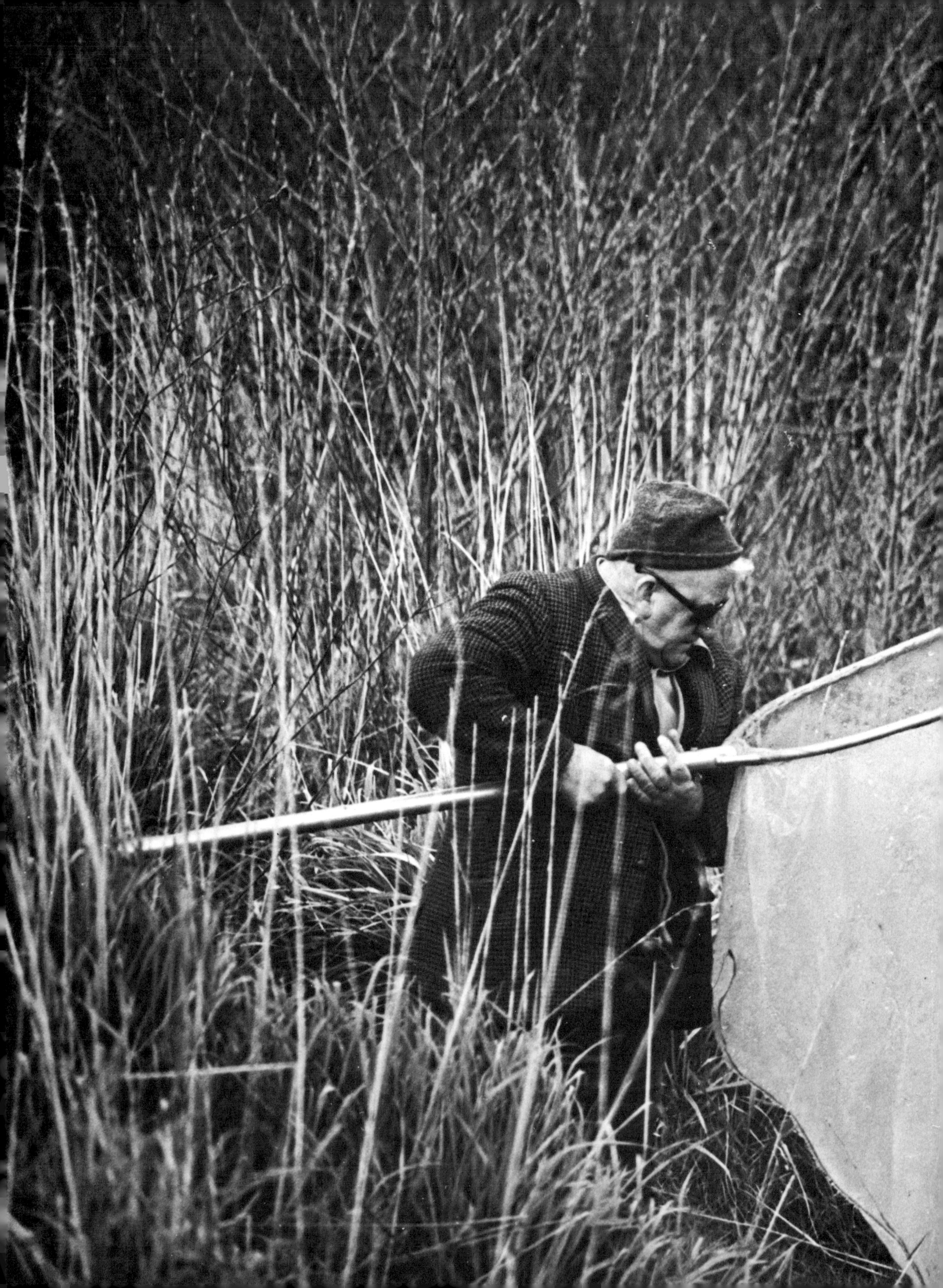

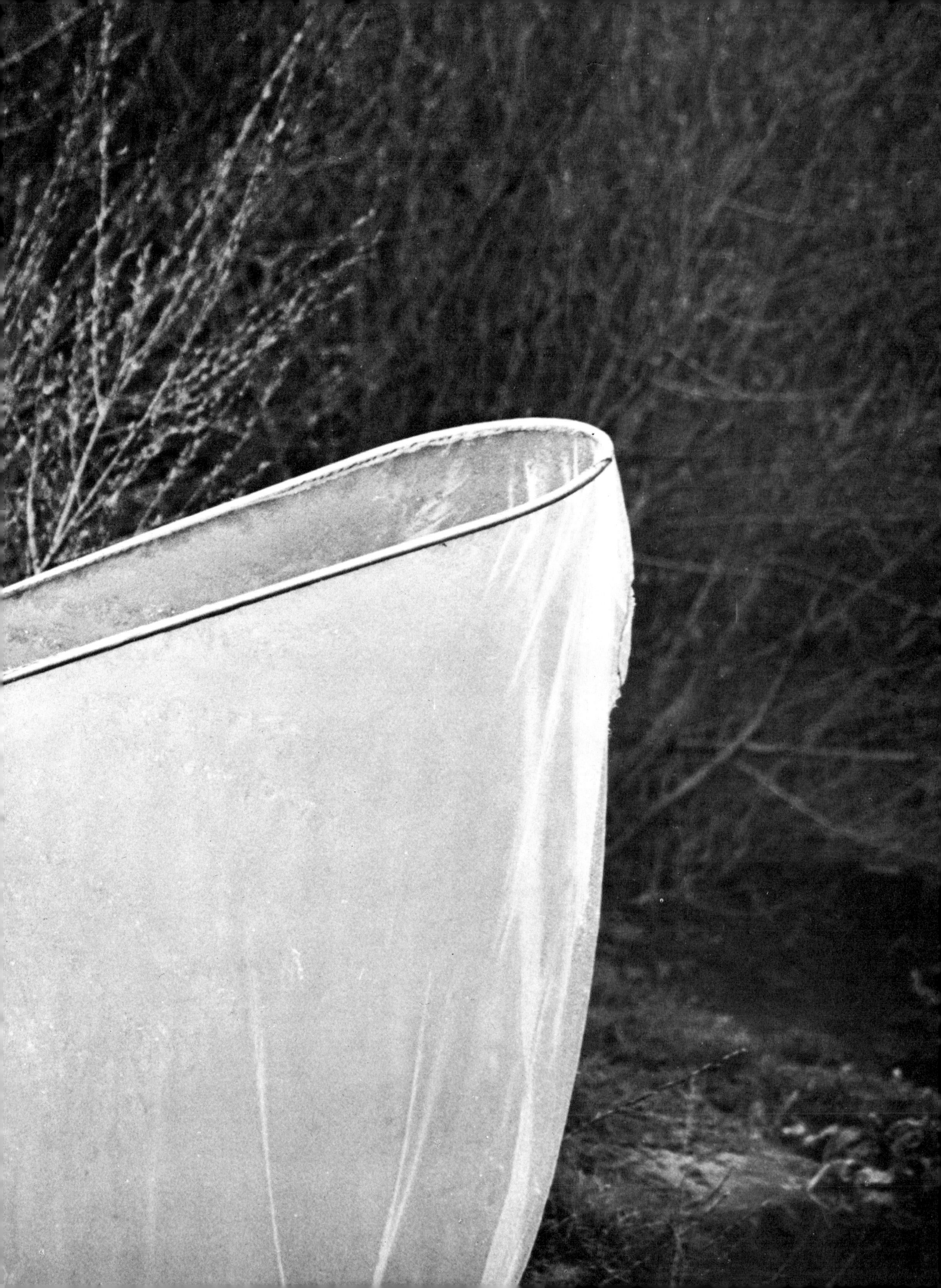

ON wool and gold the South Island provinces fattened and grew, the new cities prospered. Dunedin moved from the wooden facade of pioneer town to the weighty stone of commercial capital. Gold completed First Church in 1873, wool propped up the spire of Christchurch Cathedral in 1881. Colonial gain belatedly paid for the outward embodiment of religious ideals first touted by the settlement associations thirty years earlier. A core of early settlers had carried the moral banners forward. But only material success could build the monuments and institutions that gave them identity in a transplanted society. Wealth and high church, land and status — if not title — were sought by some as a source of security in a land which they used but scarcely understood. Yet the uneasy place of imported models on the frontier could be seen in Gothic cathedral sequestered by rough commercial buildings verandahed to keep off the colonial sun.

The needs of most migrants, and their children, centred on equal opportunity to achieve comfortable material wellbeing. Aspirations were for nothing higher than equitable middle class. Social ambition and cultural pretension were unwelcome and misplaced. Even today, most are at ease in a society that demands no more of them than material success through individual labour and a self-sufficient resourcefulness, seen as a natural inheritance.

Until the turn of the century the South Island grew ahead of the North Island in both wealth and population. The terrain was generally more suited for the rapid expansion of a pastoral industry, communications were easier, there was no 'native problem', and mineral resources yielded easily. Many of the nation's financial institutions and trading companies were founded in Dunedin, which later in the century became the centre of engineering and heavy industry. Christchurch boomed as a provincial market town closely identified with the pastoral wealth of the Canterbury high country and the diversifying agricultural pattern of the plains and downlands. An easy hinterland and good instincts for marketing saw Canterbury become the railway province, and the vitality steam gave to commercial and social intercourse did not diminish until the rise of the motor vehicle.

Nelson remained a separate identity in the South Island, caused by the isolating factor of difficult communications through the mountainous centre and north, and a terrain and climate which fostered different lines of farming development. Though stimulated by gold rushes in Golden Bay, the Sounds region and Buller during the 1860s, its growth and character depended less on the wool and gold that governed the bigger provinces to the south. Lack of vast acreages for sheep and a wide variety of land types saw development of the most diverse farming pattern in New Zealand. Exploitation of a climate which combined adequate rainfall with high levels of sunshine made Nelson one of the chief fruit-growing regions of the country, and later its only producer of tobacco and hops.

The search for more sheep country caused the early Nelson settlement to spill eastwards into the dry river plains and hills of what later became the province of Marlborough. Similarly in the south, the need for more and better country for pastoral expansion beyond the confines of the original Otago settlement began the growth of Southland into the richest sheepfarming region of New Zealand.

Westland, with few areas suitable for farming amid the rugged bush spurs of the Southern Alps, and connected to the markets and ports of the east by tenuous road and rail links, has never found a secure economic base for development. Coal mining provided income and employment as the value of gold production slipped, but the shift to oil and hydro electricity as sources of power pushed this industry into decline too. Westland's economic hopes for the future rest on a renewed demand for coal in a power hungry world and the timber resources of its huge forests. Now its population hovers uneasily at a figure well below the gold boom time of the 1860s.

After the turn of the century, as good communications became assured across the centre of the North Island, as the dairy export industry found its feet, as Wellington grew as the political and administrative capital, as Auckland became the commercial and industrial centre, the balance of population, wealth and influence moved inexorably from the South Island to the north. By the early 1970s more than twice as many New Zealanders lived in the north as in the south. This shift of population slowed industrial and commercial development, particularly processing and consumer industries which became further and further removed from the main markets in the north.

The effects of the northward drift have been felt throughout the South Island. Westland's intrinsic natural barriers to progress seemed doubly severe as markets became more distant. Otago and Dunedin, with less security in farming than either Canterbury or Southland, never recovered economic and financial leadership. Nelson grew slowly and independently through the sheer diversity of its agricultural, mineral and timber resources. Only Southland and Canterbury, with a sure footing in healthy pastoral export industries, maintained growth rates at all comparable to North Island regions.

Today Canterbury is more than the physical centre of the South Island. It is the agricultural and cropping centre of New Zealand as well as a major producer of meat and wool. More than a third of the South Island's population of 840,000 live in the greater Christchurch area which fosters not only industries allied to farming but major manufacturing industries geared to a New Zealand market.

Christchurch and Canterbury may be secure but the economic wellbeing of the South Island as a whole may largely depend on governmental regional development policies that view its future as more than a vast grain and sheep farm, or source of hydro power, in a tourist setting of mountains and bush. Yet economic development for its own sake, once the prime concern of a new colony, may be less important in the future than the maturing growth of community values within a superb and largely unspoilt environment. Lack of population as well as room to move may be the South Island's ultimate fortune.

The landscape of the South Island has provoked superlative descriptions since the inception late last century of an industry that had no place in the plans of pioneers and that has grown far beyond the dreams of its early promoters. Tourism now is an important part of South Island economy, based on the scenic and sporting attractions of rugged mountain and forest country first deemed useless, even in the eyes of enterprising sheepmen and prospectors. When leisure became part of the colonial vocabulary, a few who saw physical and spiritual refreshment in mountains and lakes began to tackle the Milford Track (from 1889), the 'greatest walk in the world'; or take the alpine air at Mount Cook (from 1884), setting foot on the Tasman Glacier, 'the longest glacier in the temperate regions of the world'. From small beginnings grew a profitable network of tourist facilities that now caters not only for New Zealand holidaymakers but also for a quarter of a million foreign visitors annually.

It was seen early that the priceless assets of South Island landscape had to be protected against indiscriminate exploitation, whether by farmer, bushman, miner or tourist operator. National parks were created — seven out of ten in New Zealand in the south — areas that 'contain scenery of such distinctive quality or natural features so beautiful or unique that their preservation is in the national interest' (National Parks Act 1952). The seven parks contain much that is the essence of South Island landscape: bush-fringed beaches and sea inlets of Golden Bay; the sweeping beech forests of the eastern flanks of the Southern Alps; the high alpine regions of Mount Cook and the glaciers that descend to the forest within a few hundred metres of sea level in the west; the unique bushed fiords and lakes of the southwest.

Yet the system of national parks and reserves does not yet encompass the violent contrast in landscape and climate that is the outstanding feature of a long (850 km), high (to over 3700 m) island lying 1600 km from the nearest major land mass. Prevailing westerlies blow against the high mountain spine of the island, release heavy rains over West Coast forests and are then transformed into dry, sapping fohn winds that bleach the tussocks of the eastern basins and foothills and bluster their way to the eastern seaboard. Rainfall in the west can be as much as 6500 mm annually; in Central Otago in the east little more than 300 mm; and in Christchurch double that, chiefly from cooling southerly winds, the lifegiving antidote to the scorching nor'westers.

It can be said that the Southern Alps are the South Island. Ridges from the central ranges reach out to the sea on the north, west and south; the eastern hills are precursors to greater heights, the valleys, lakes and basins within them created by long-gone glaciers; the eastern plains formed from mountain debris. No matter where one lives or moves in the island there is a presence of mountains, through both their landscape and the climate they have created. Today, though one is more likely to approach the South Island by air than by sea, Abel Tasman's description of over three centuries ago is still the most apt — 'a large land, uplifted high'.

THE LAND...

...and its people,
finding and celebrating abundance
in valley and plain, mountain and seashore,
discovering a natural and human heritage ...

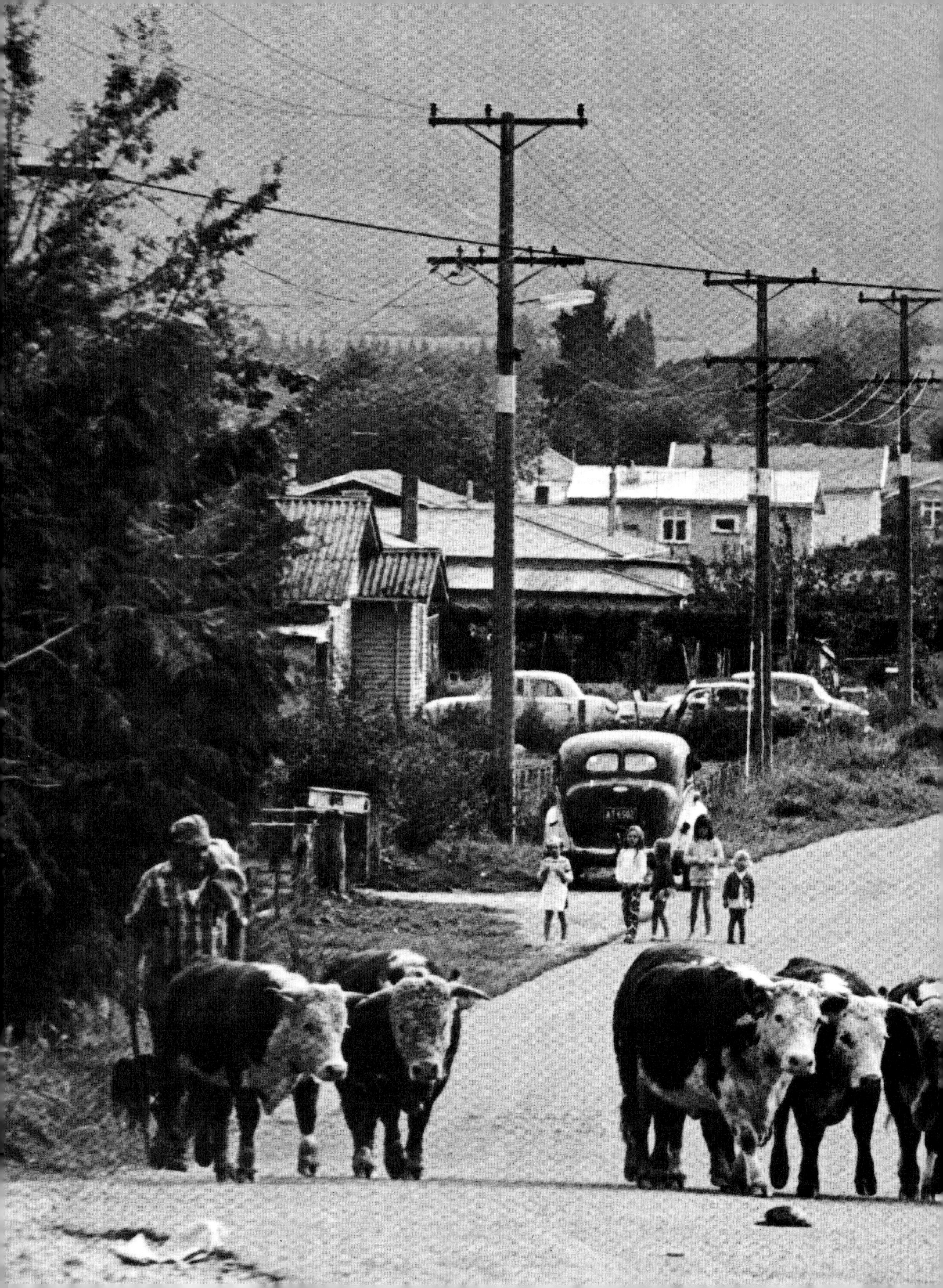

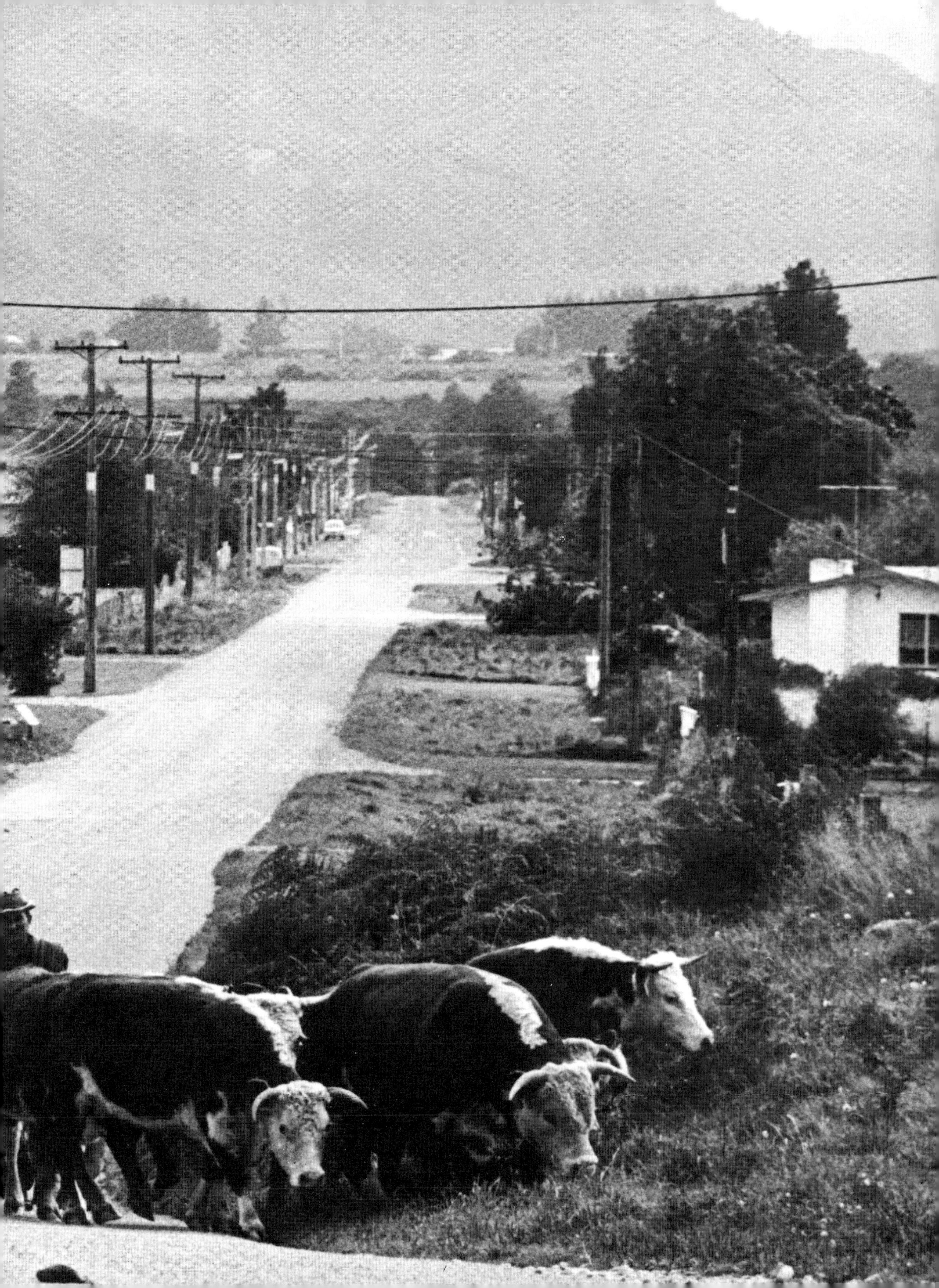

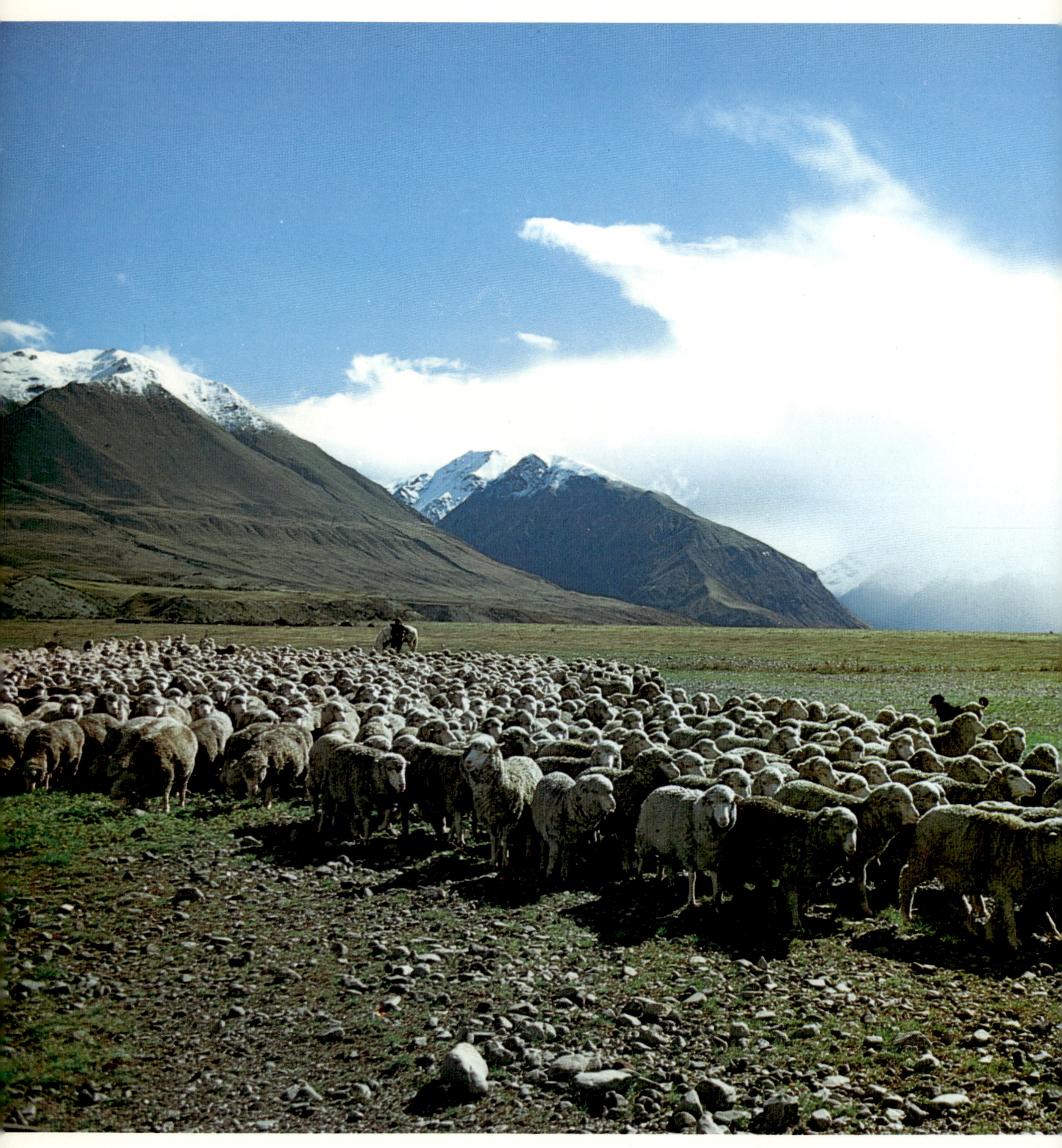

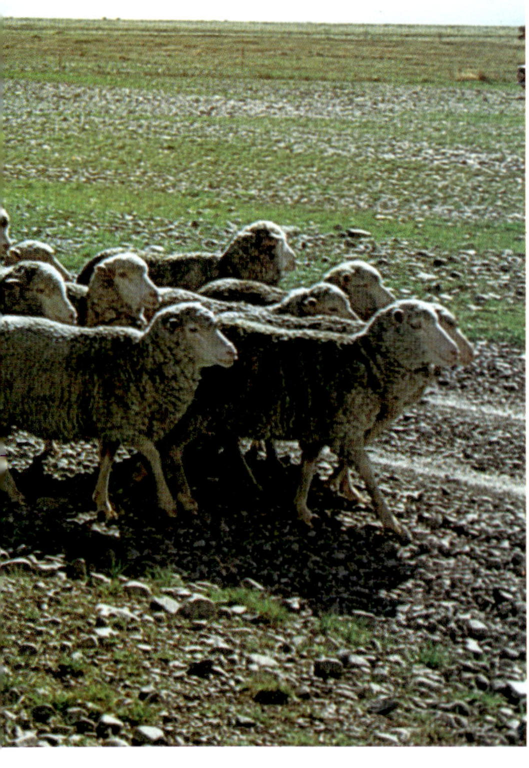

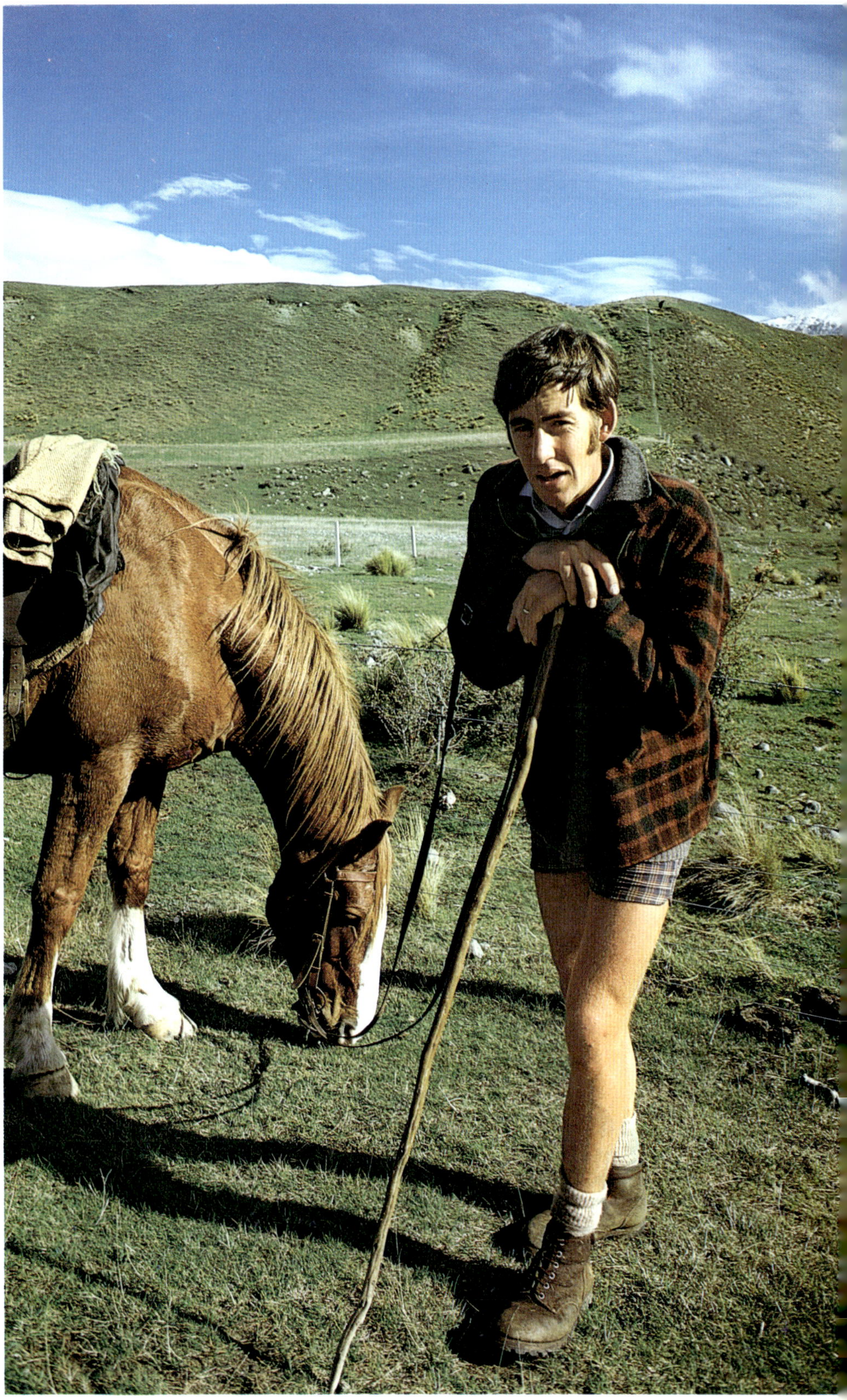

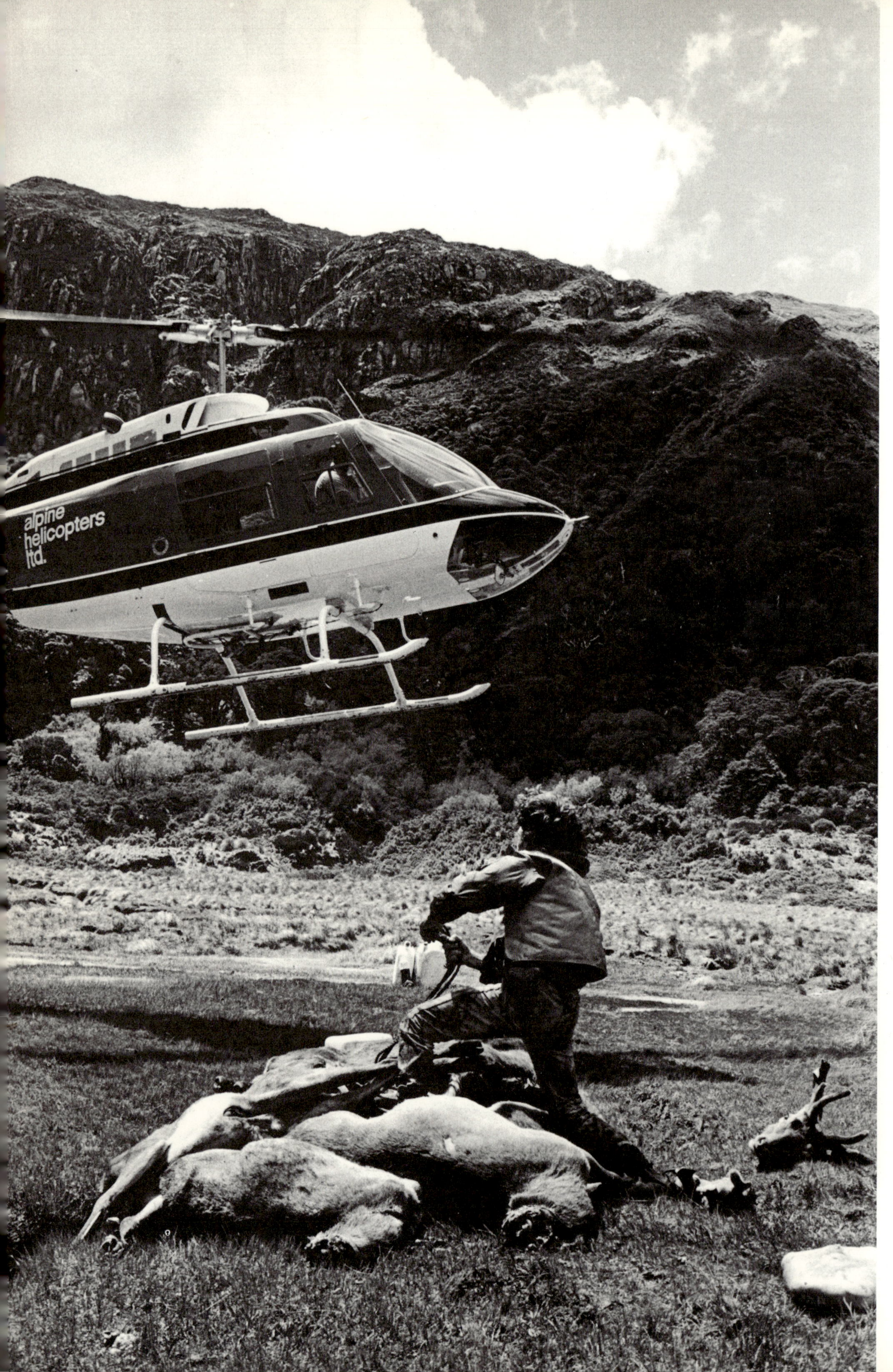

alpine
helicopters
ltd.

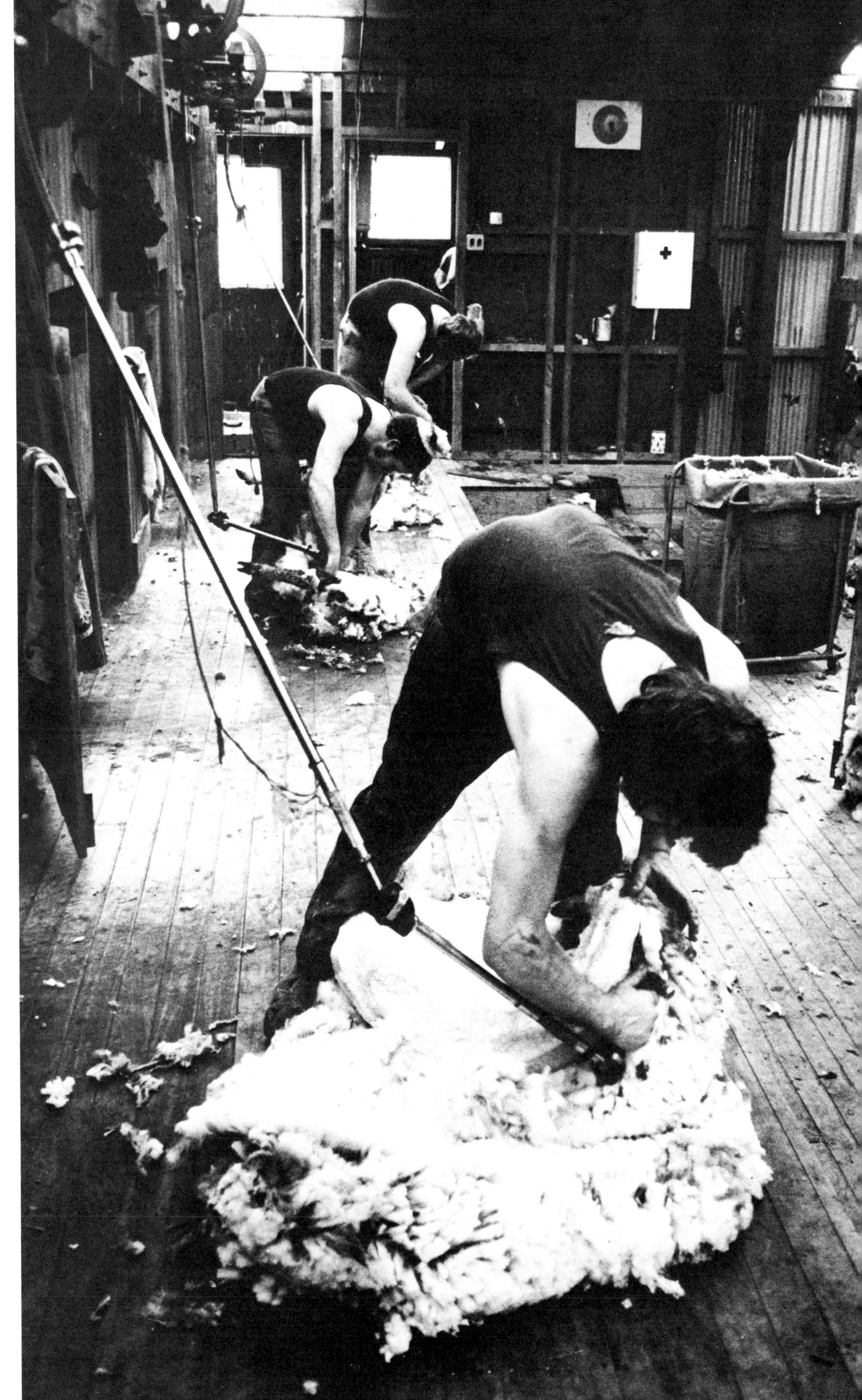

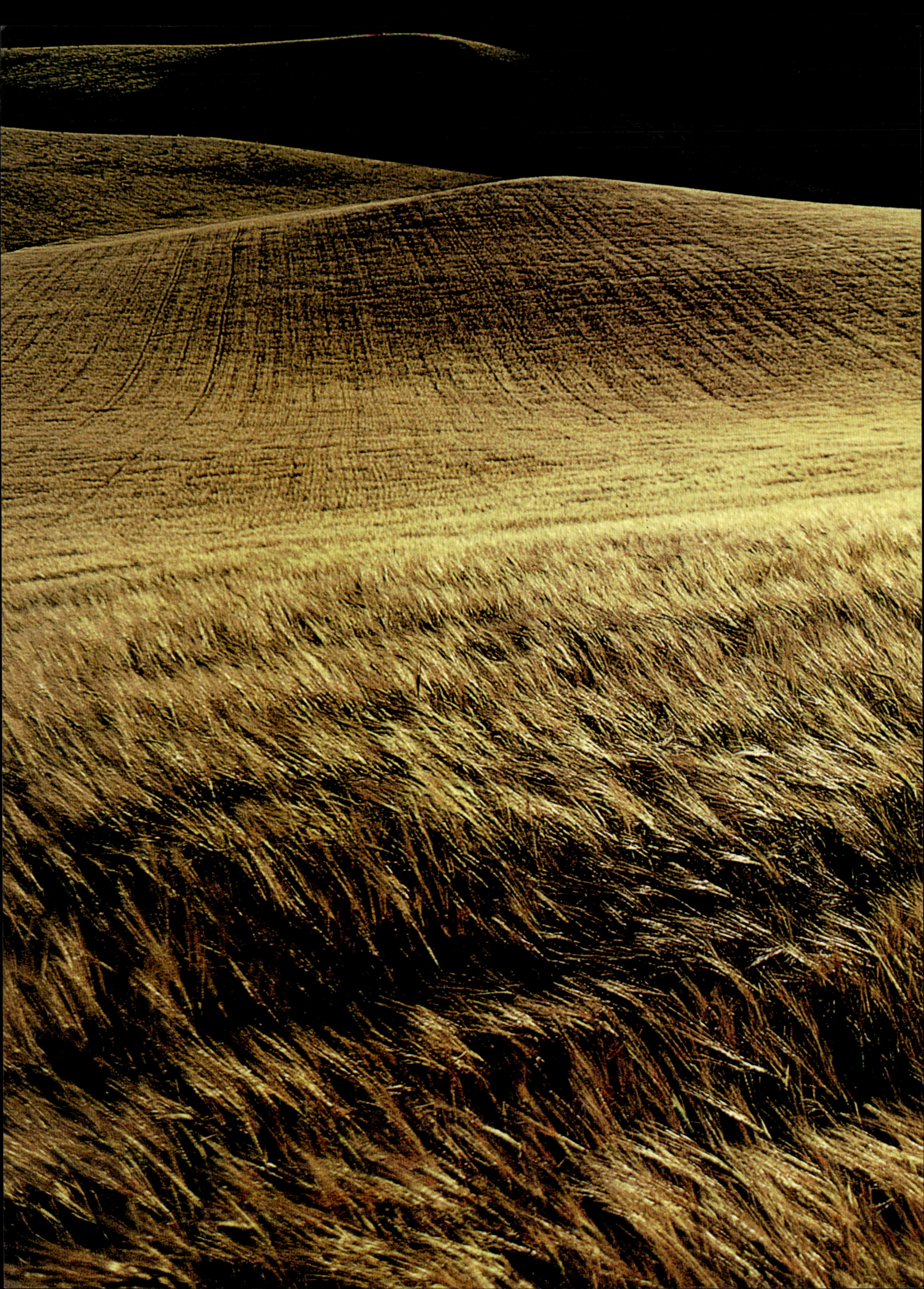

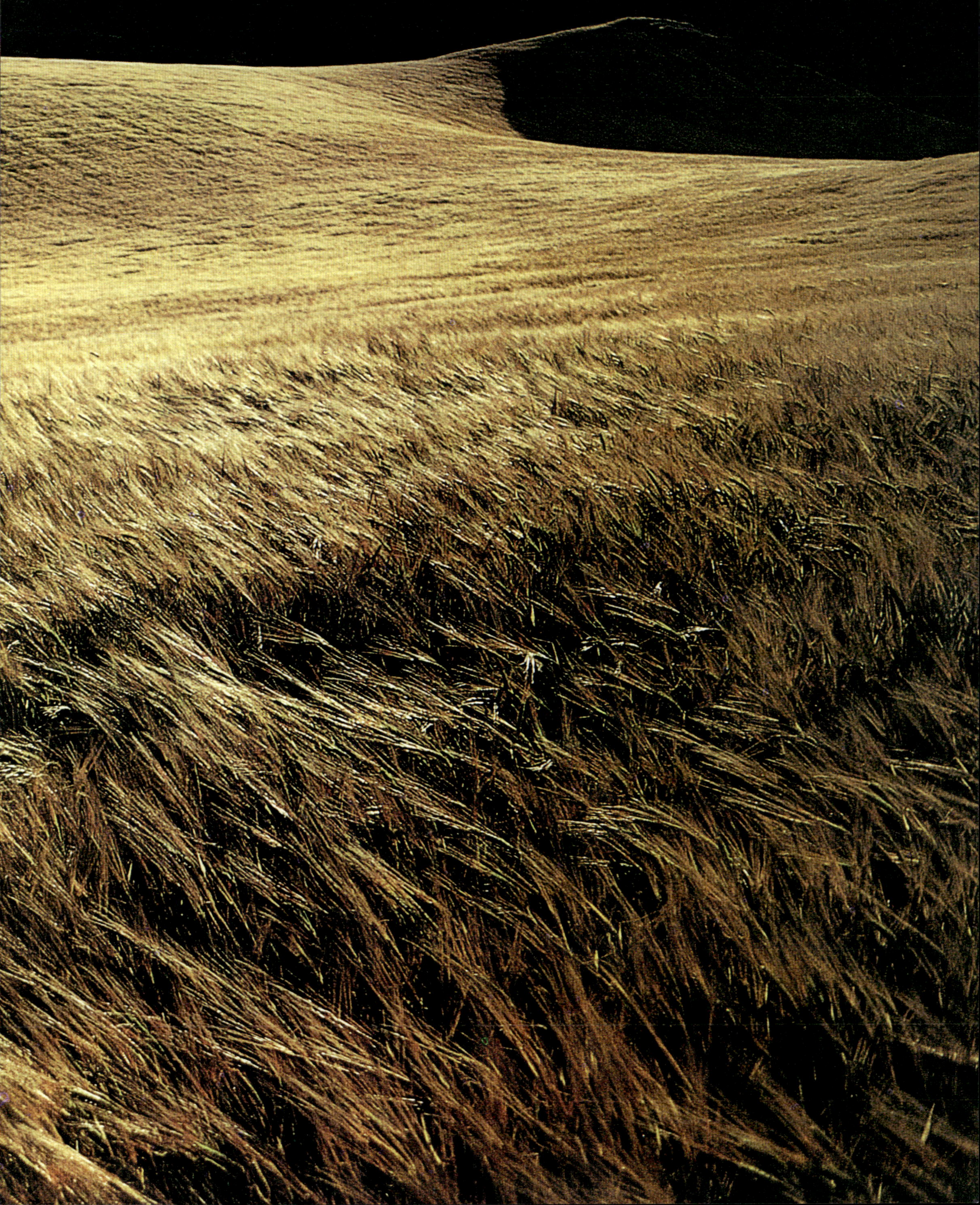

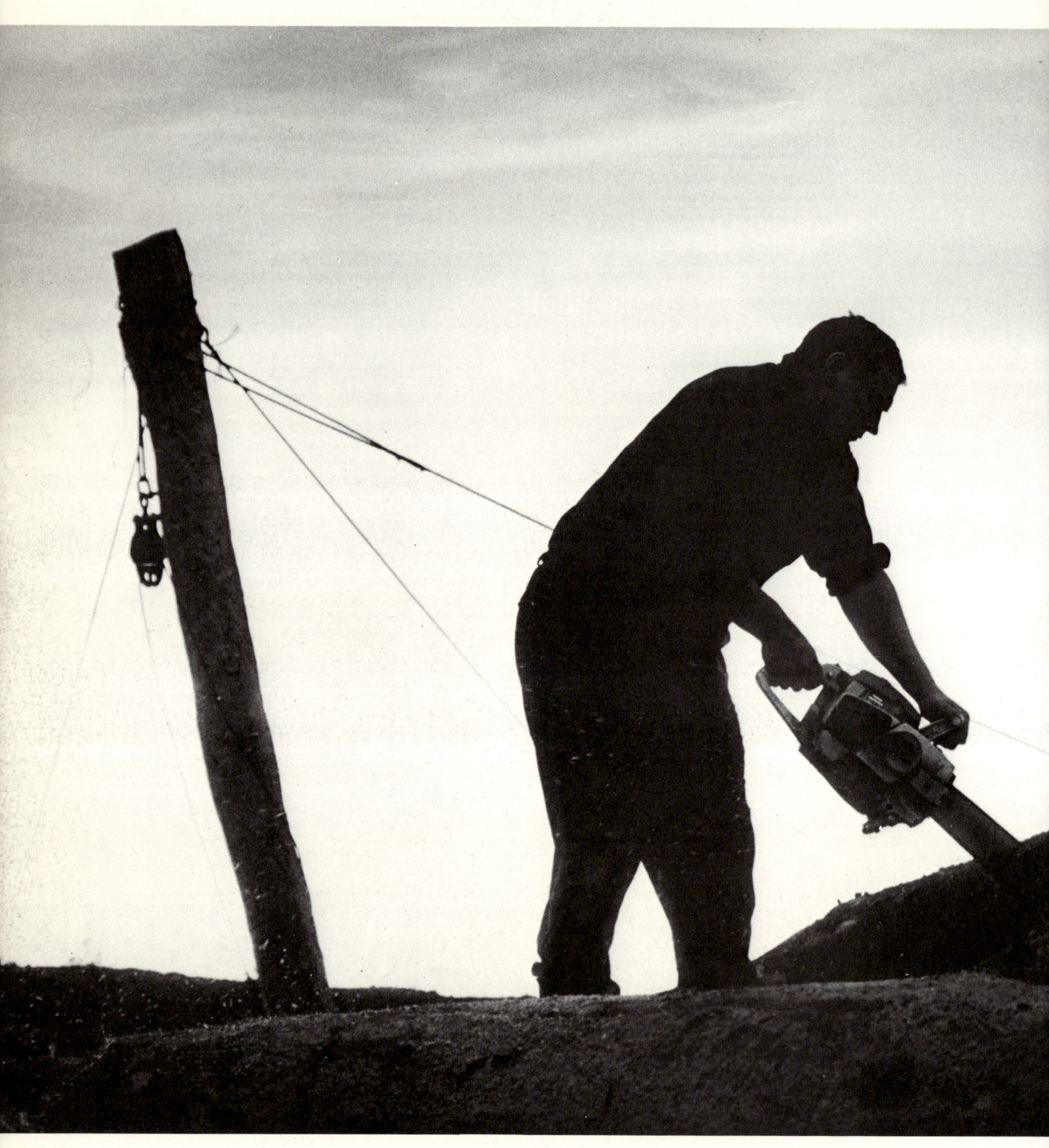

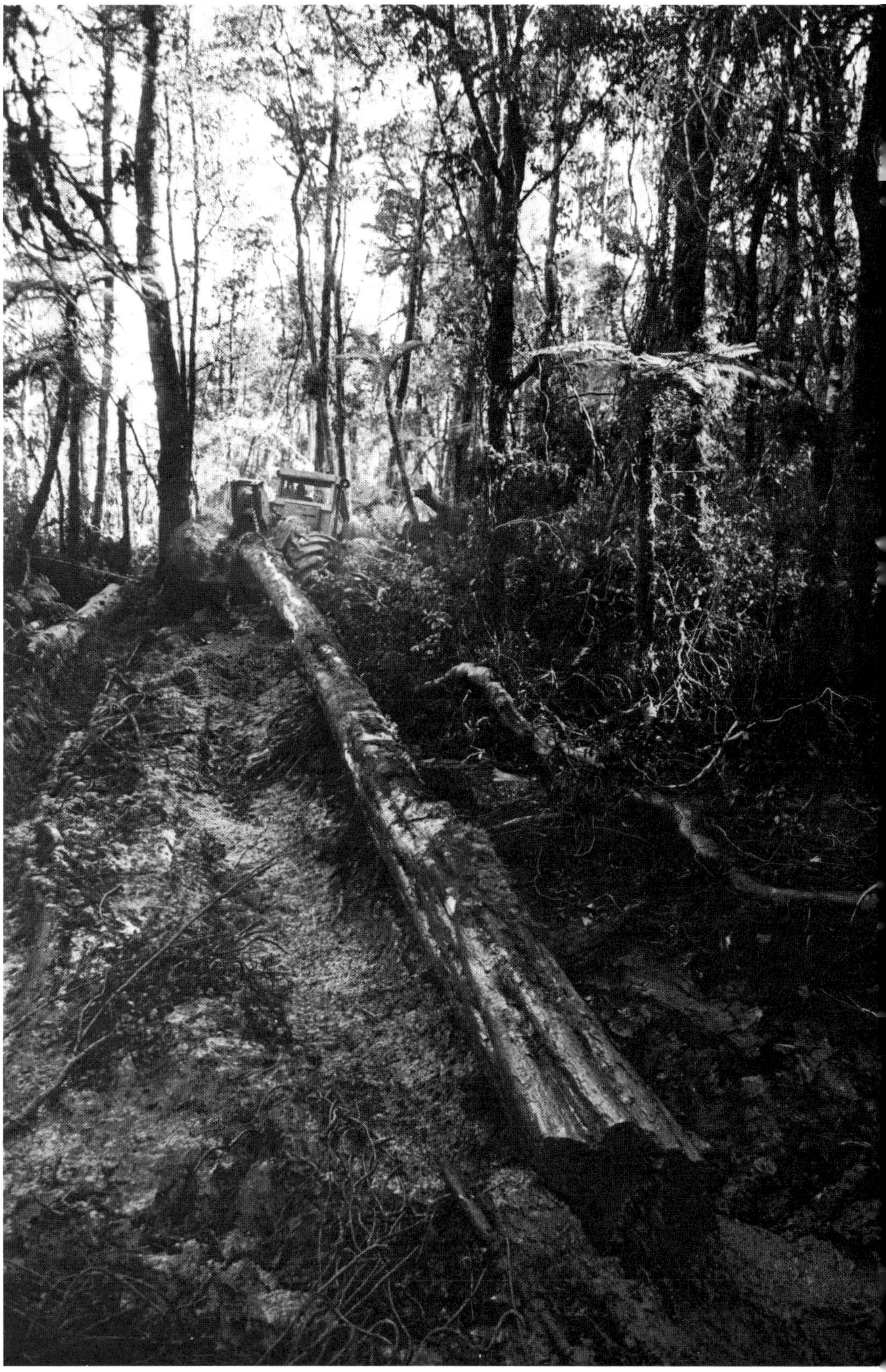

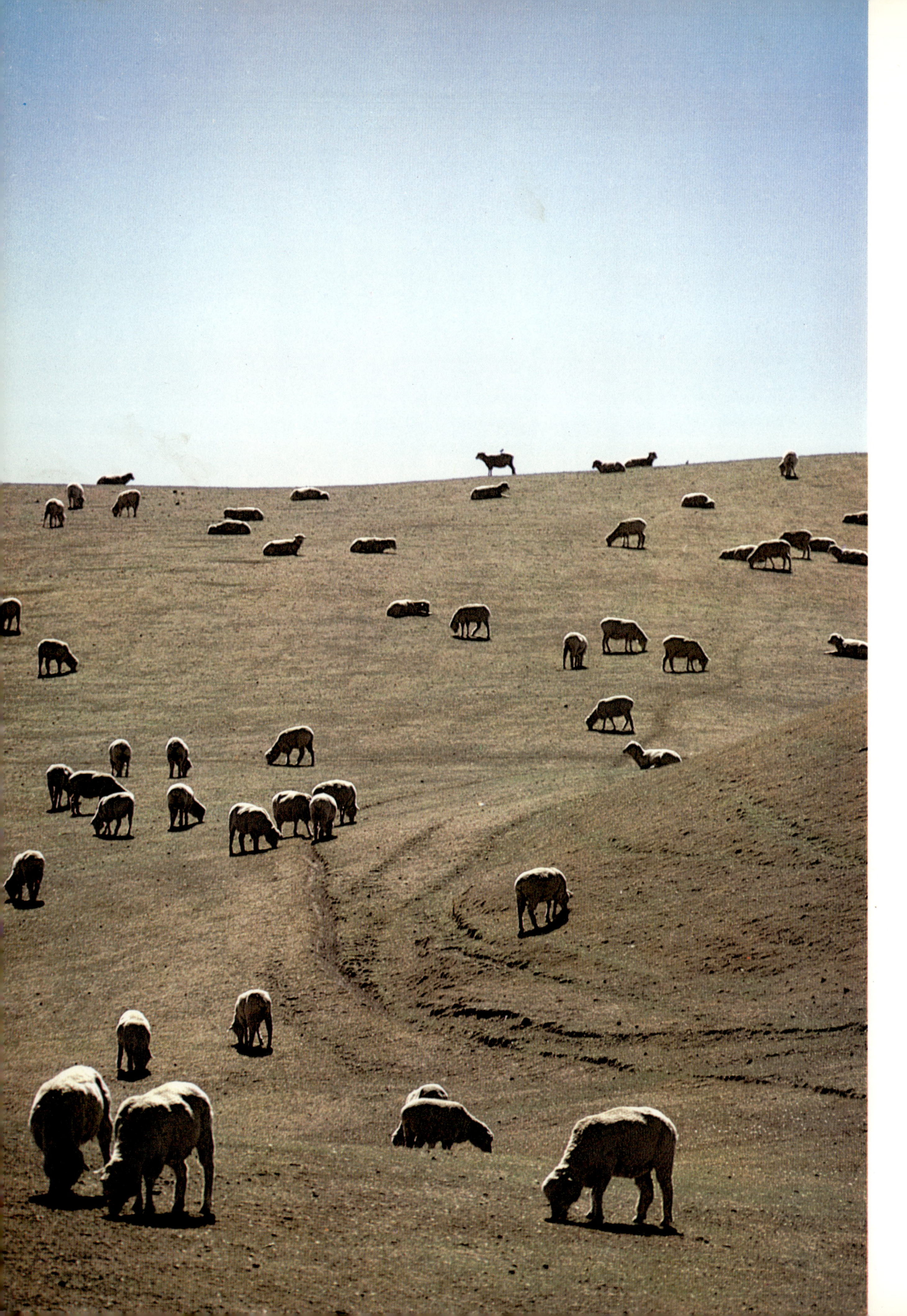

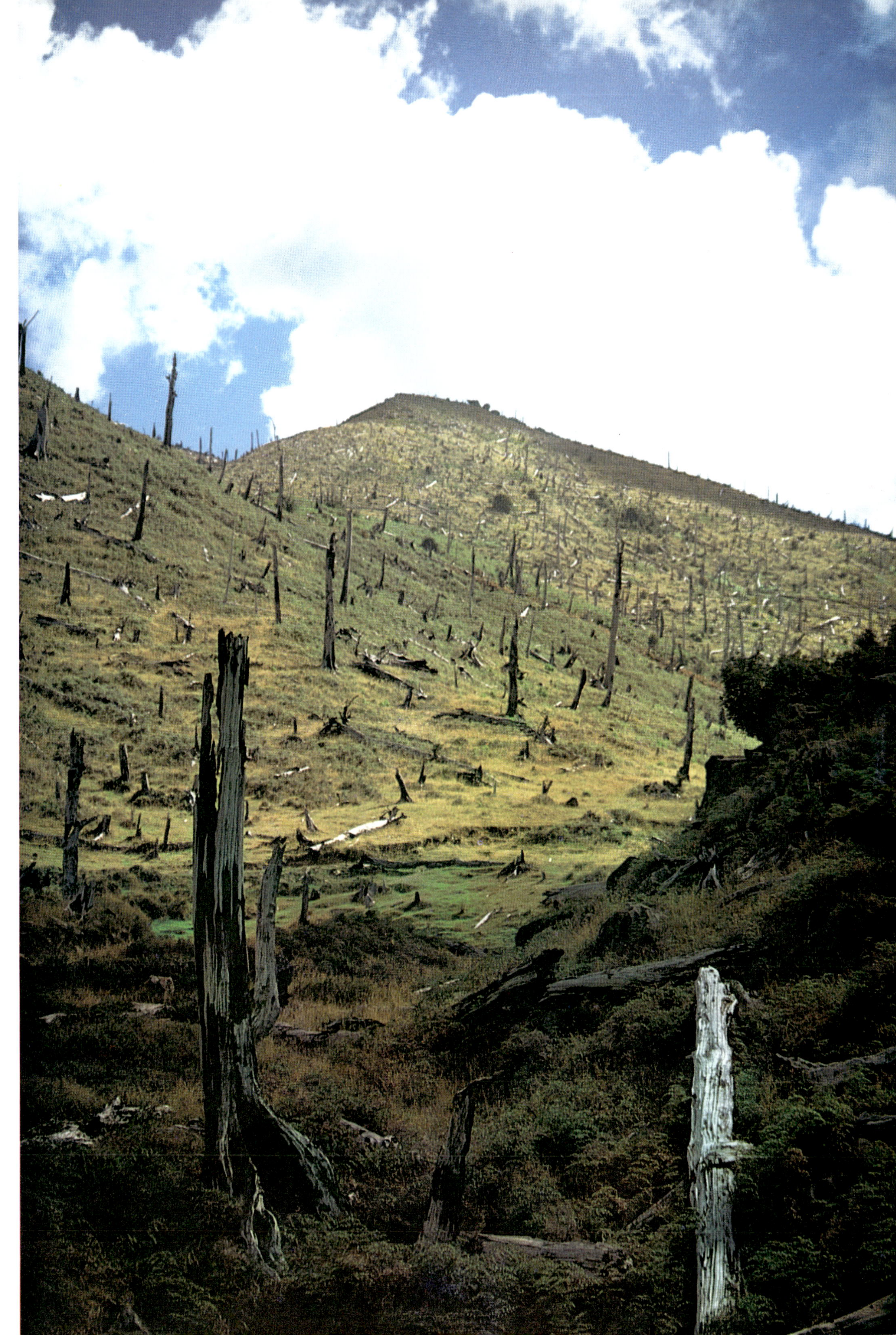

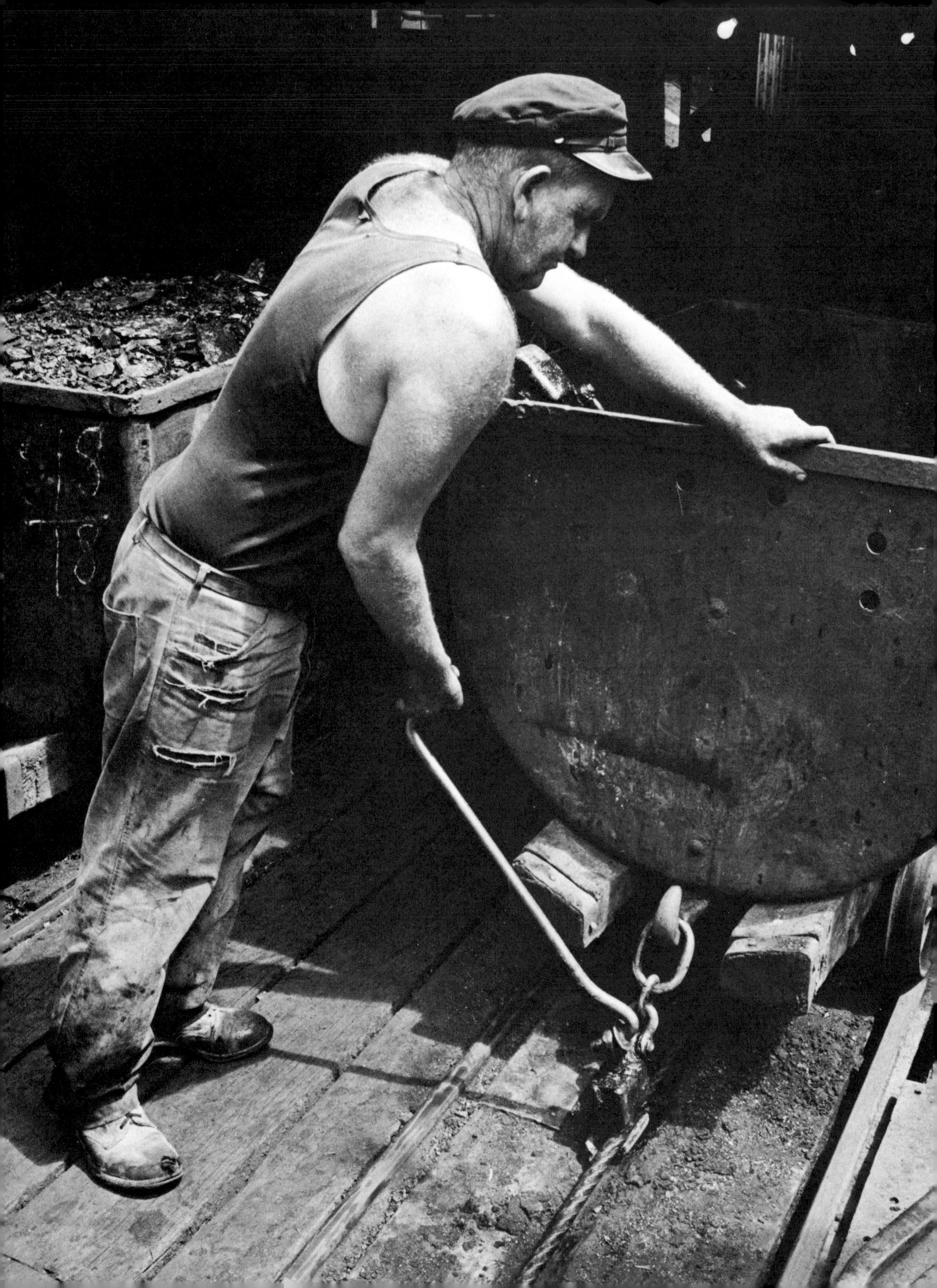

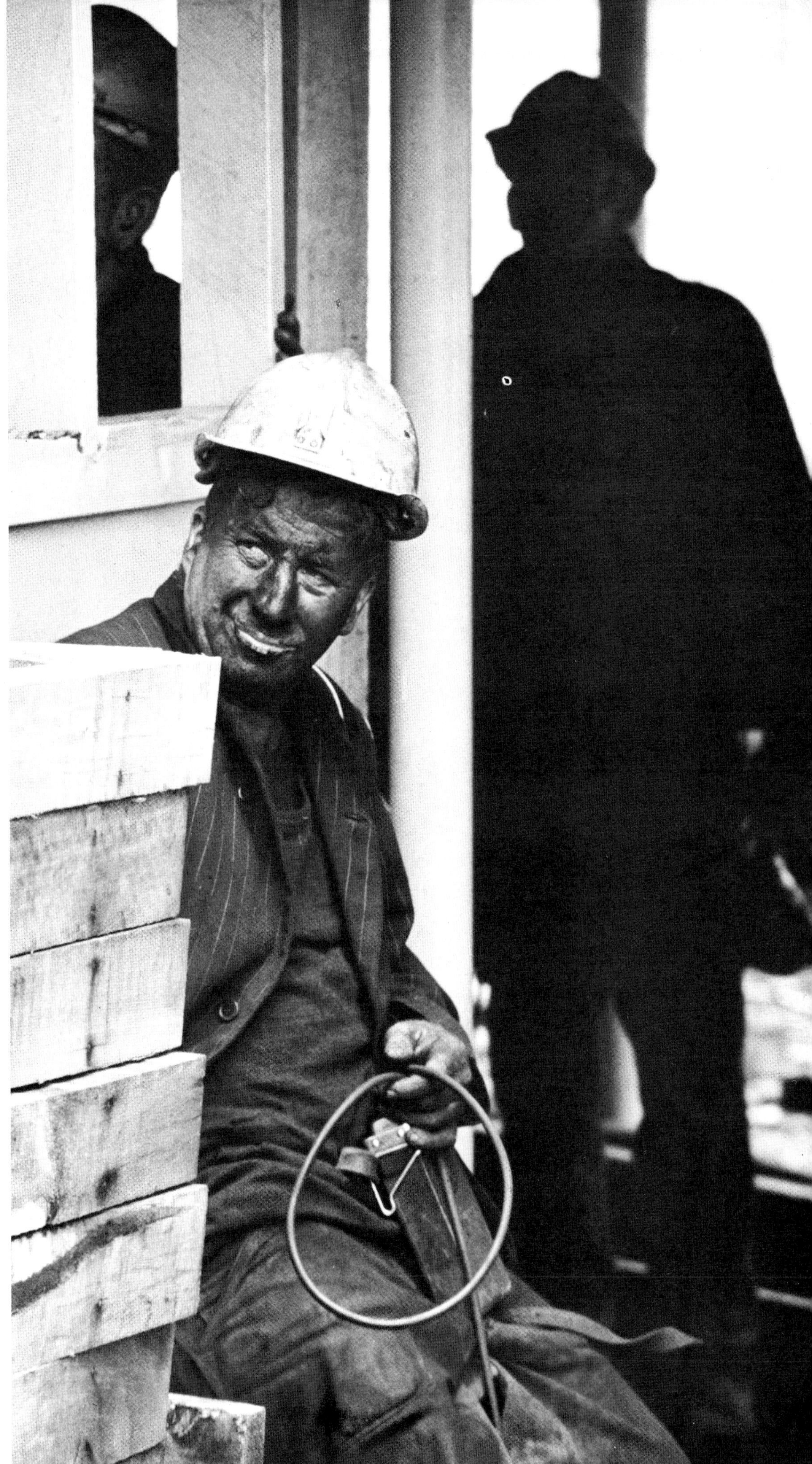

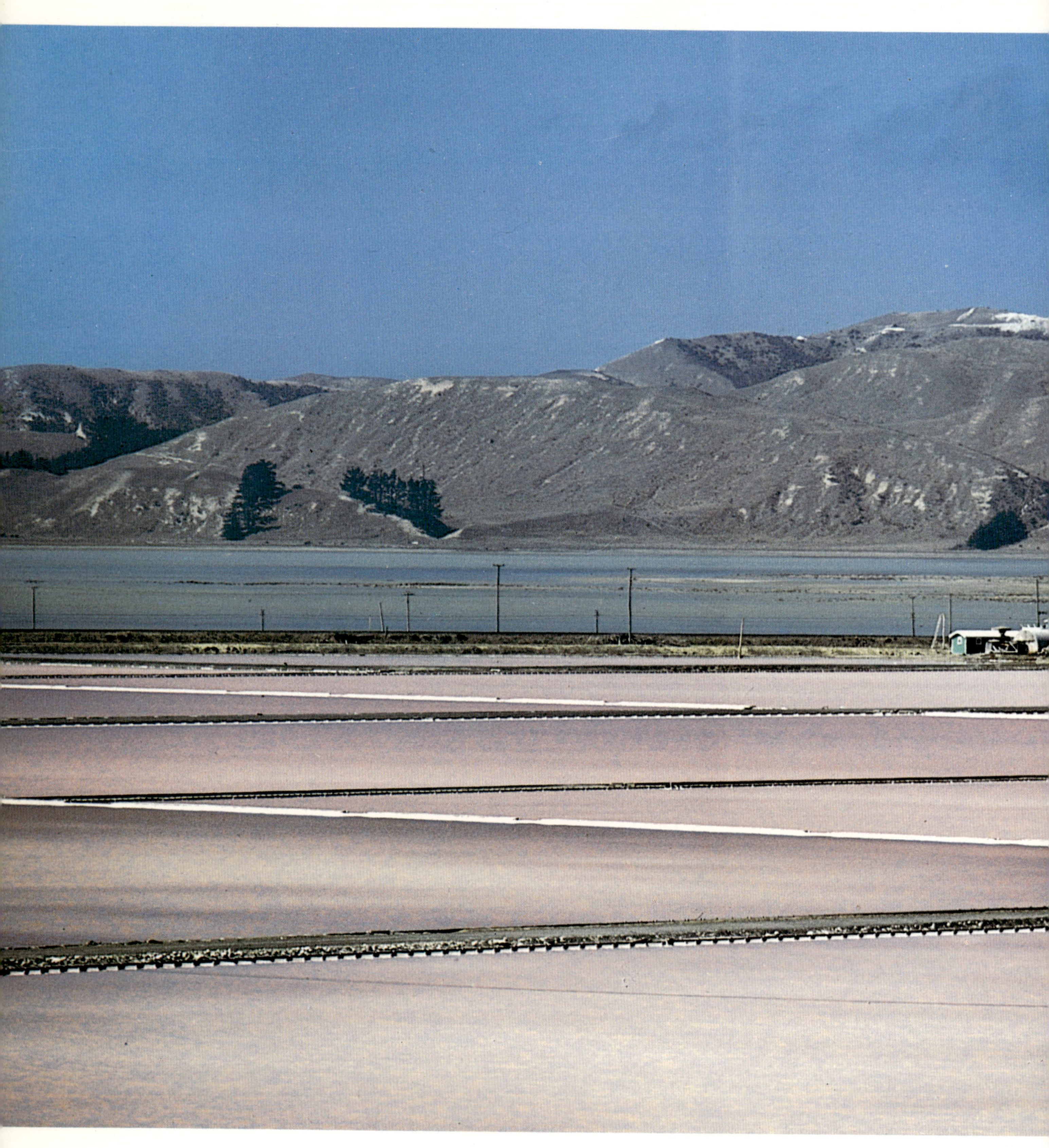

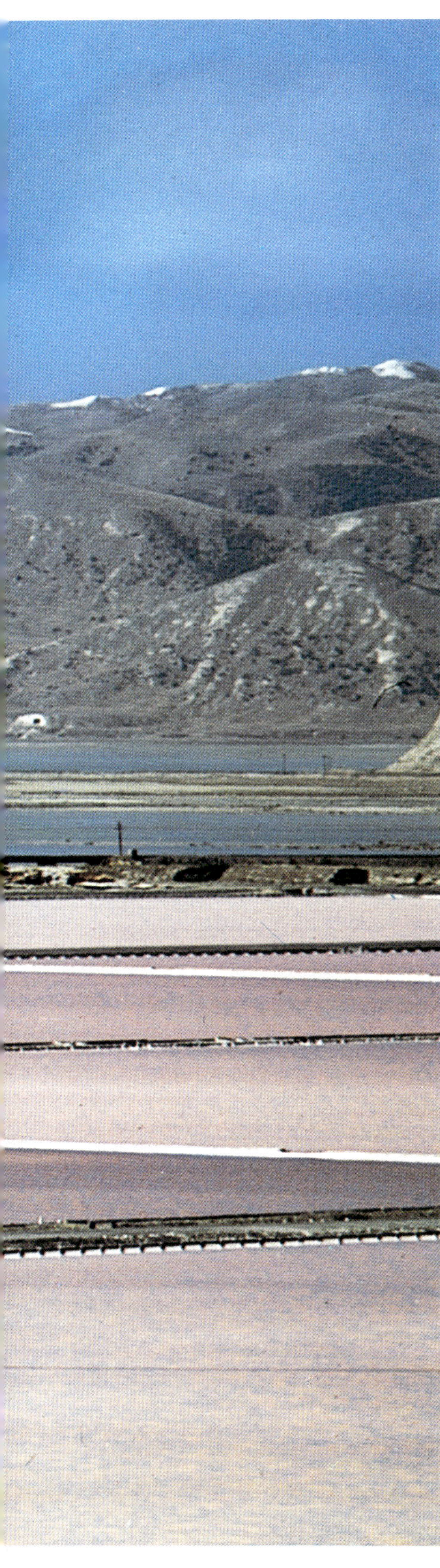

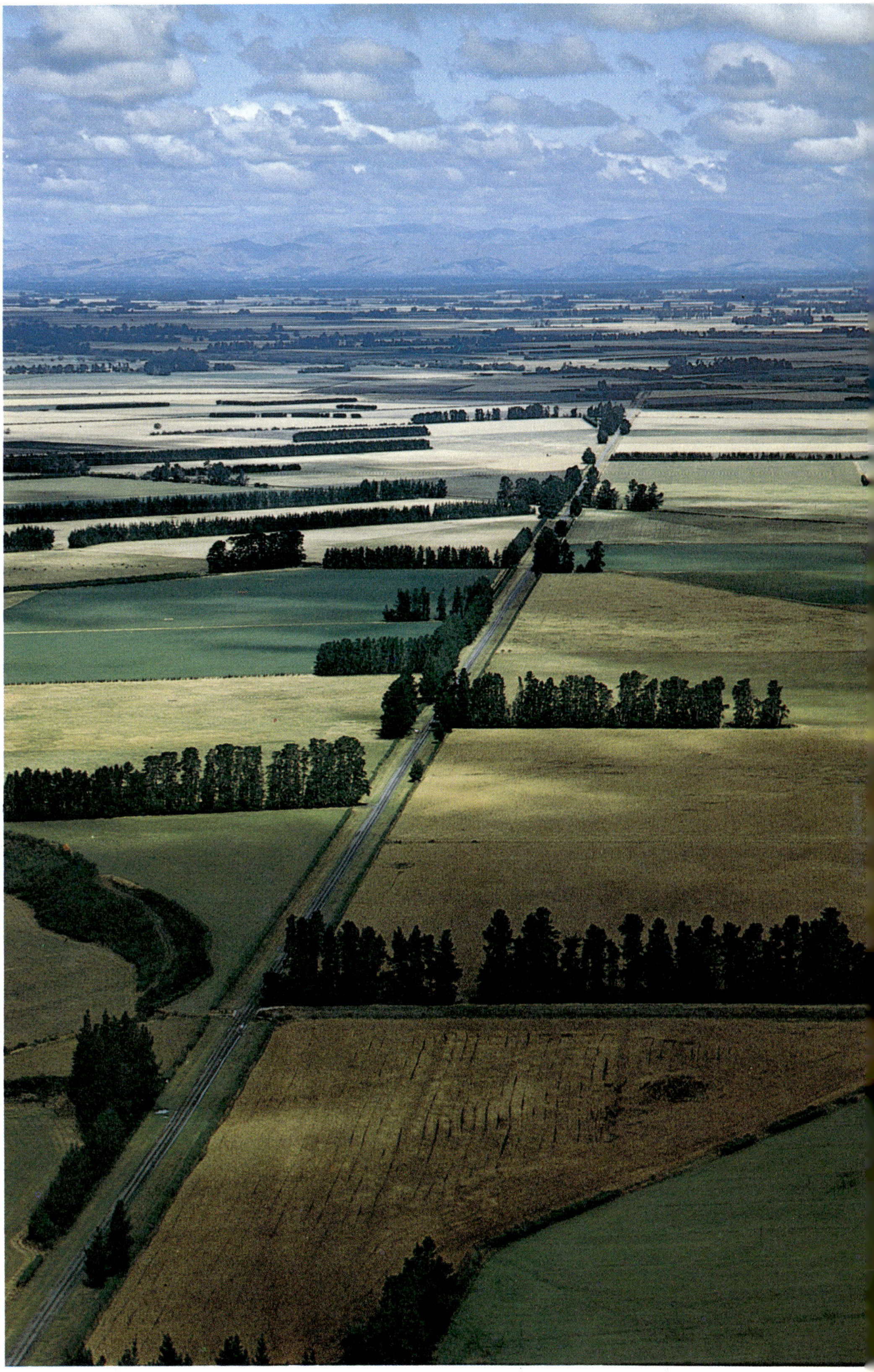

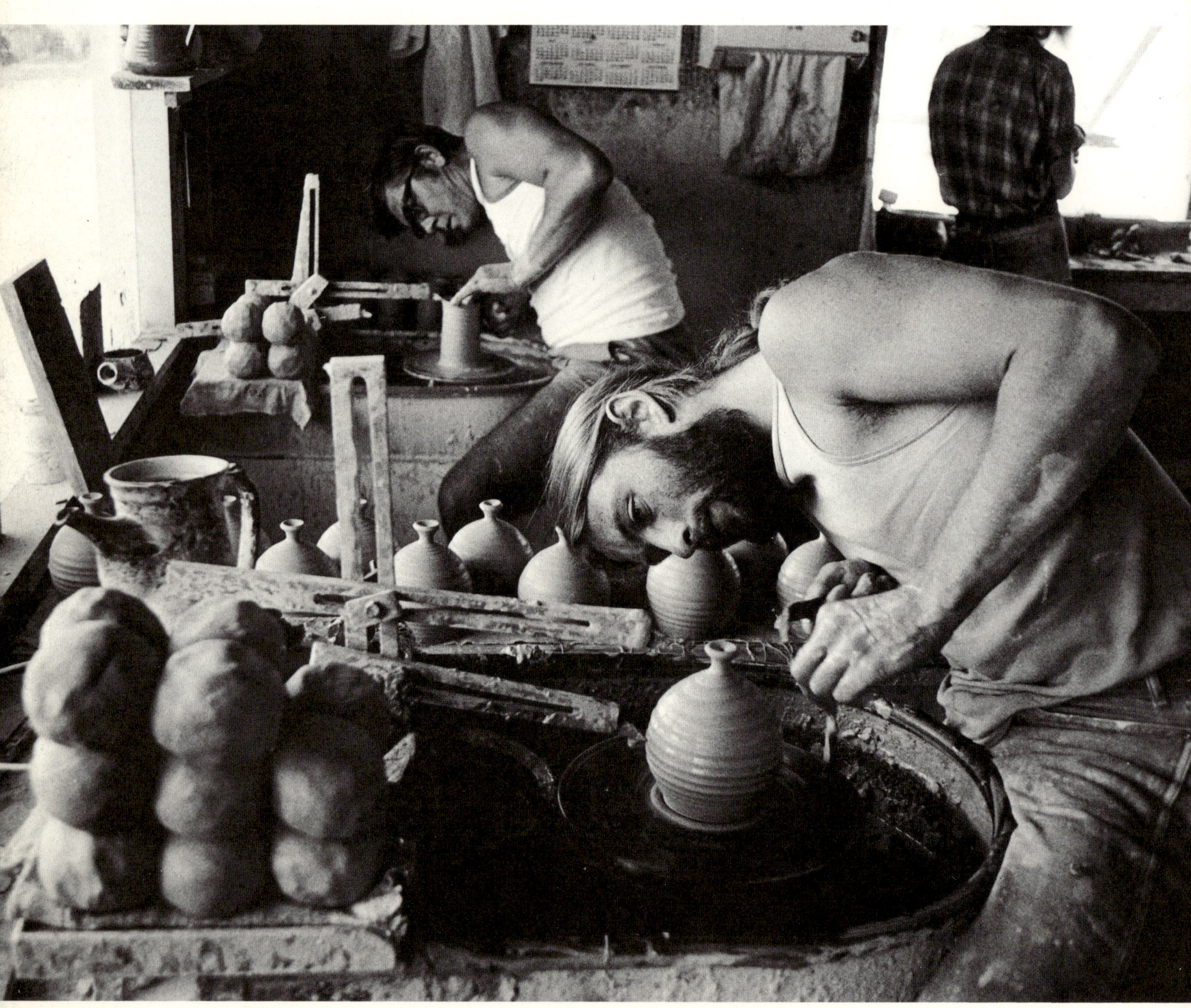

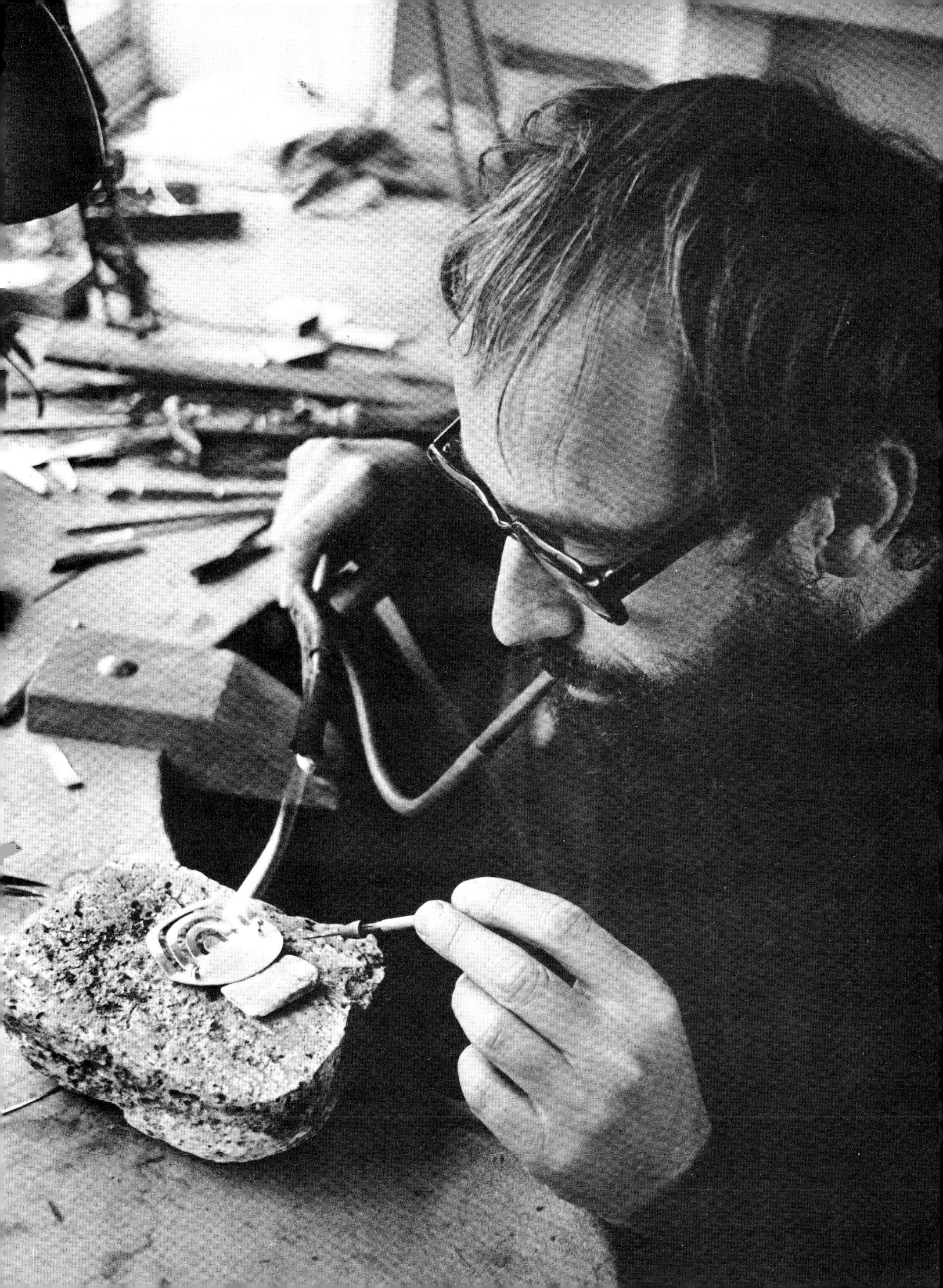

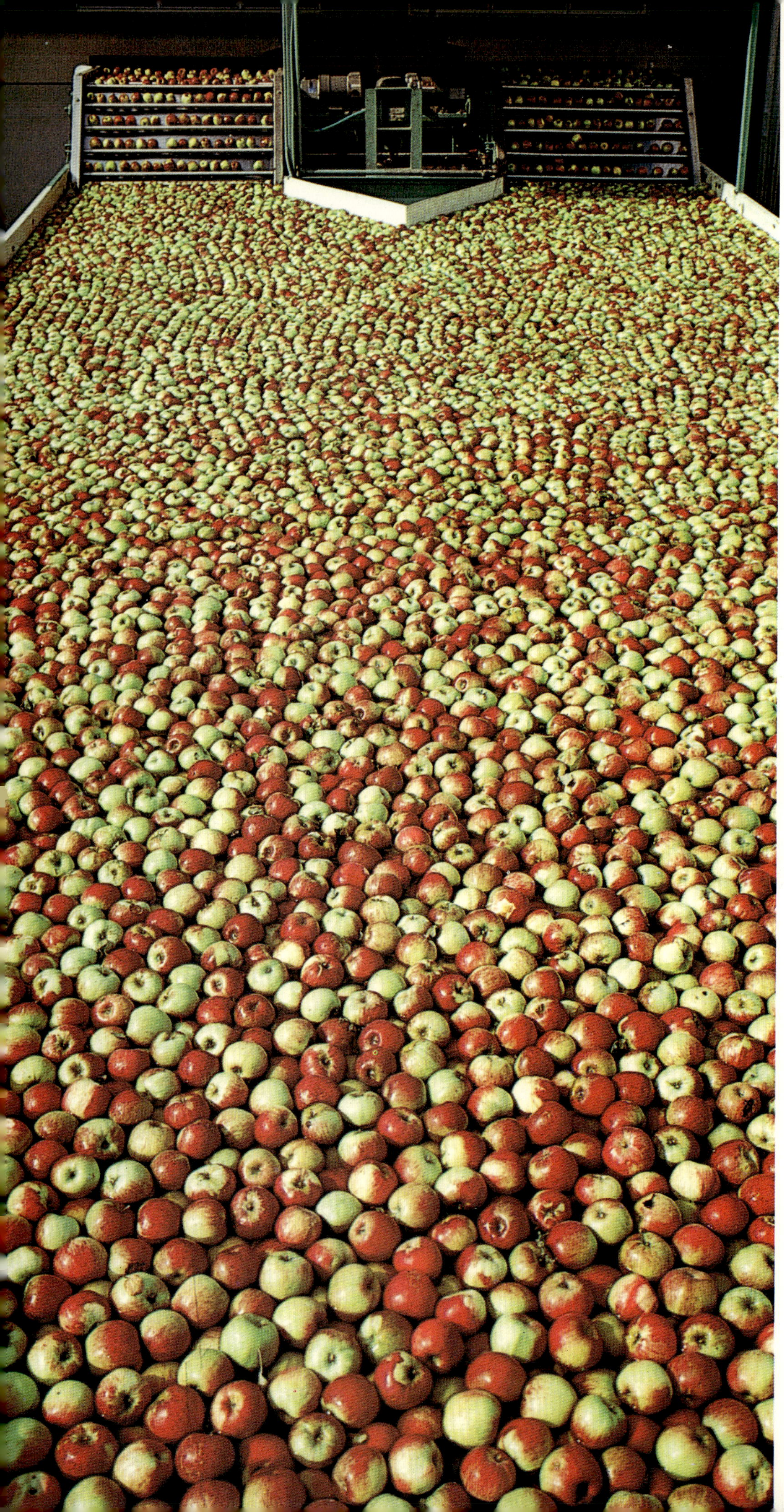

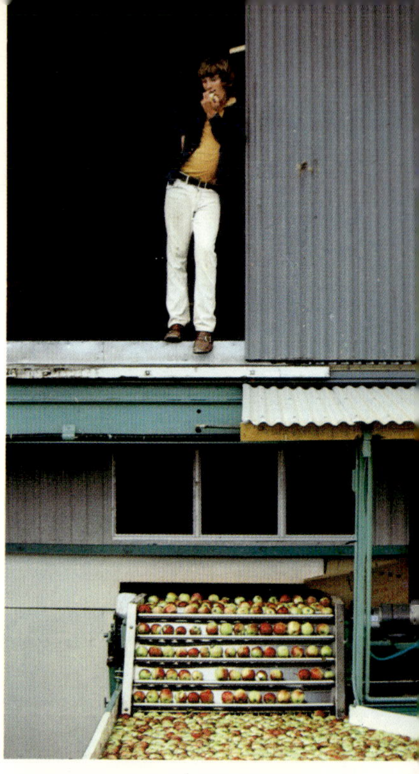

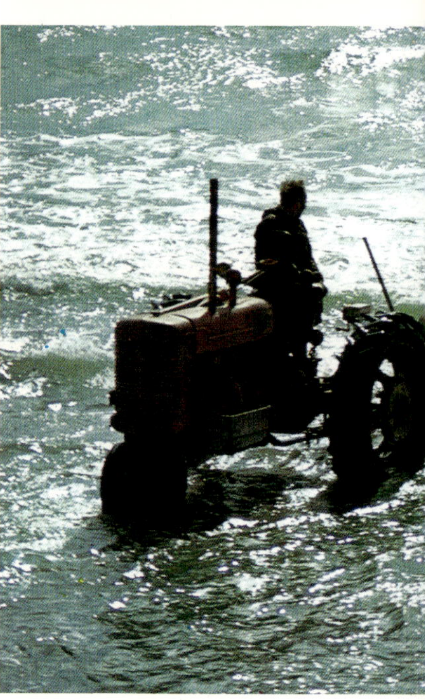

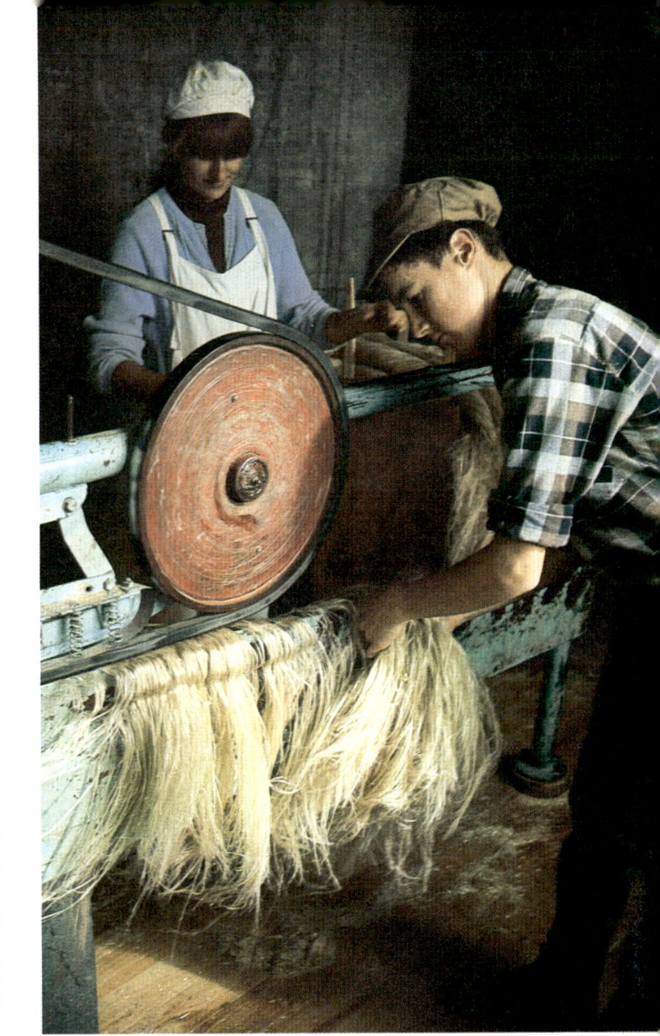
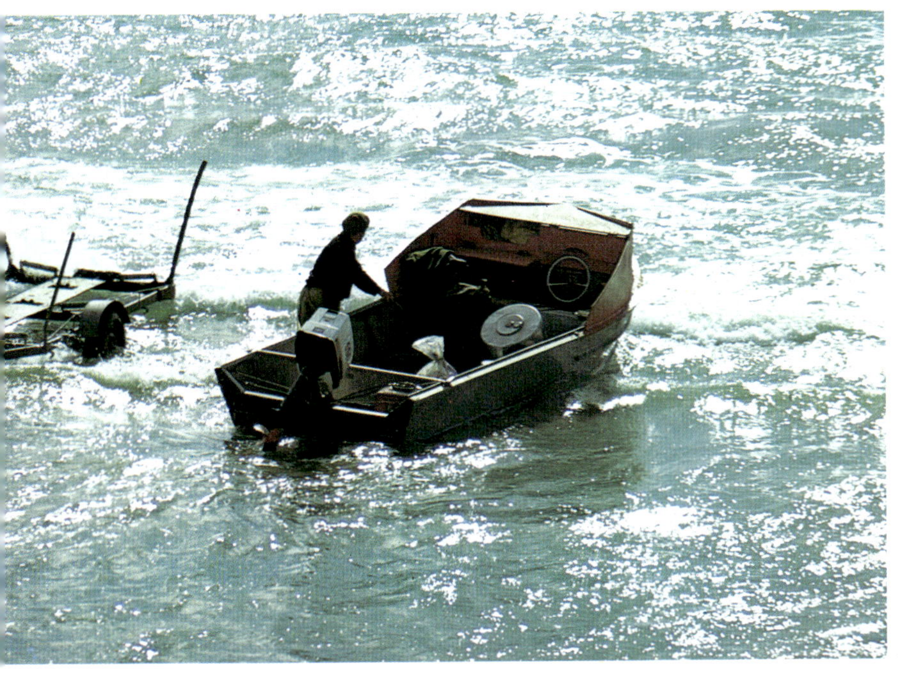
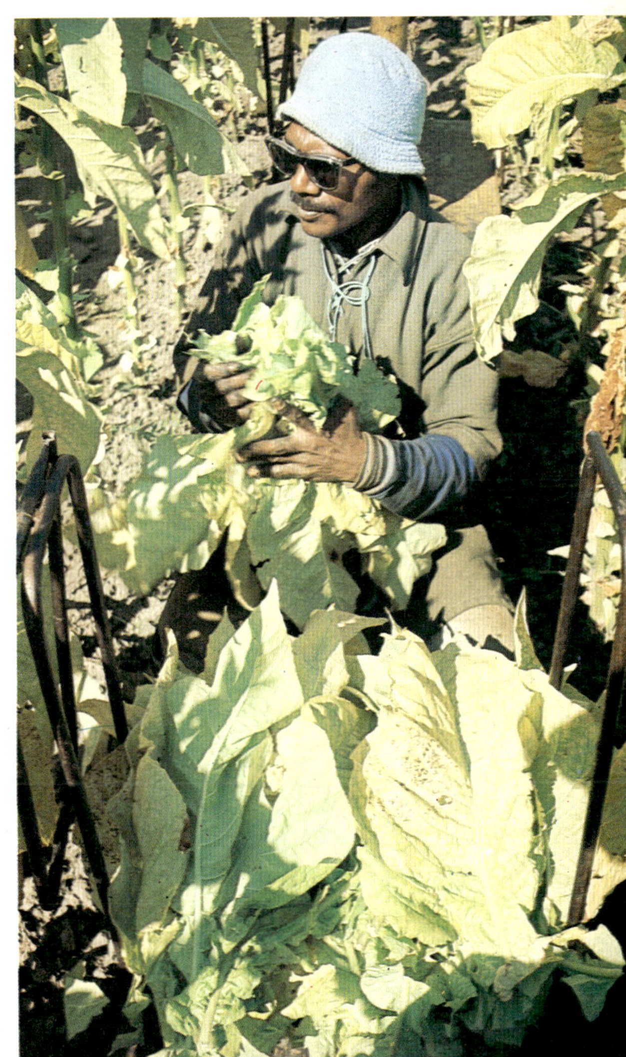
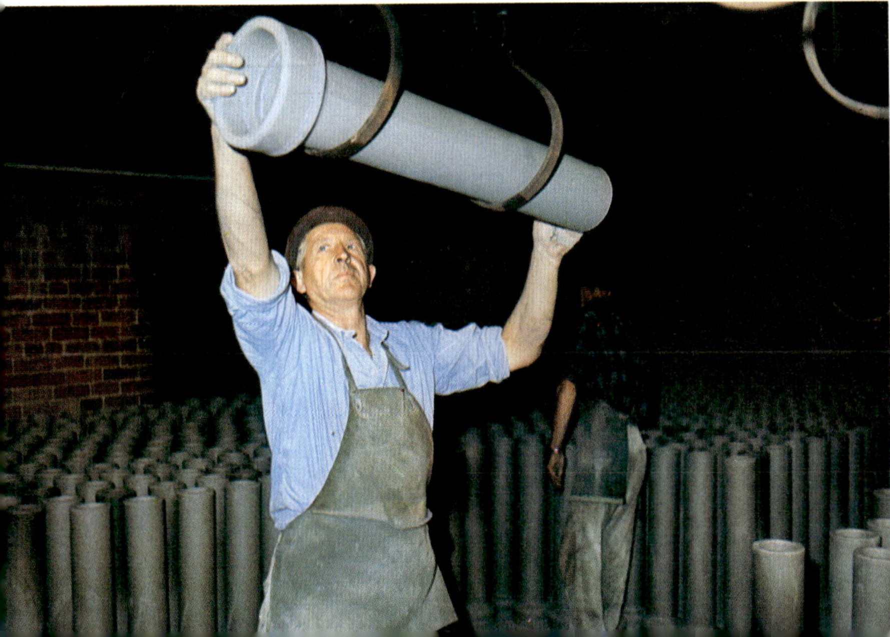

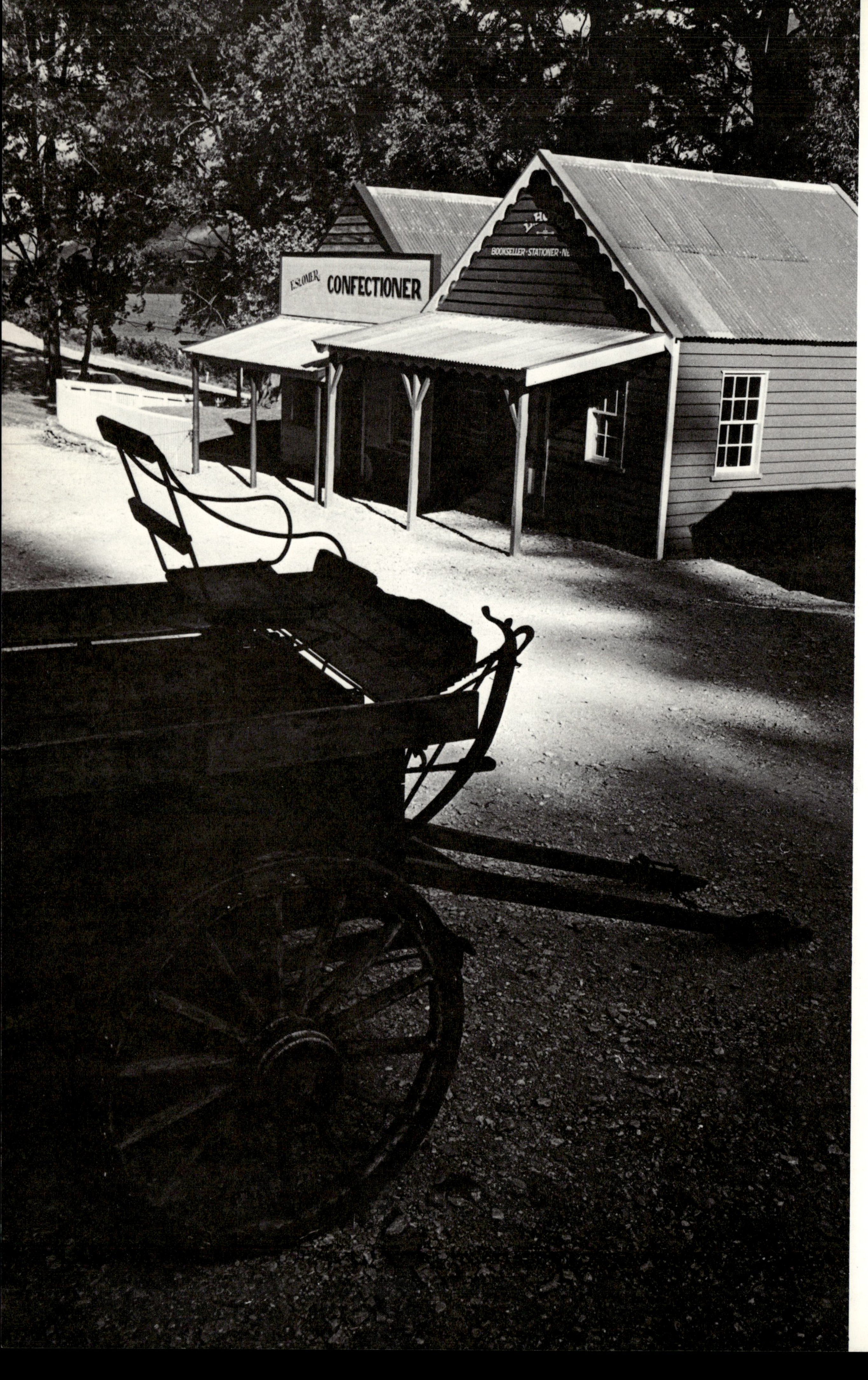
E.St.OMER CONFECTIONER
BOOKSELLER · STATIONER · NE

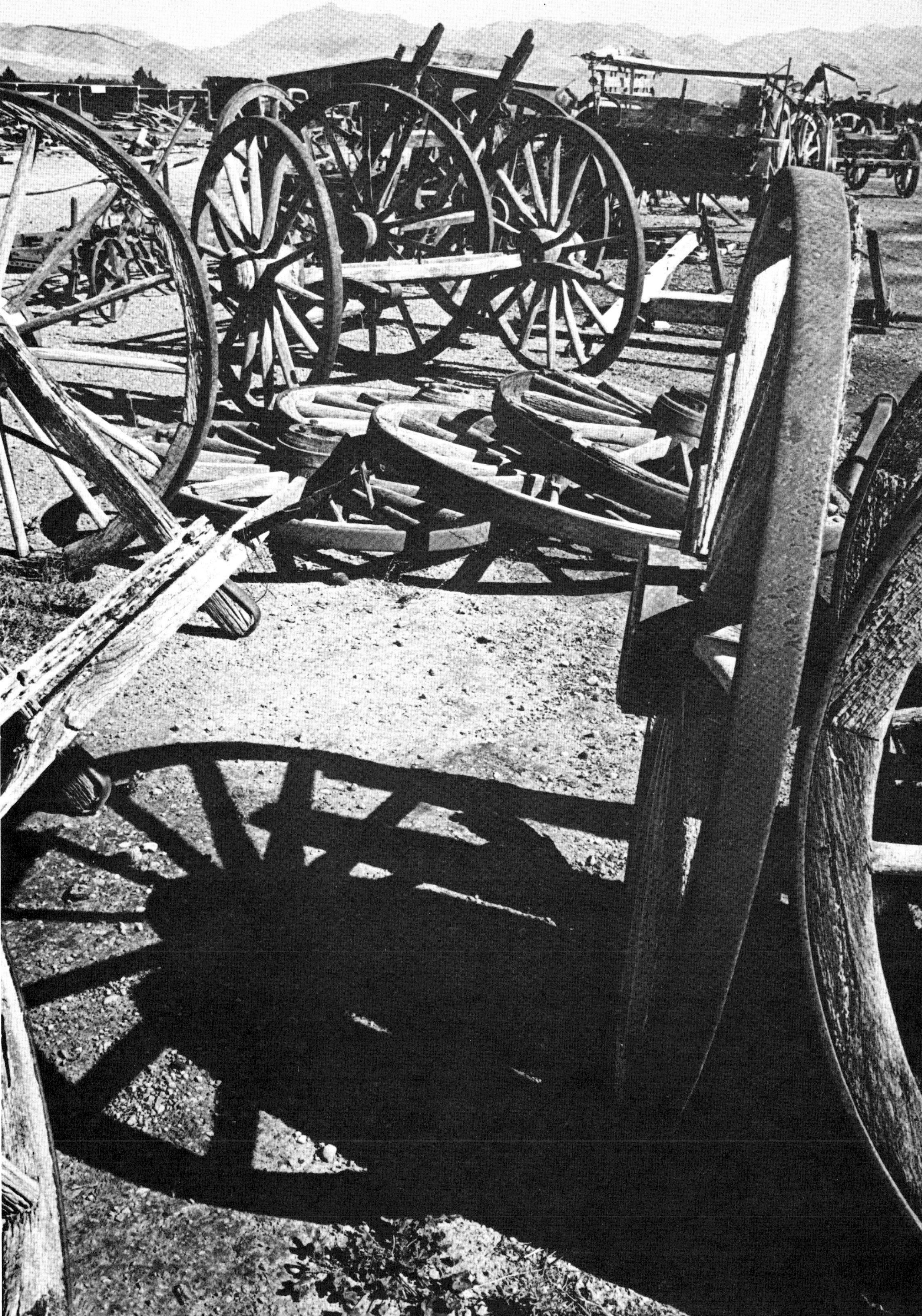

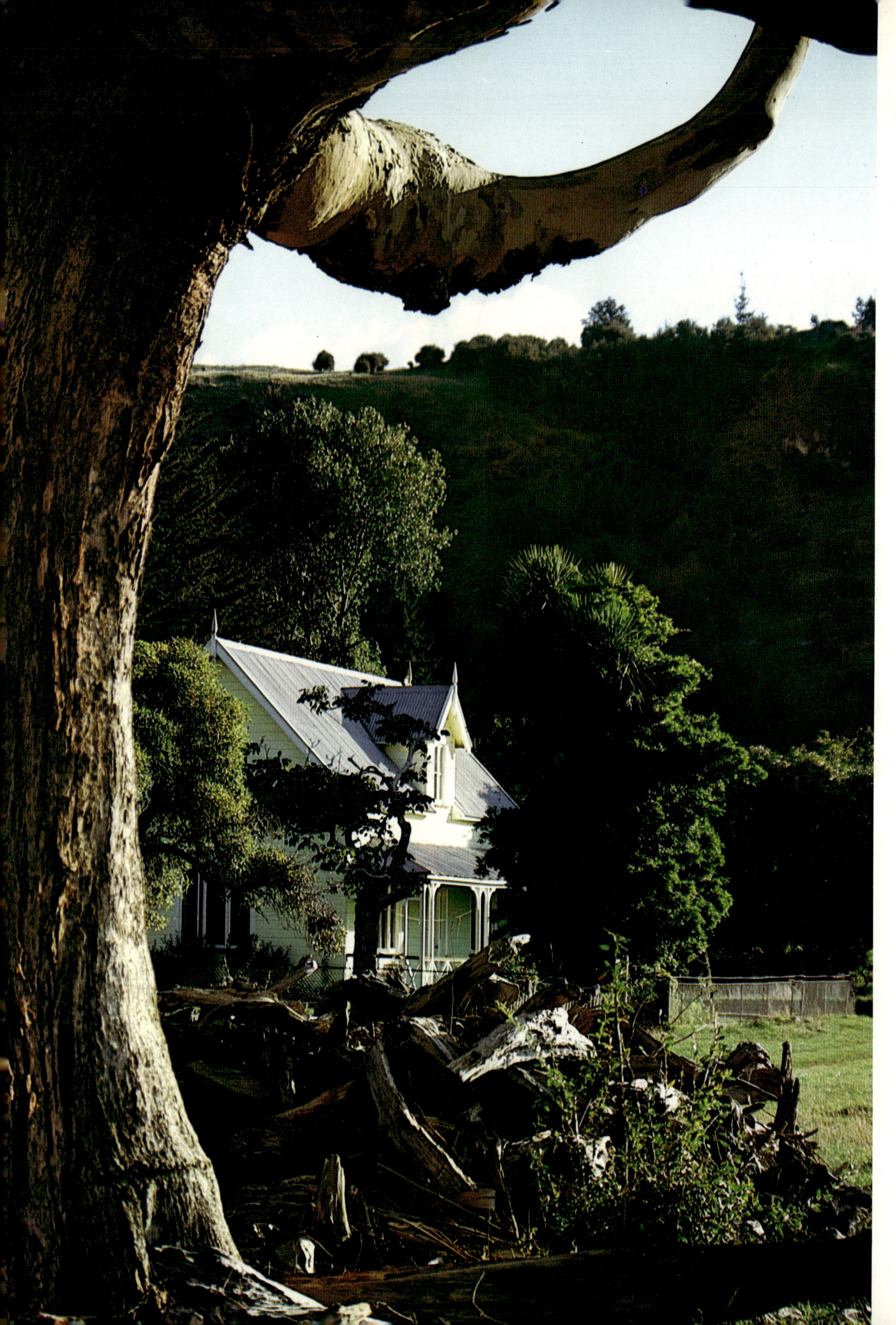

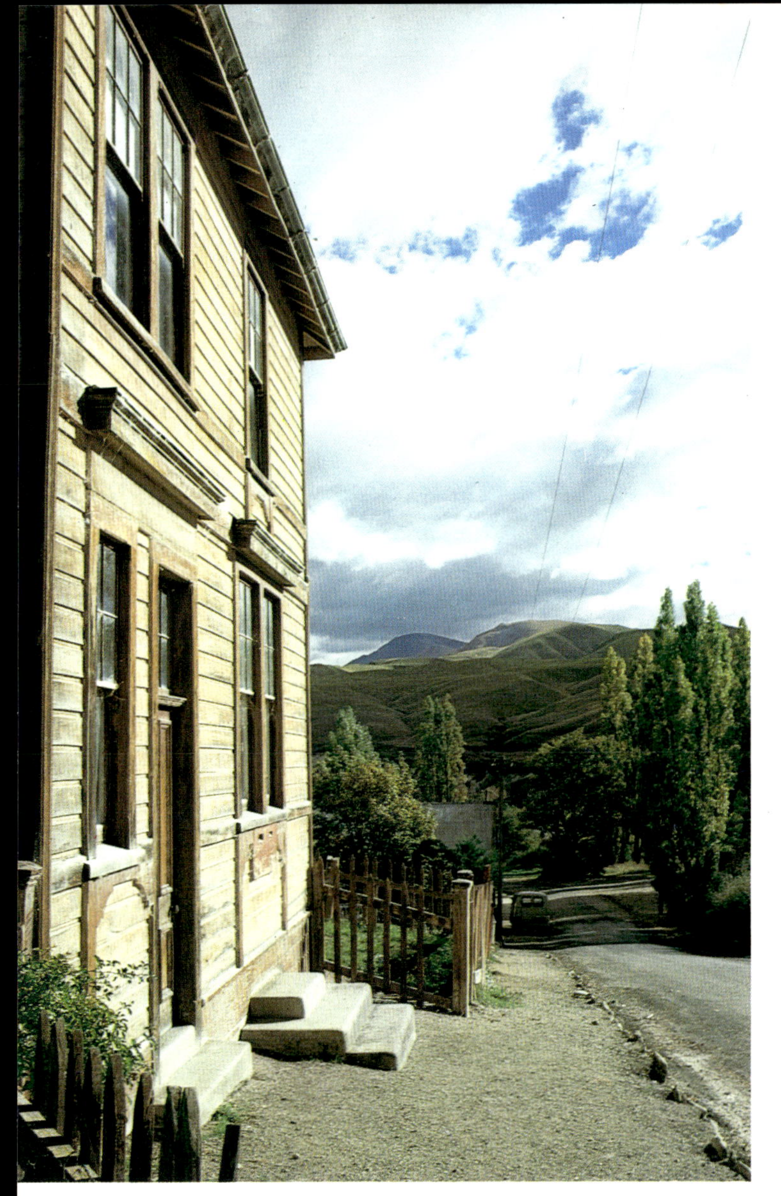
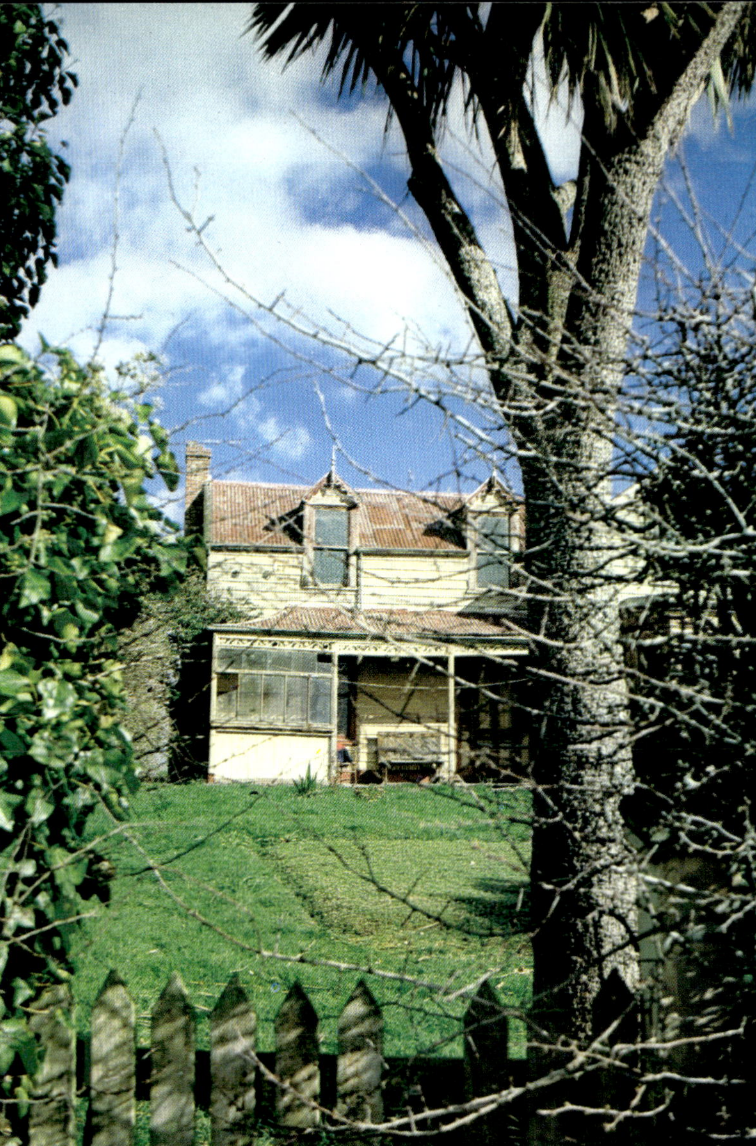

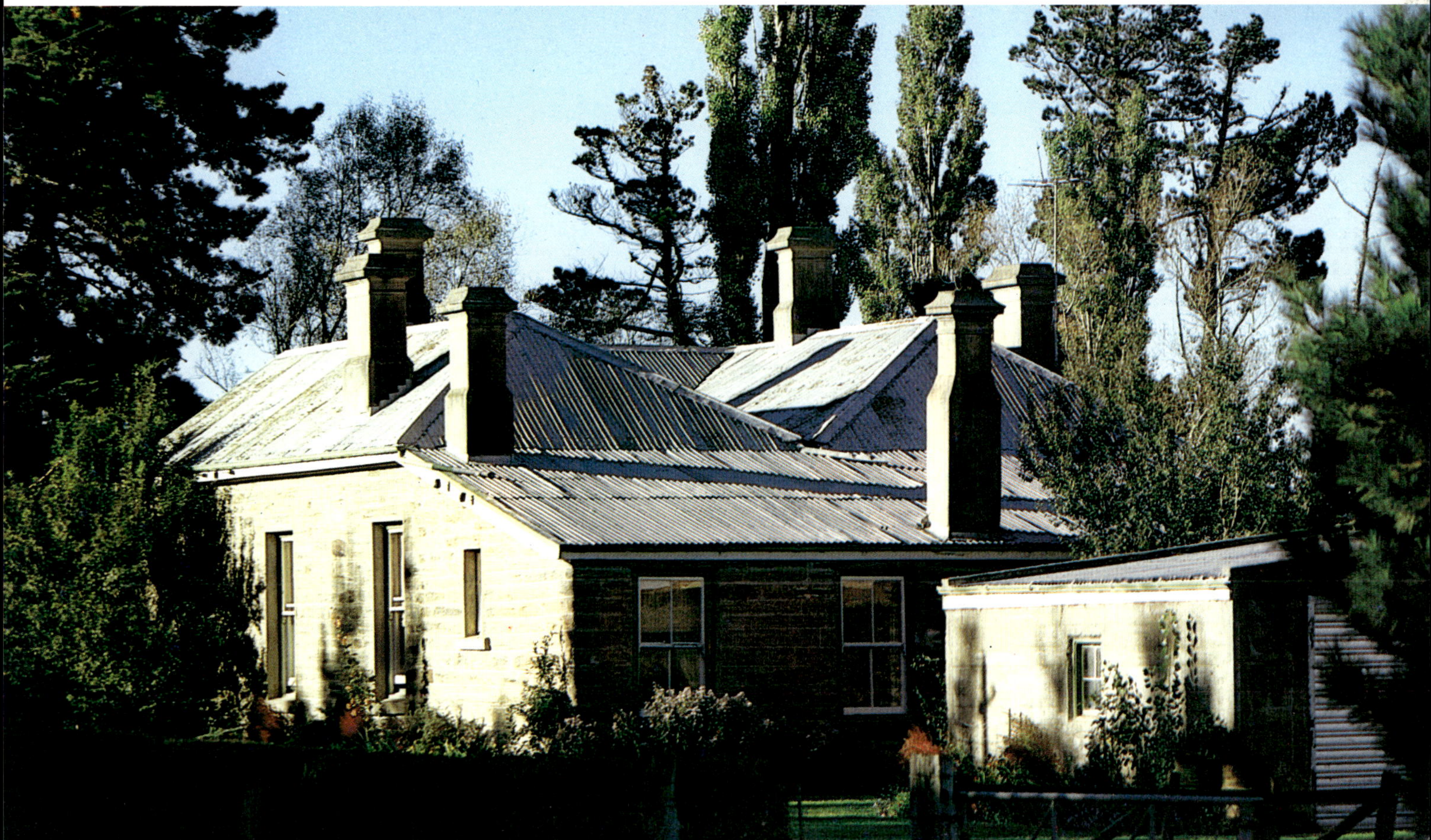

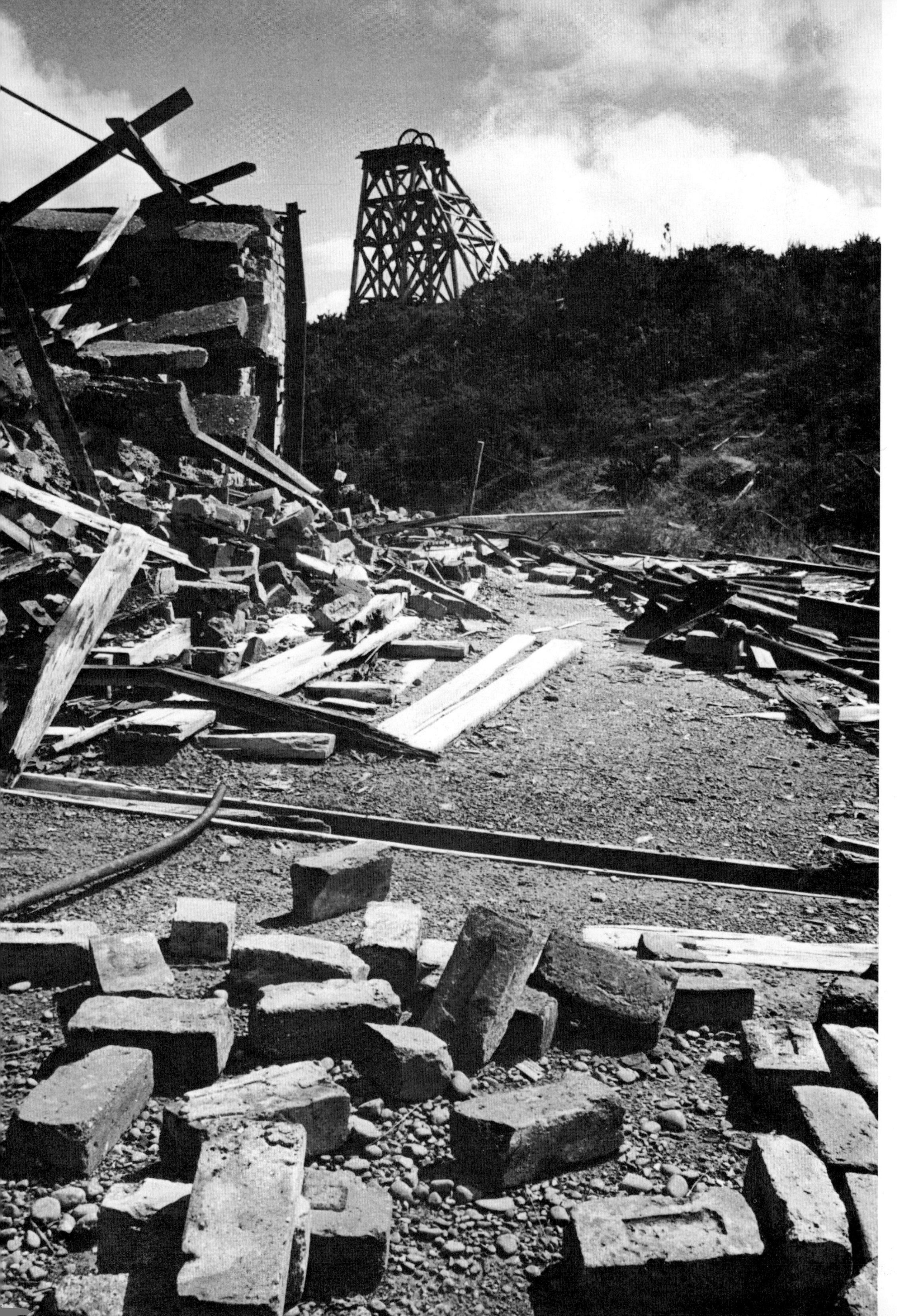

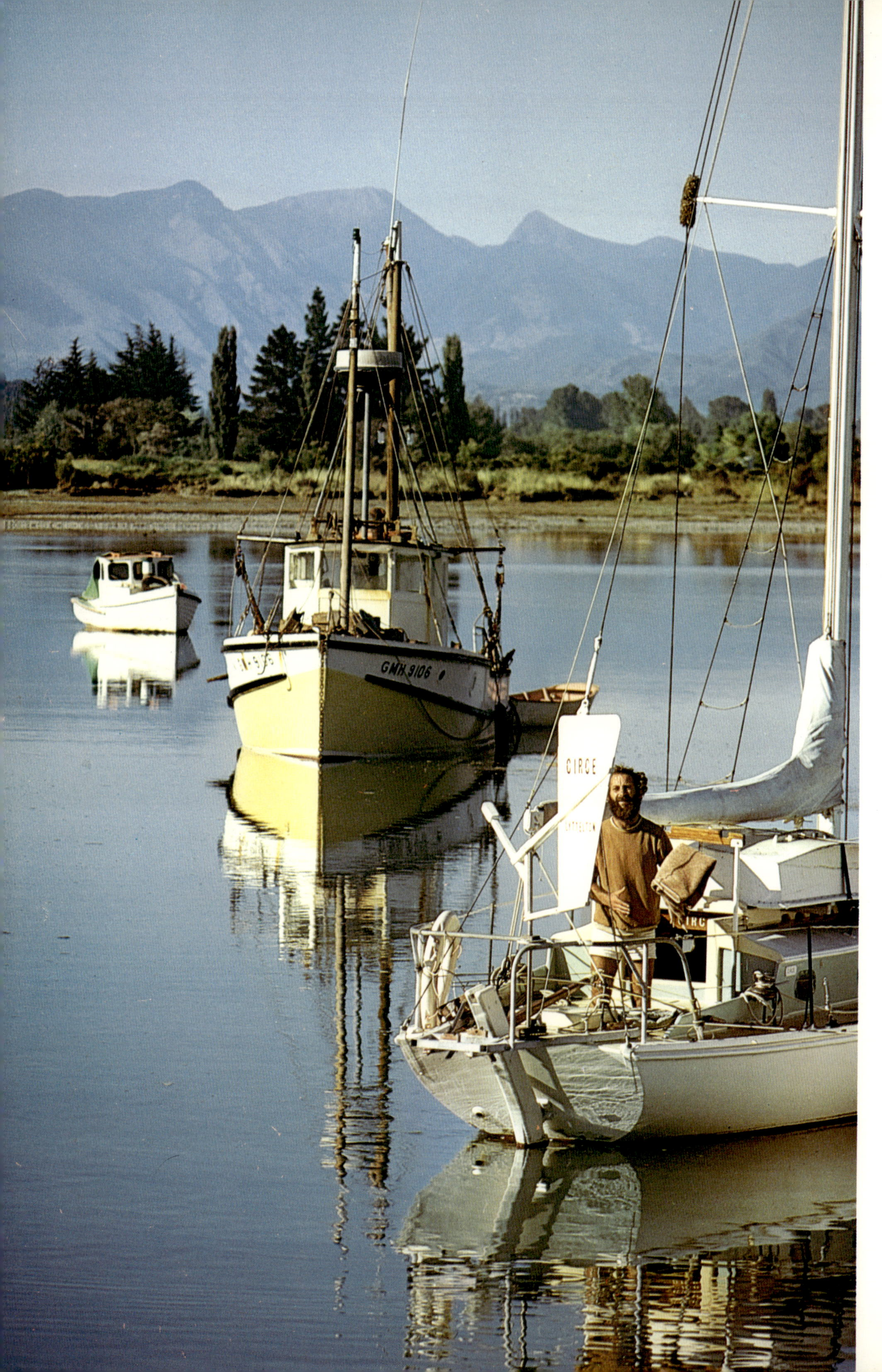

GMH 9106
CIRCE

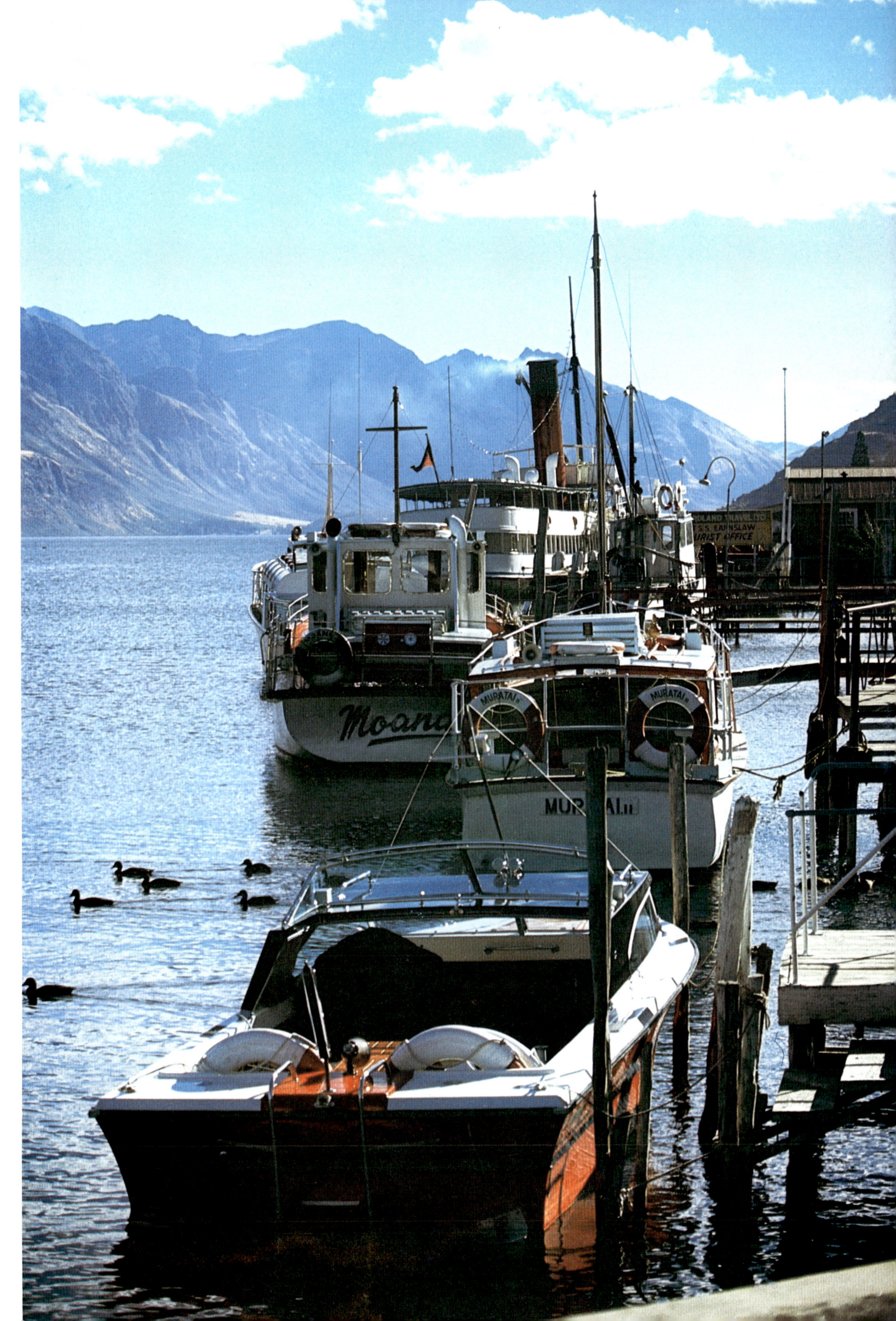

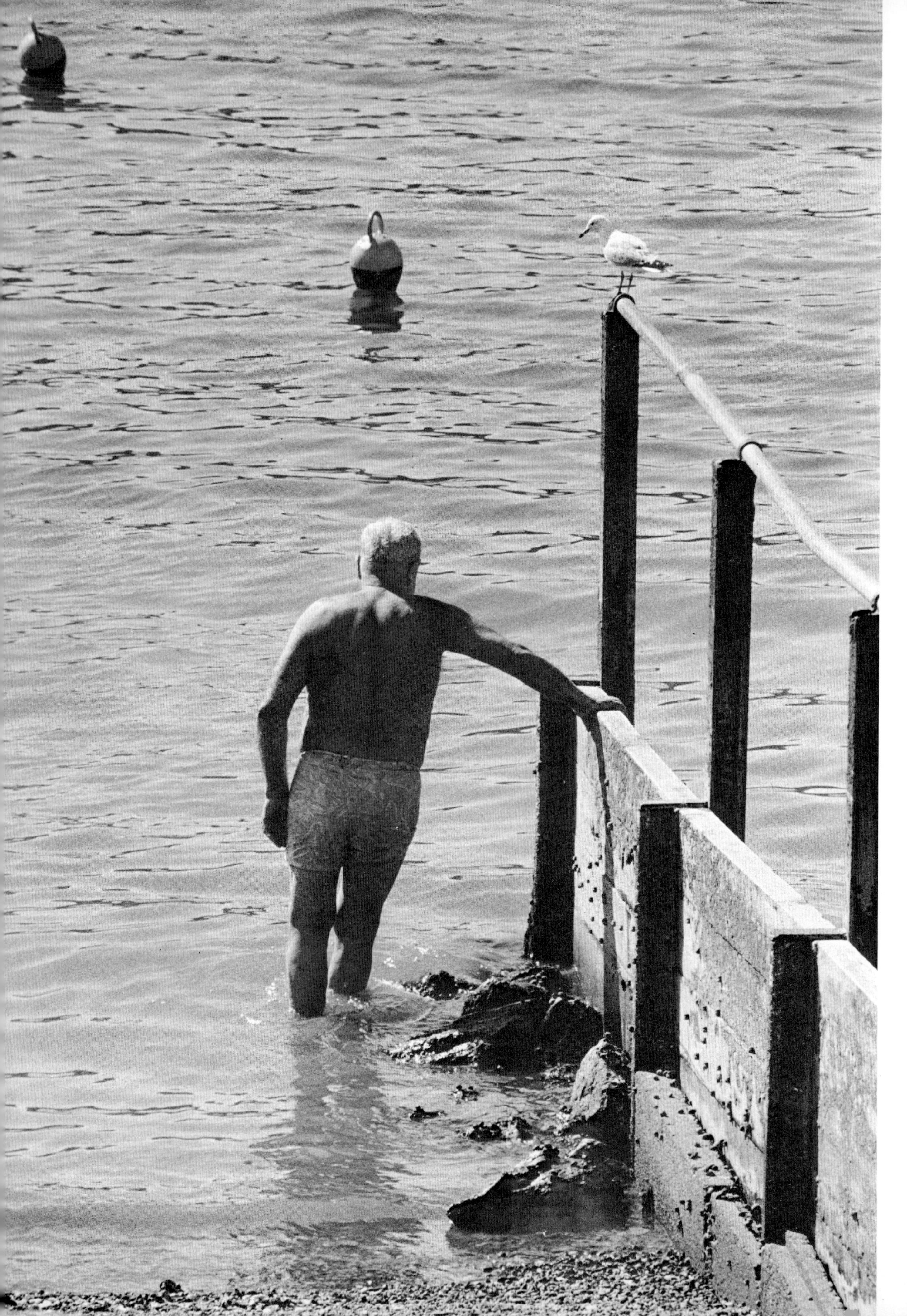

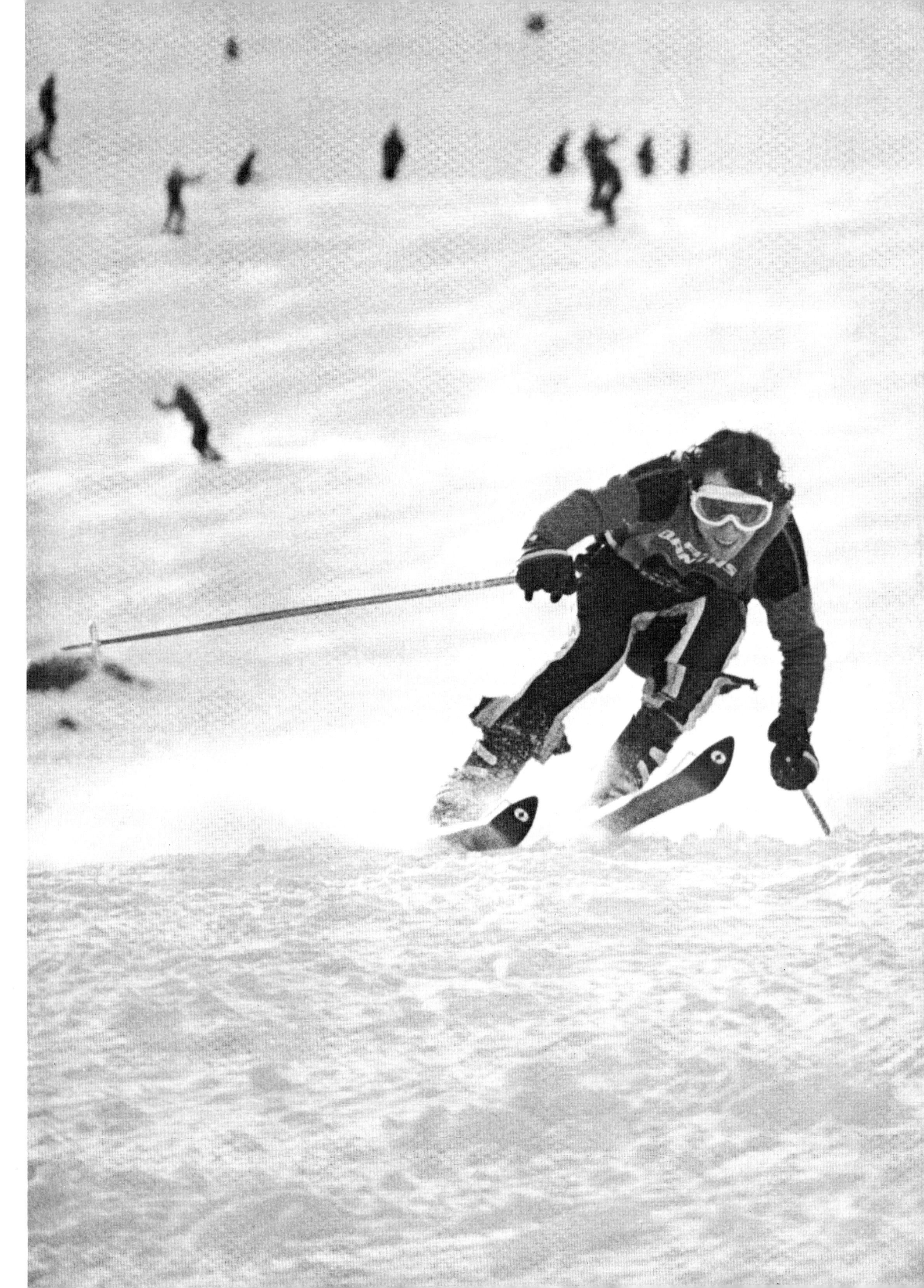

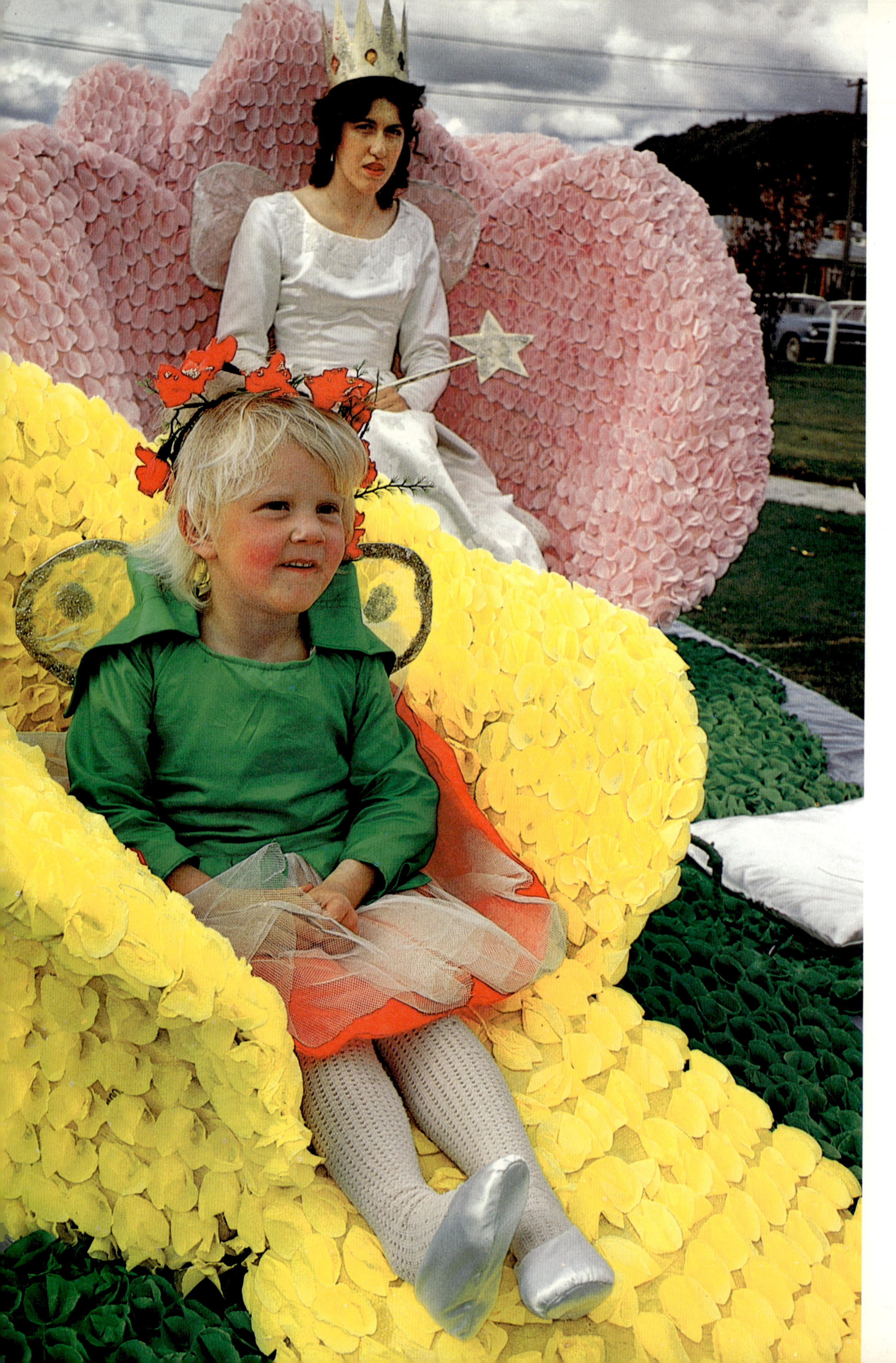

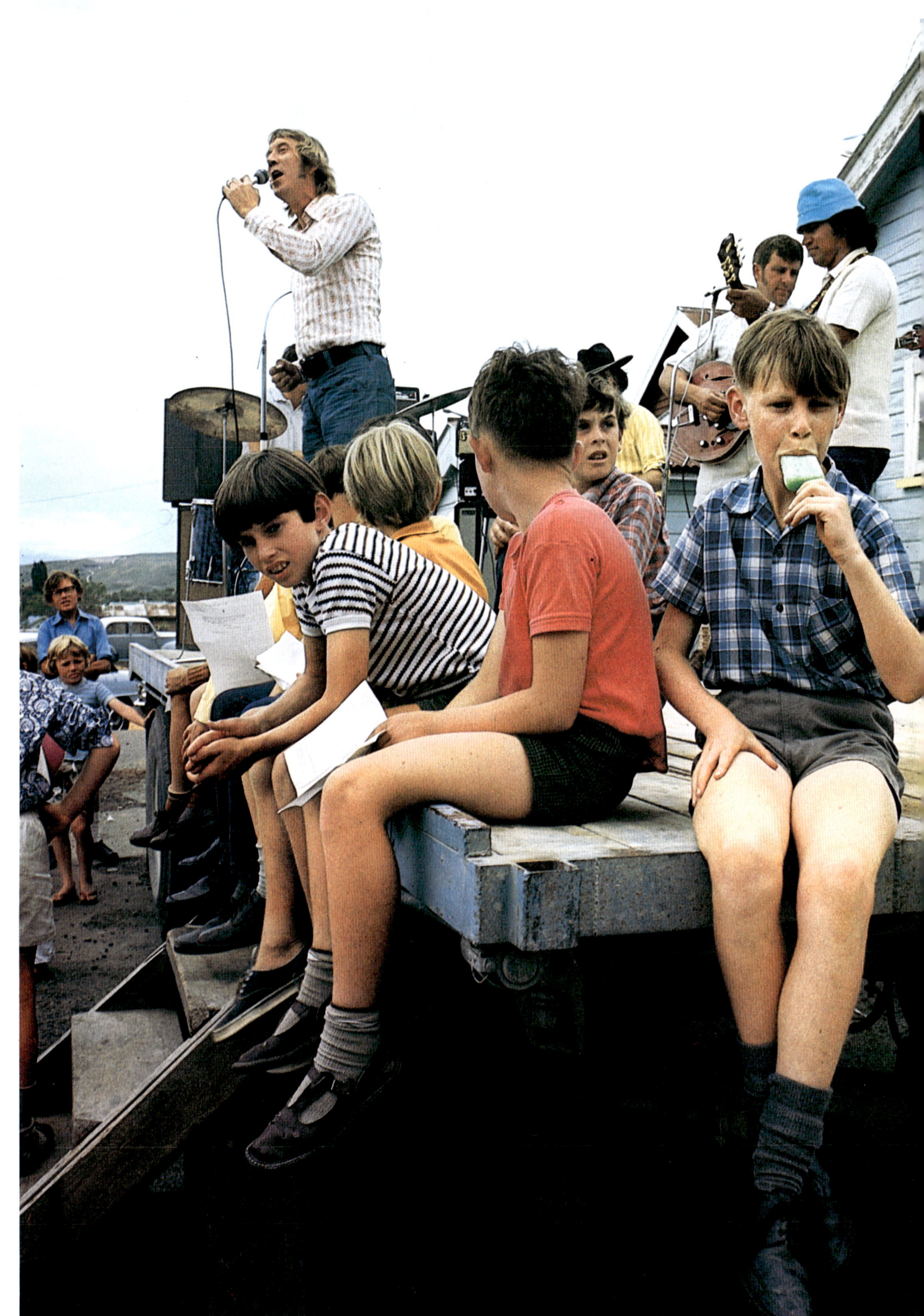

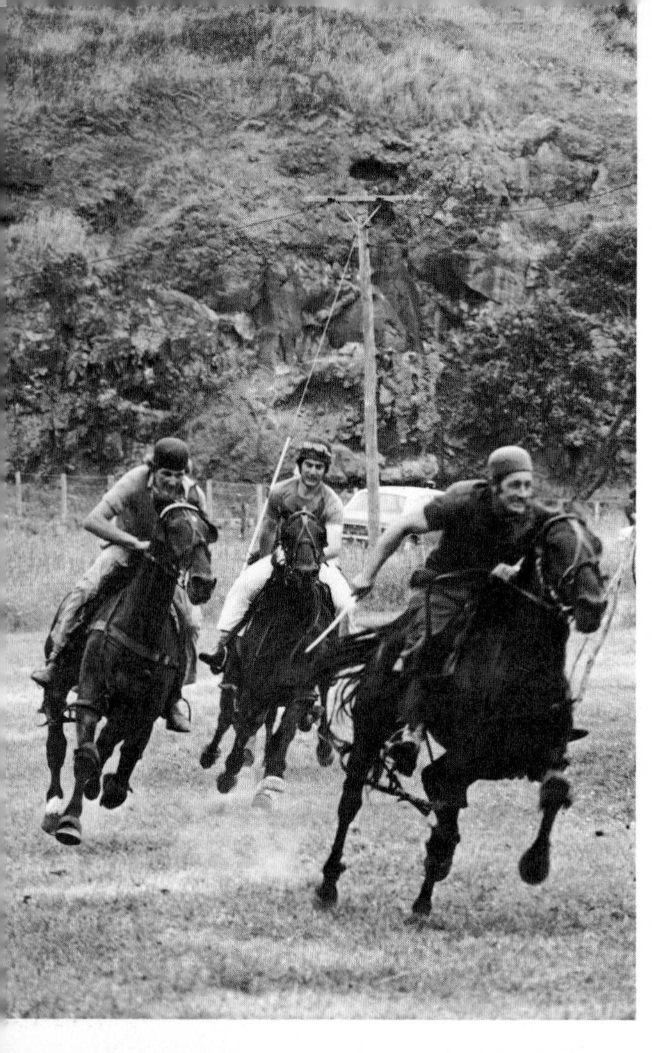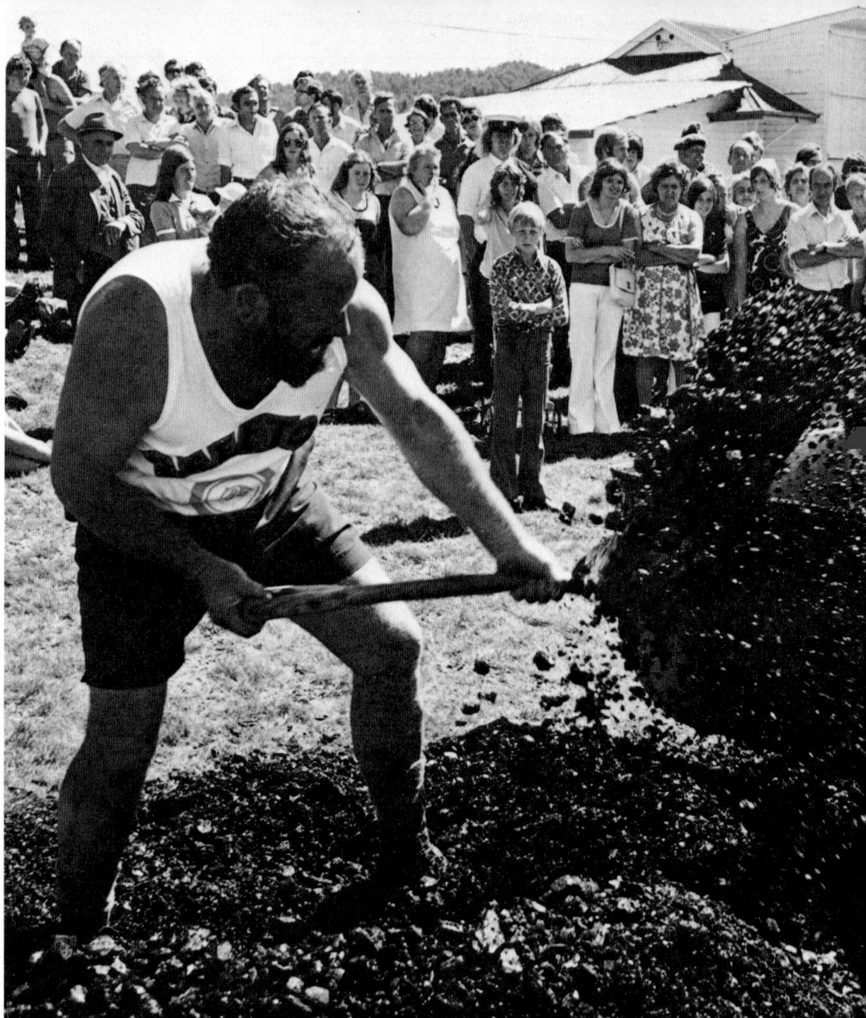

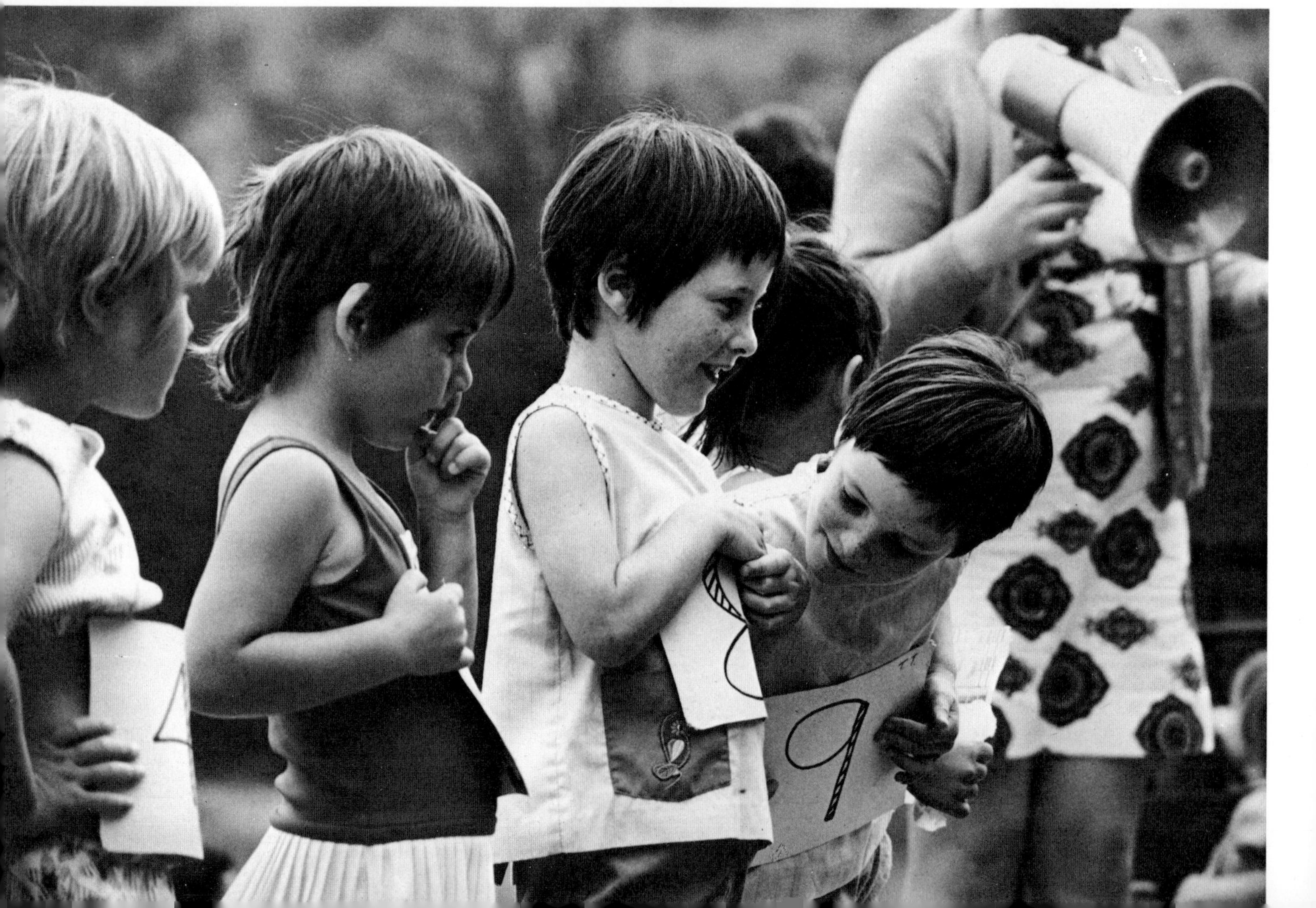

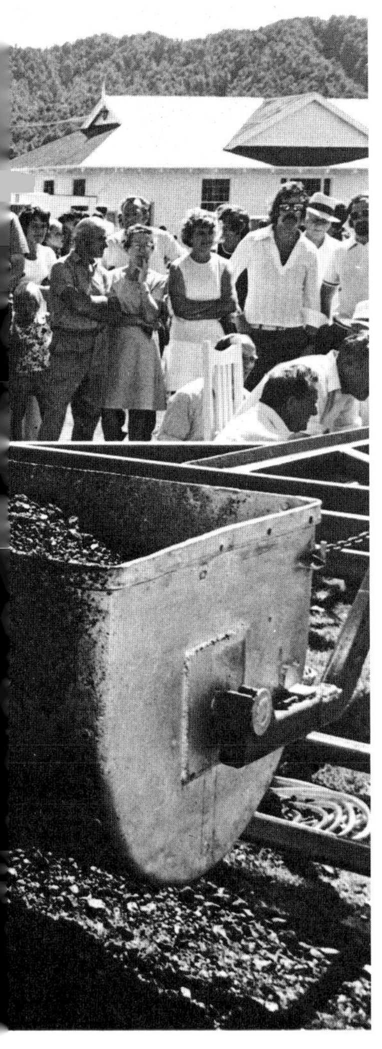
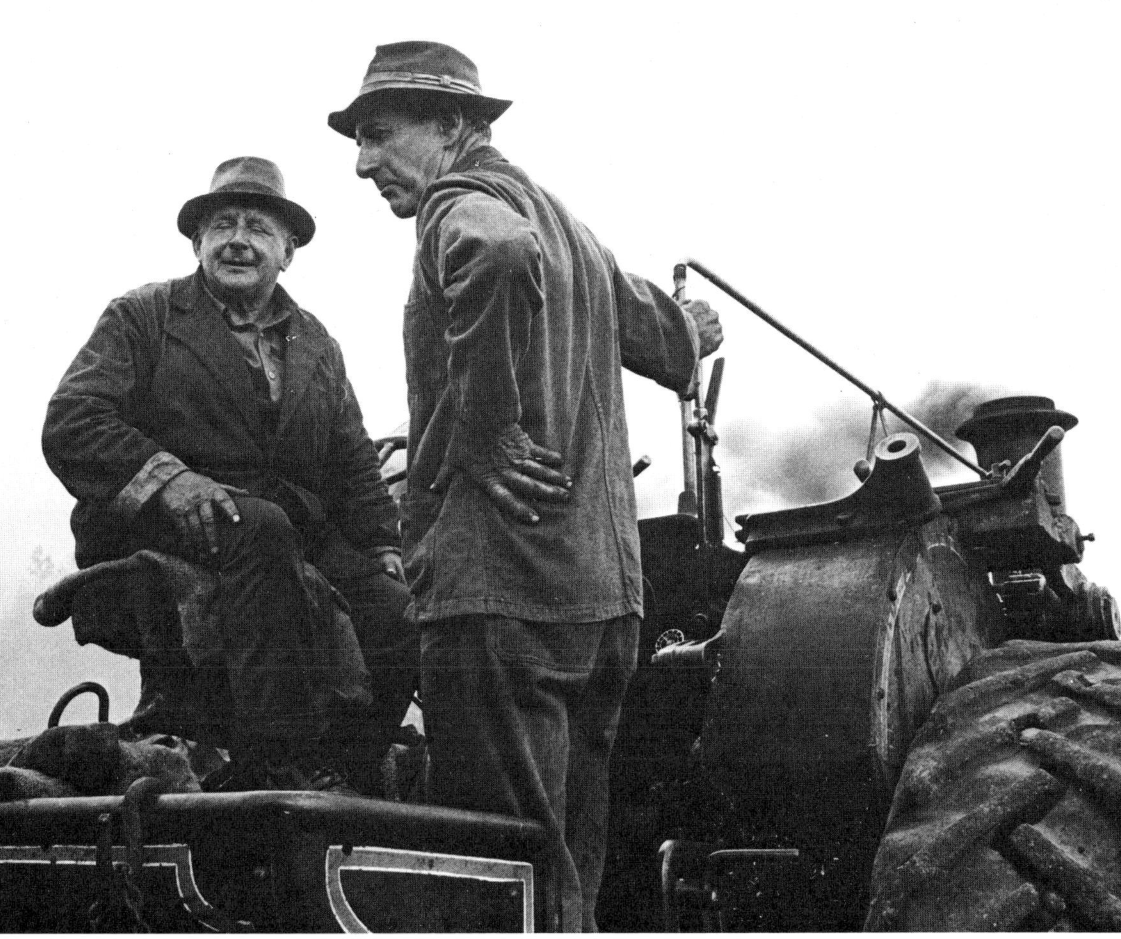

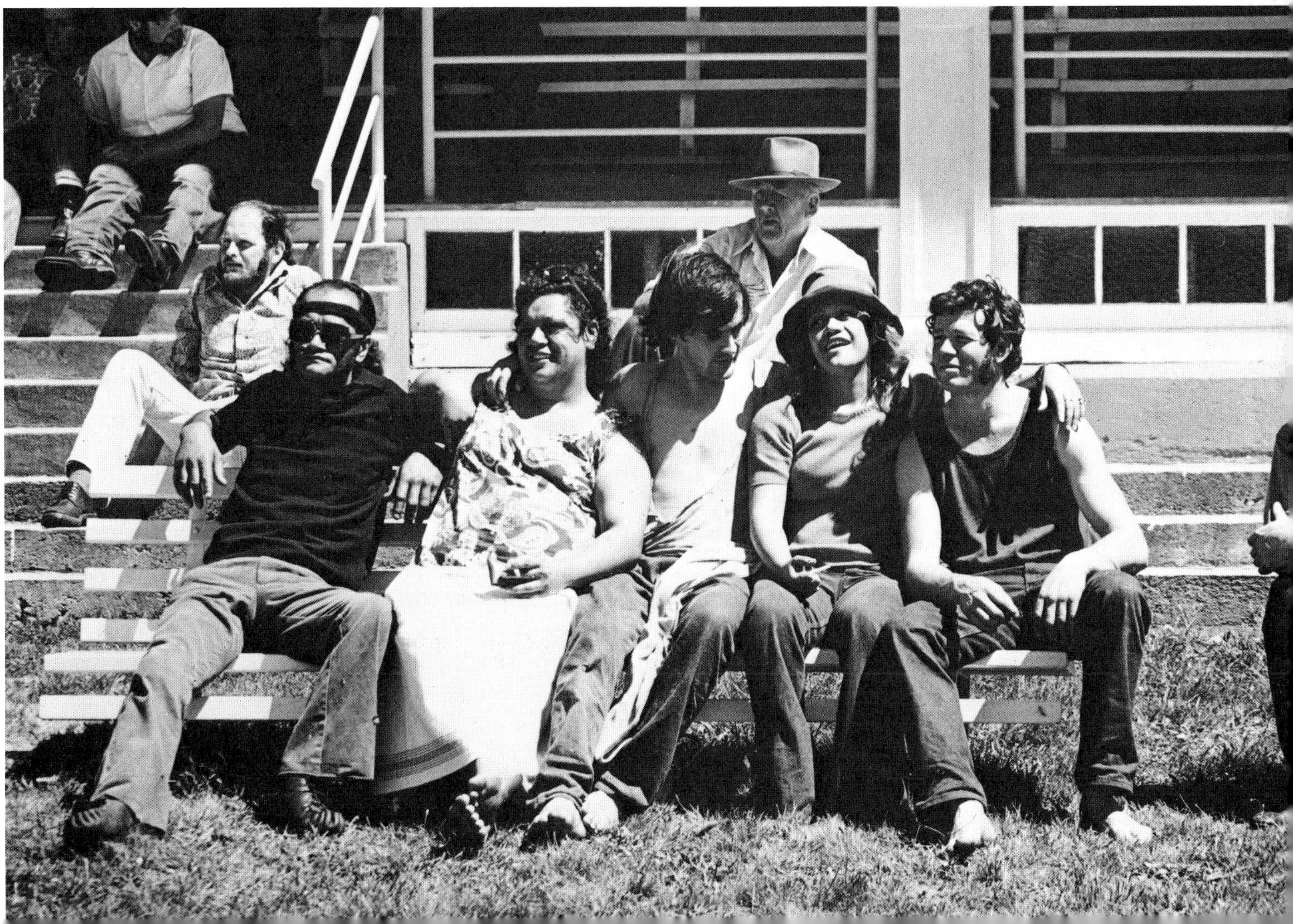

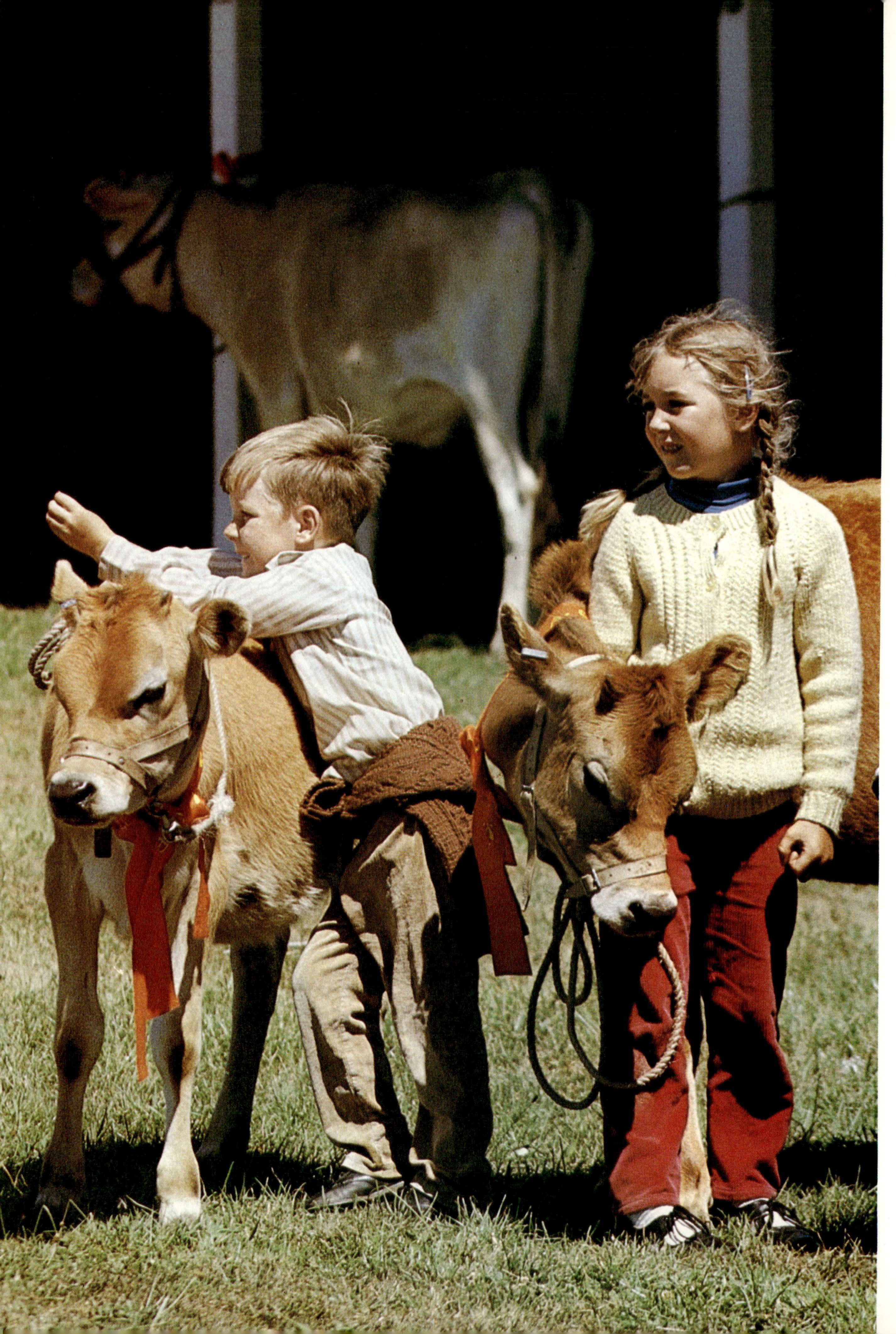

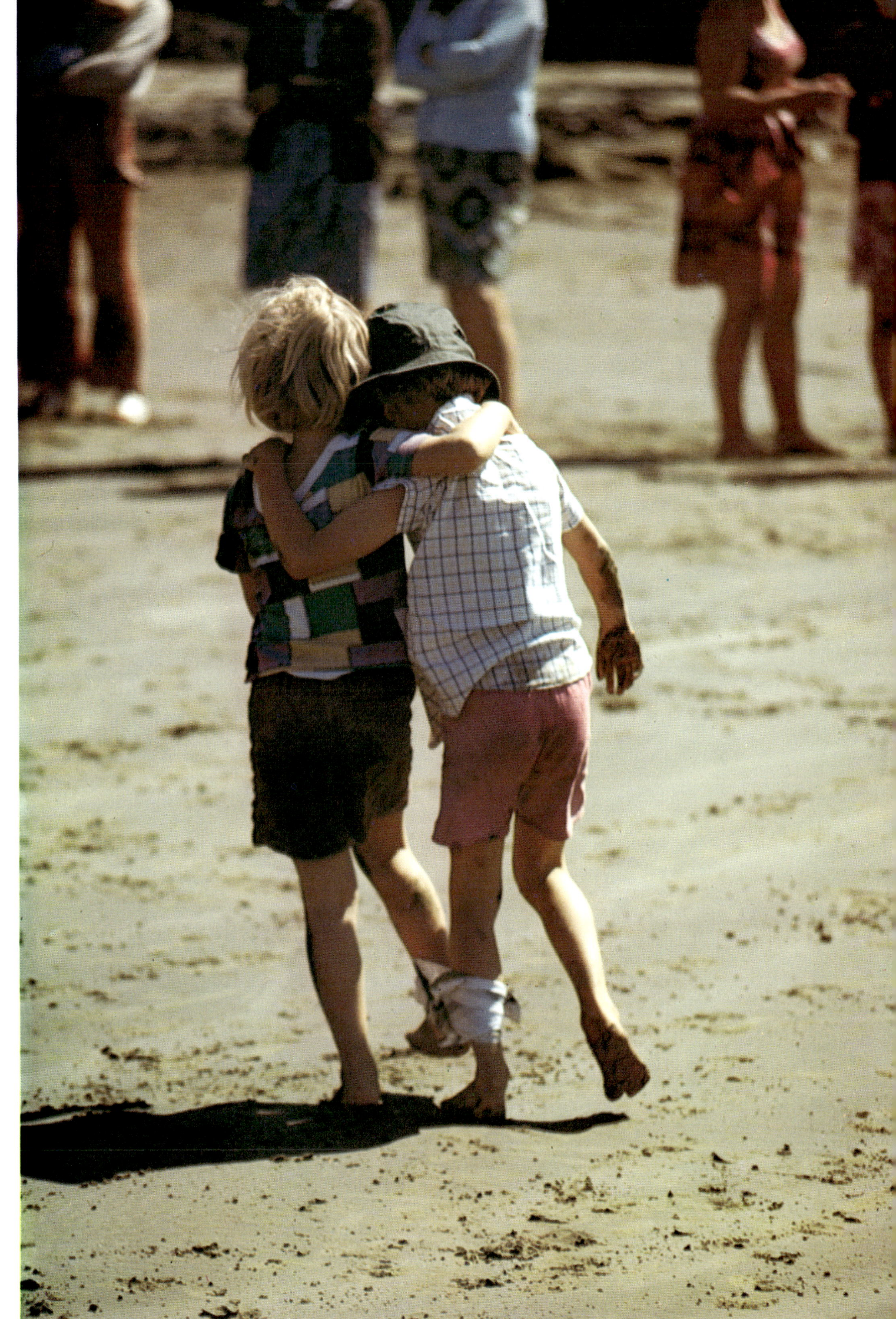

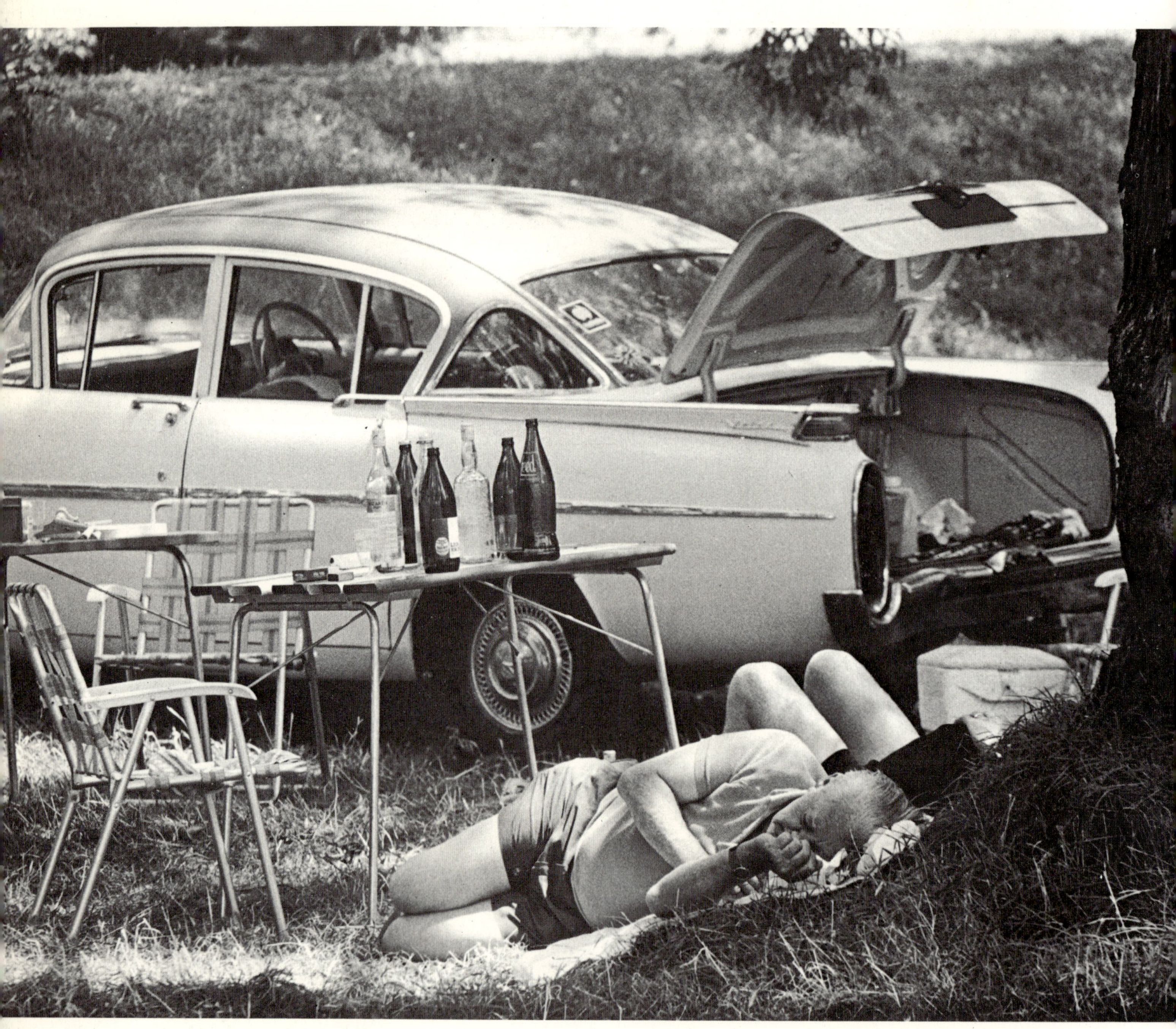

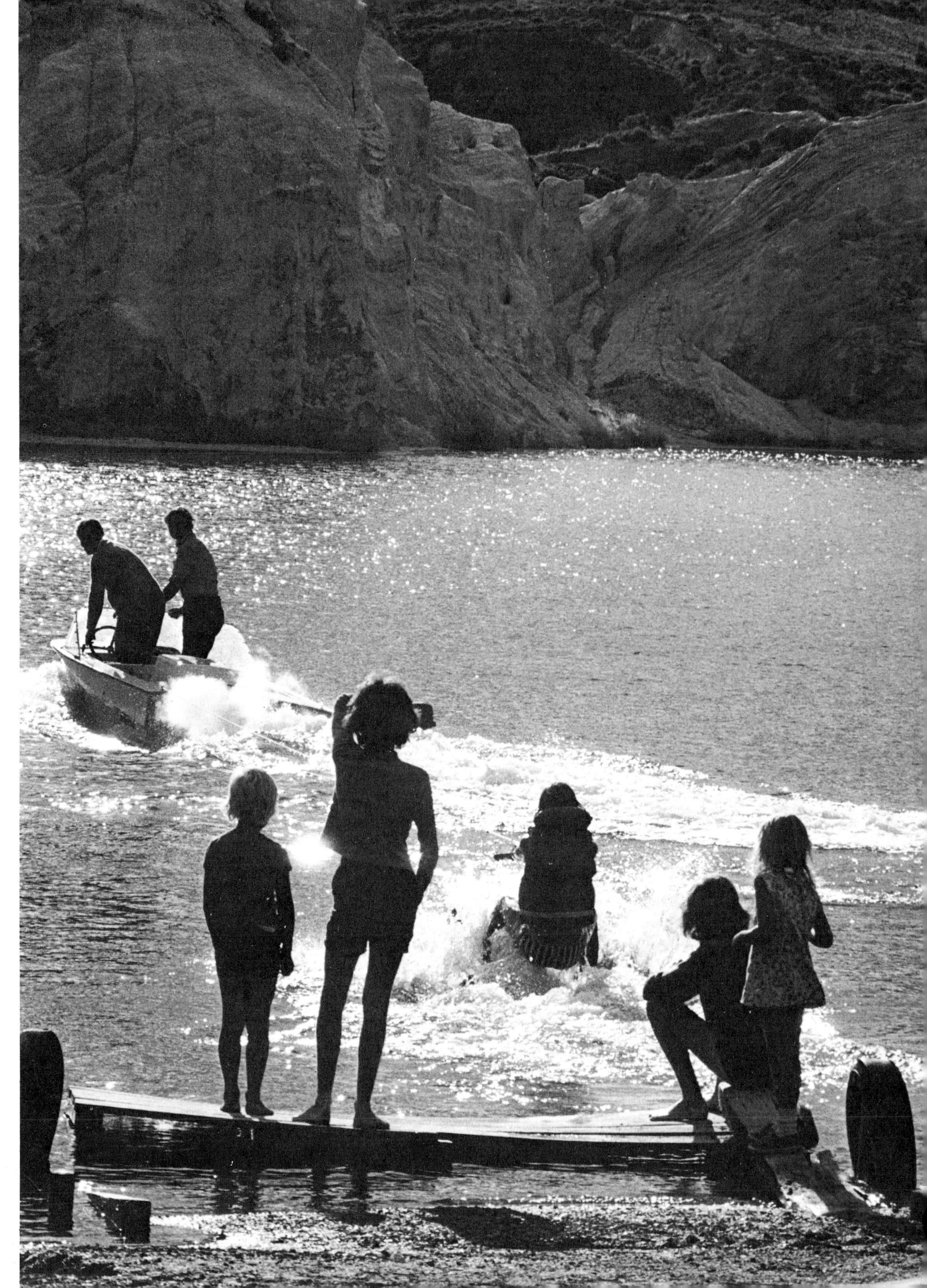

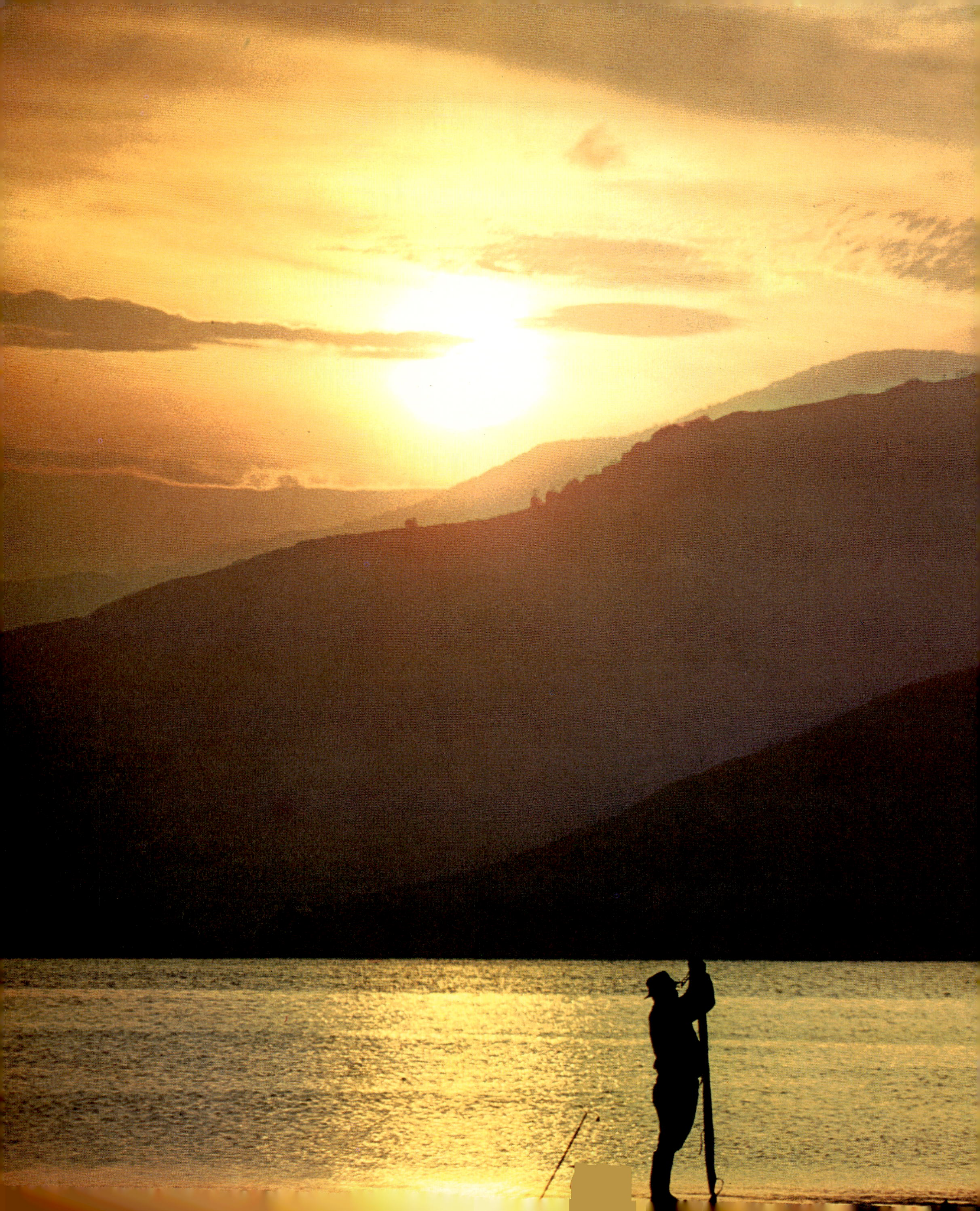

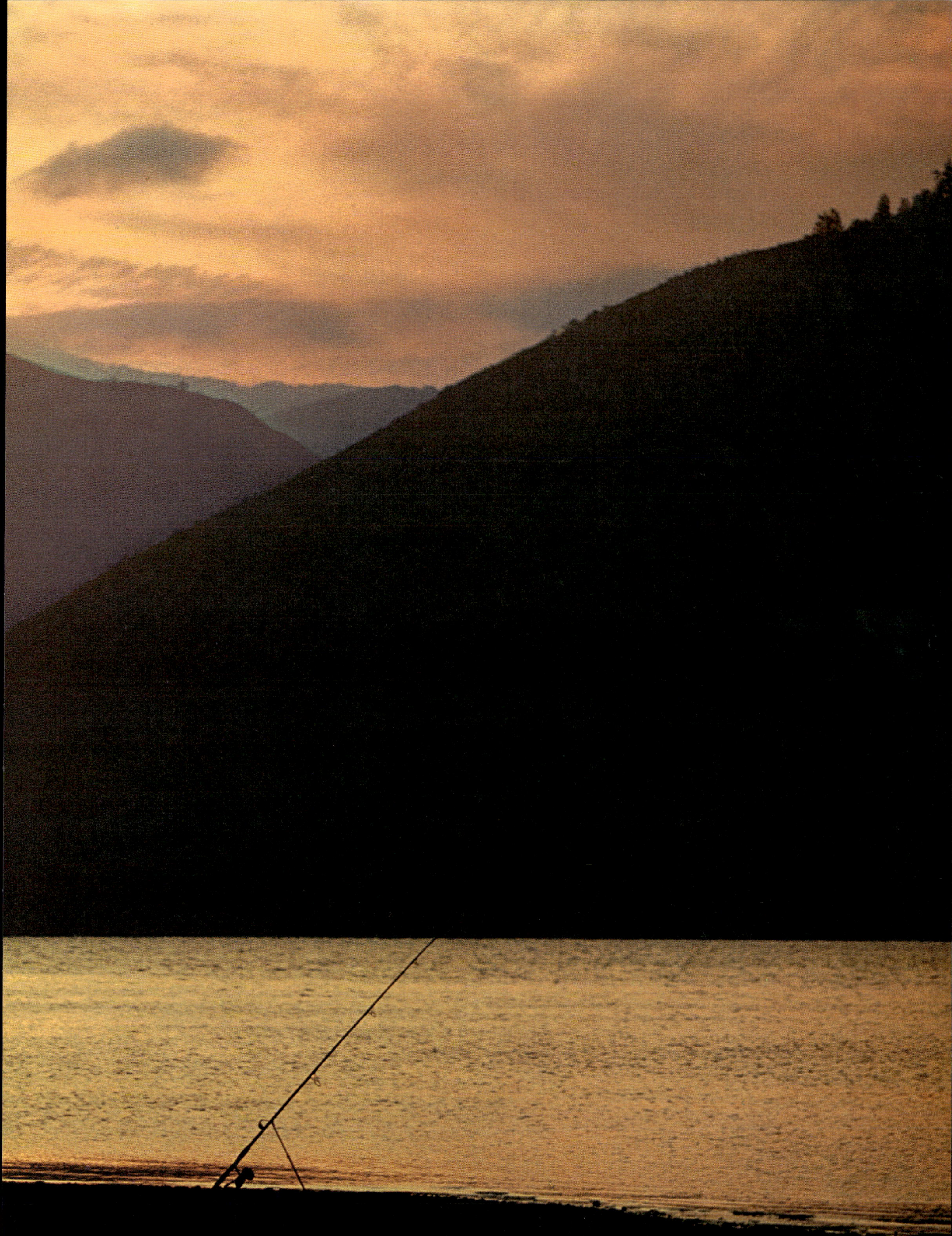

'*A large land,
uplifted high . . .*'

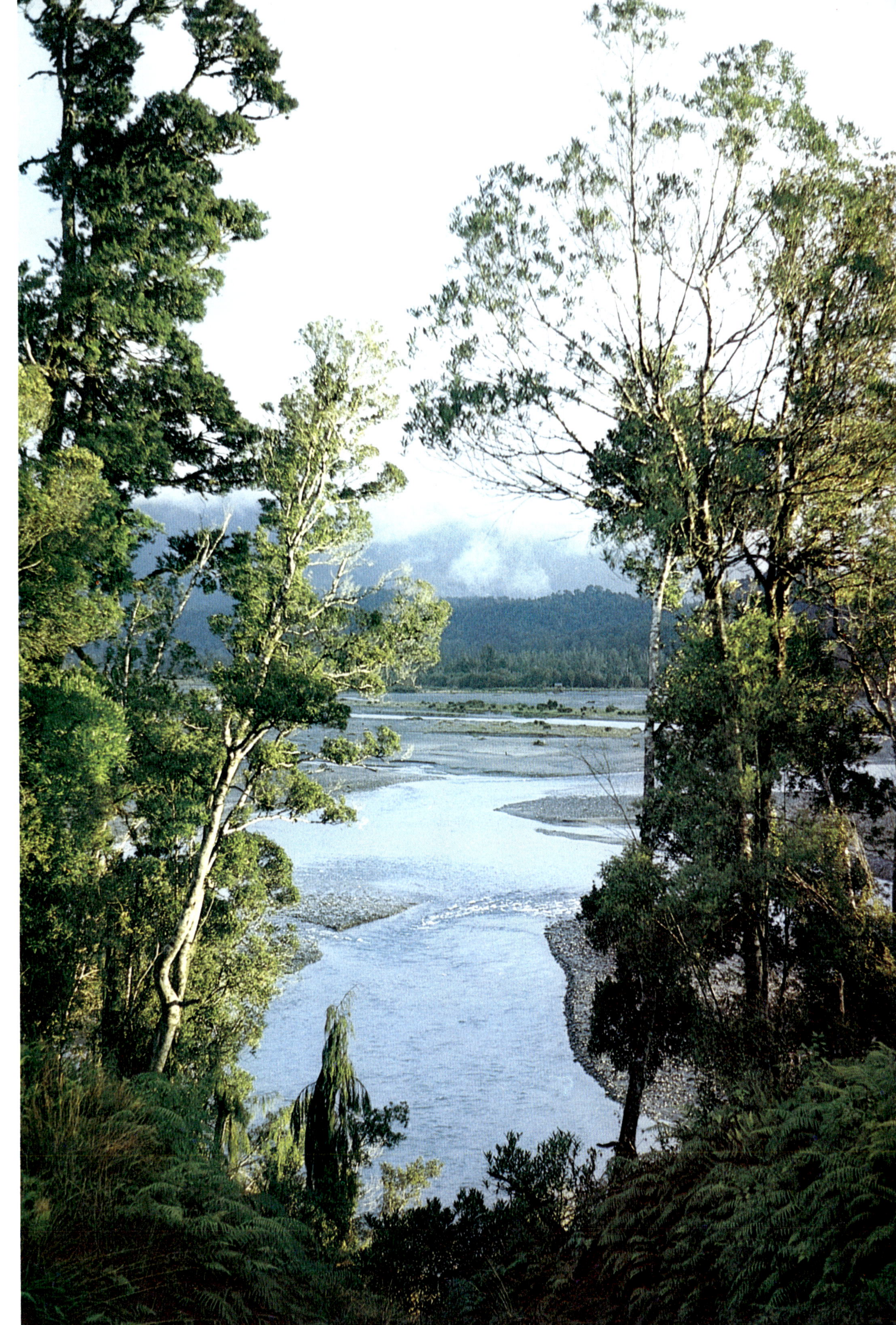

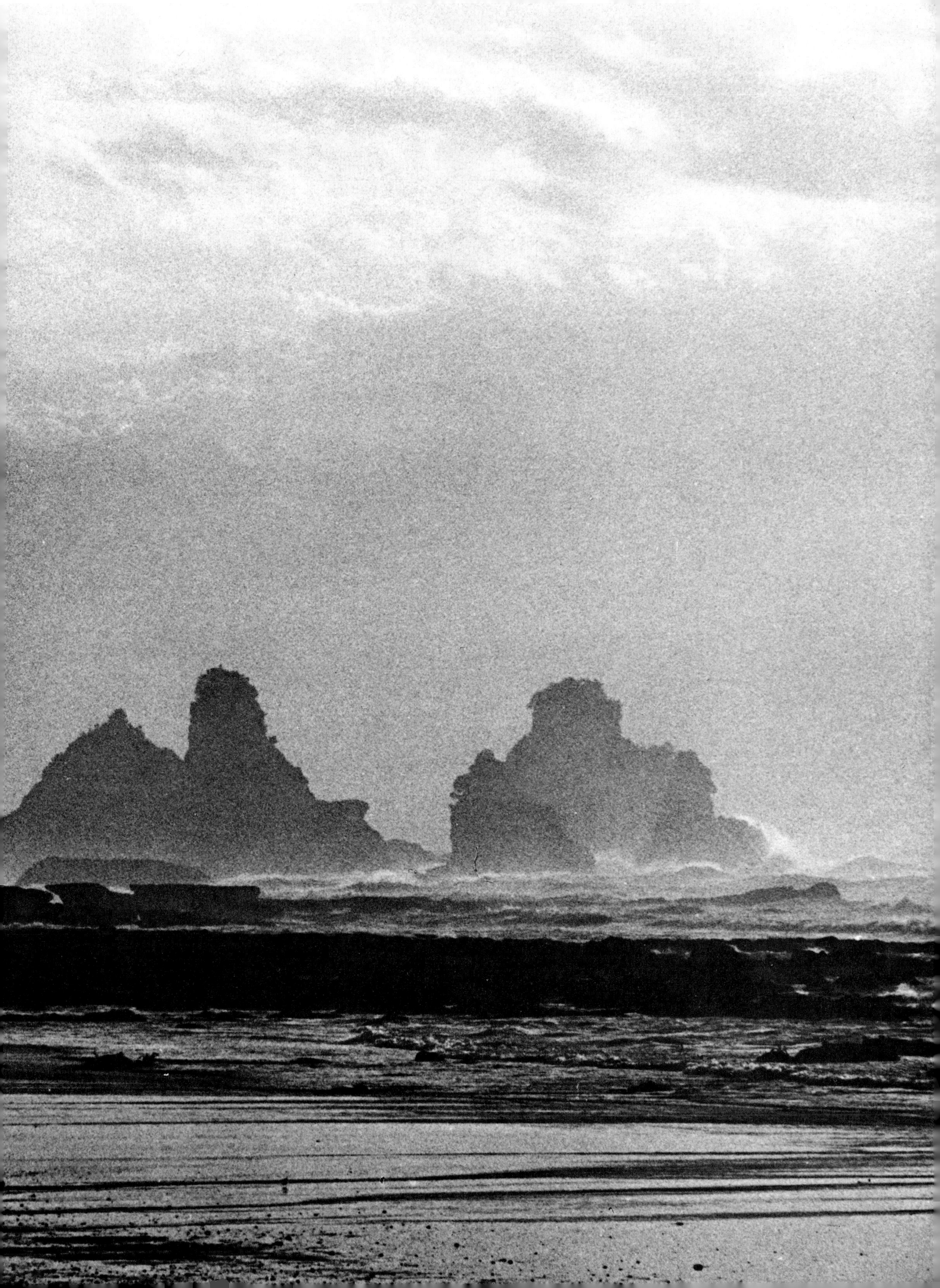

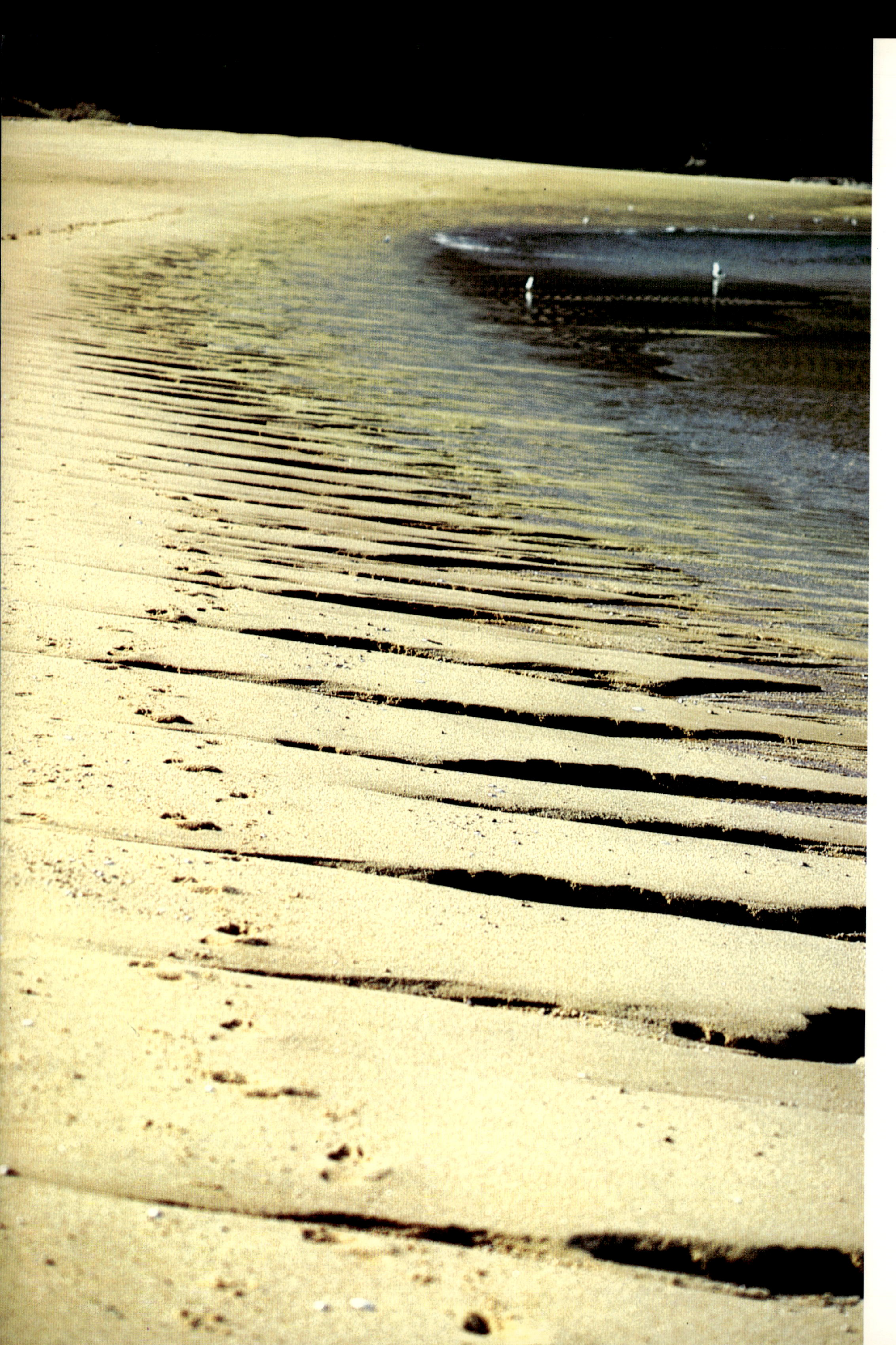

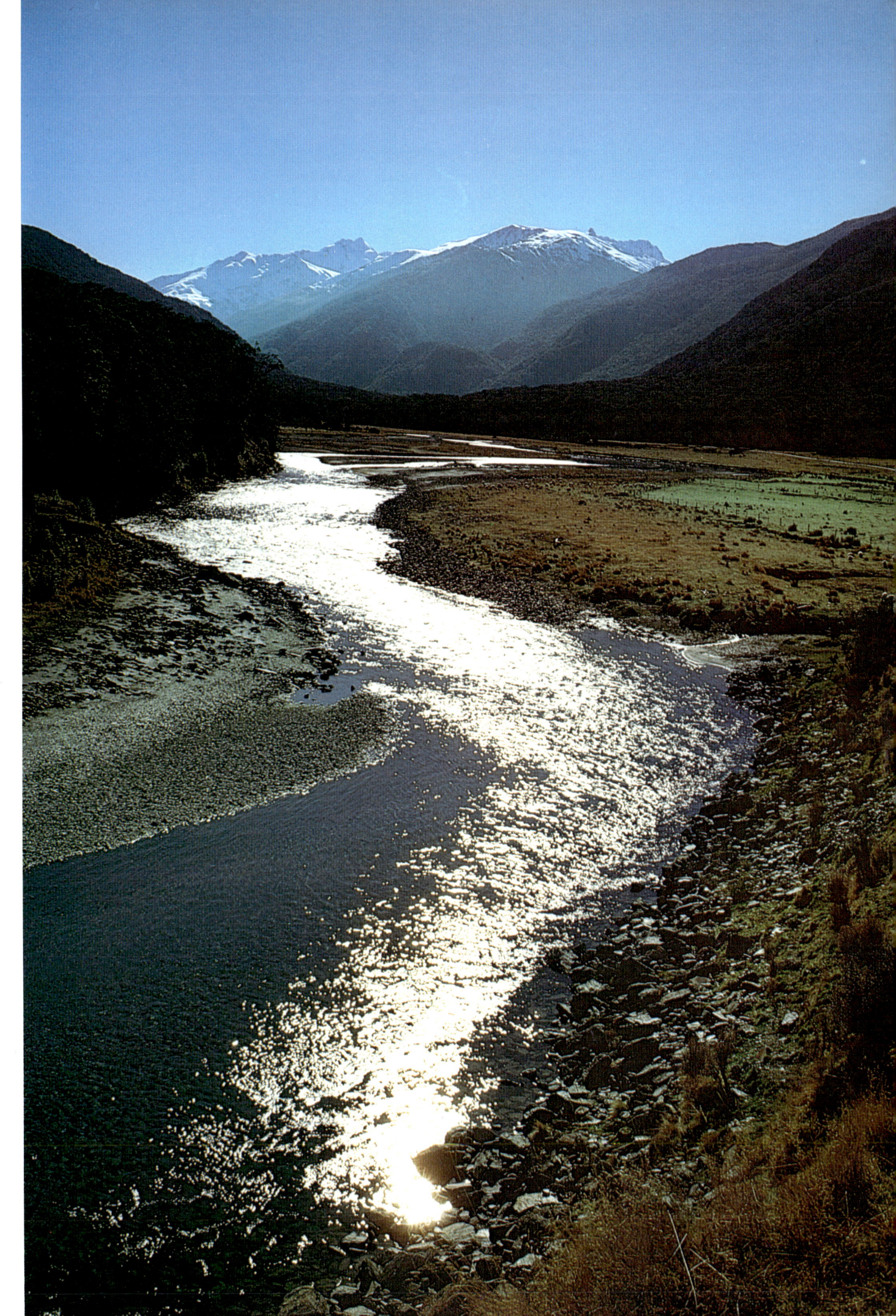

133

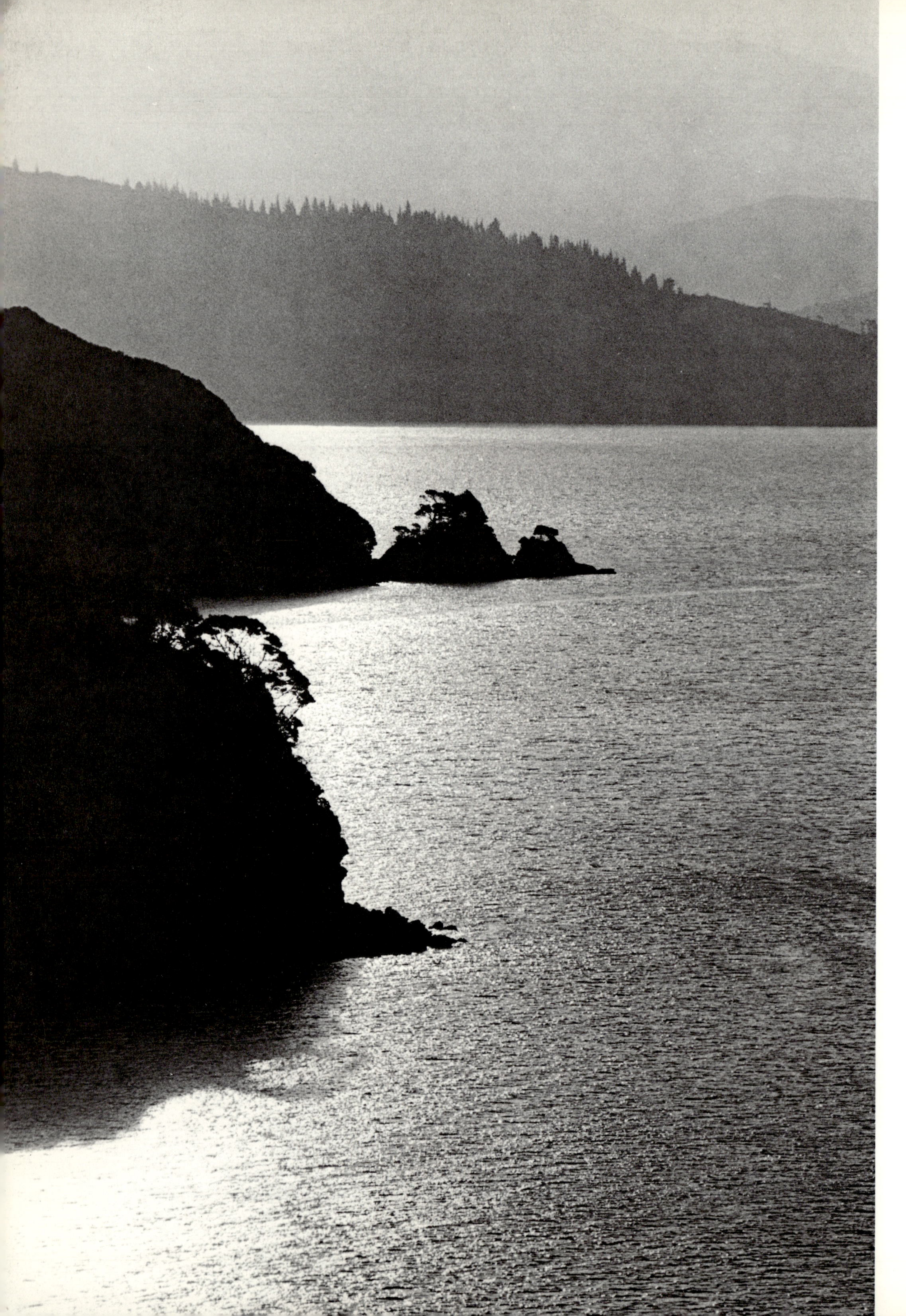

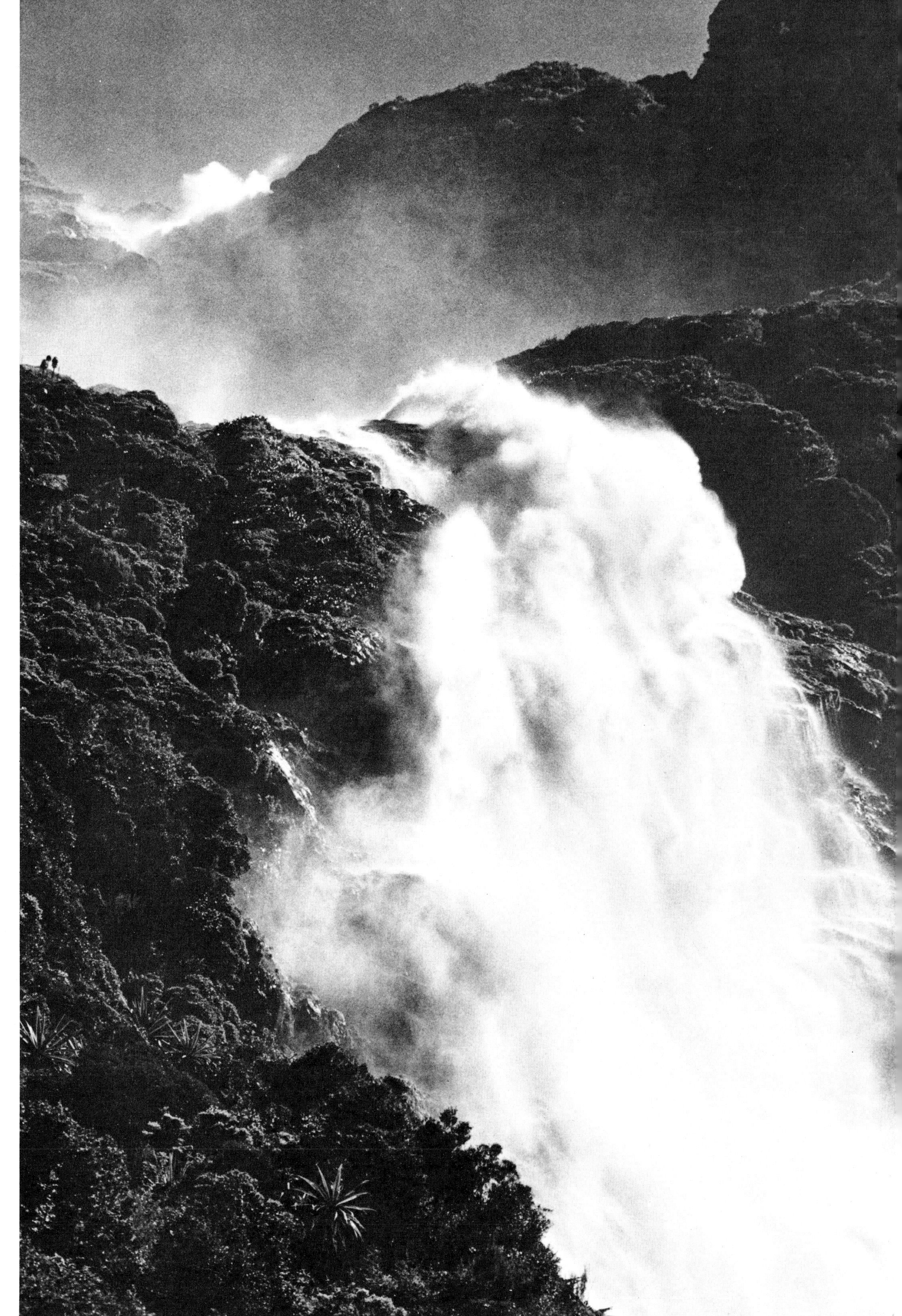

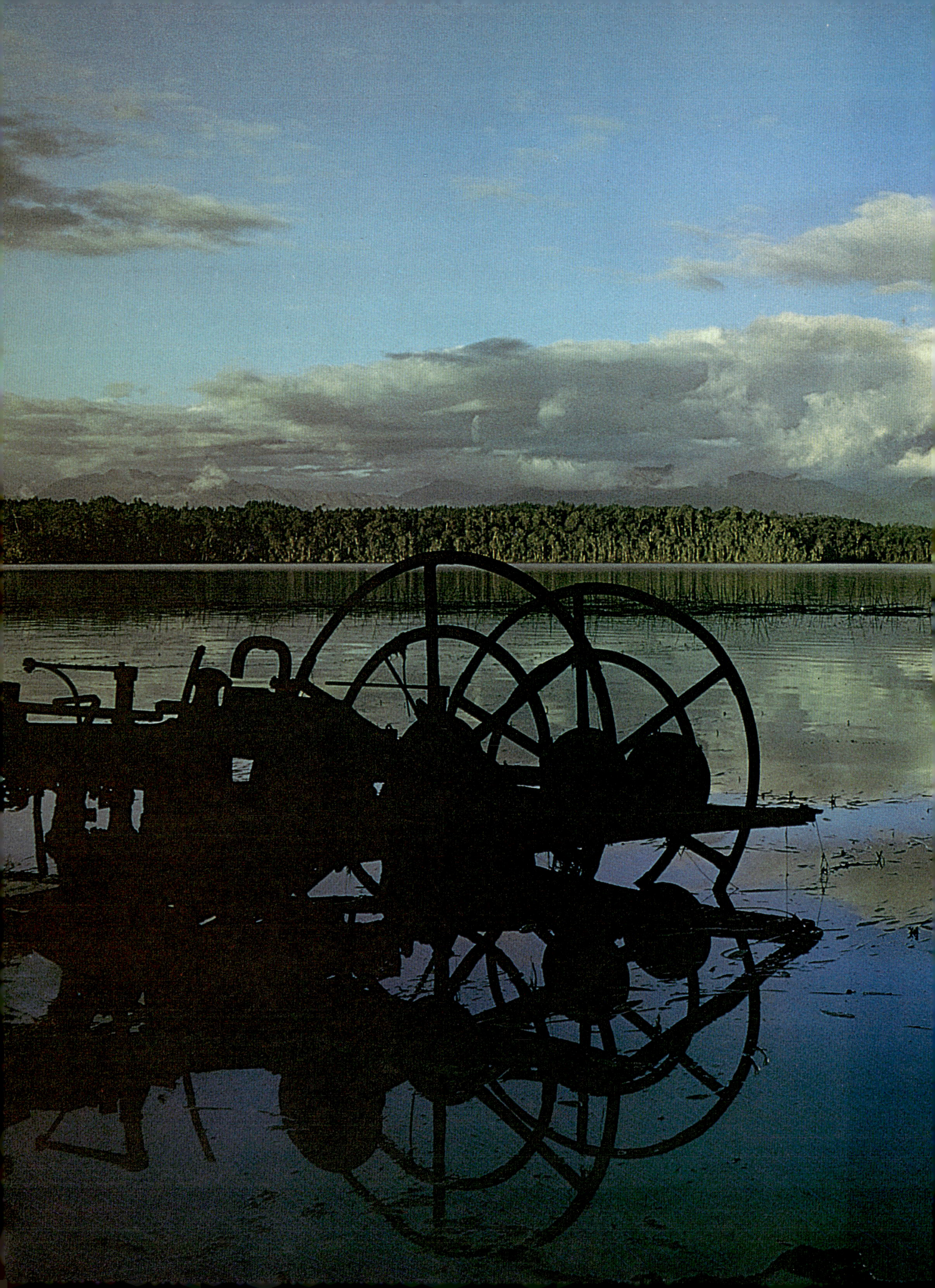

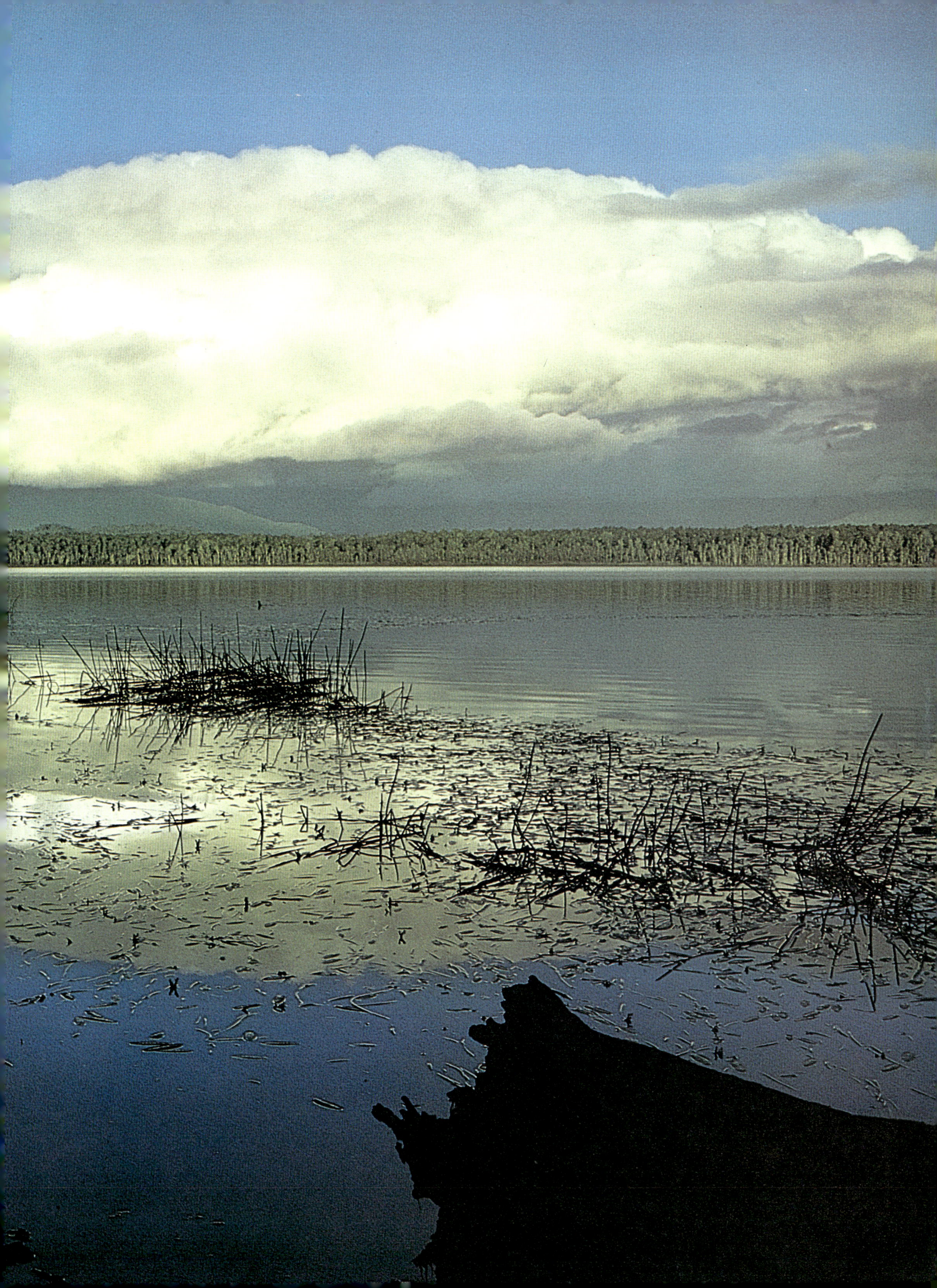

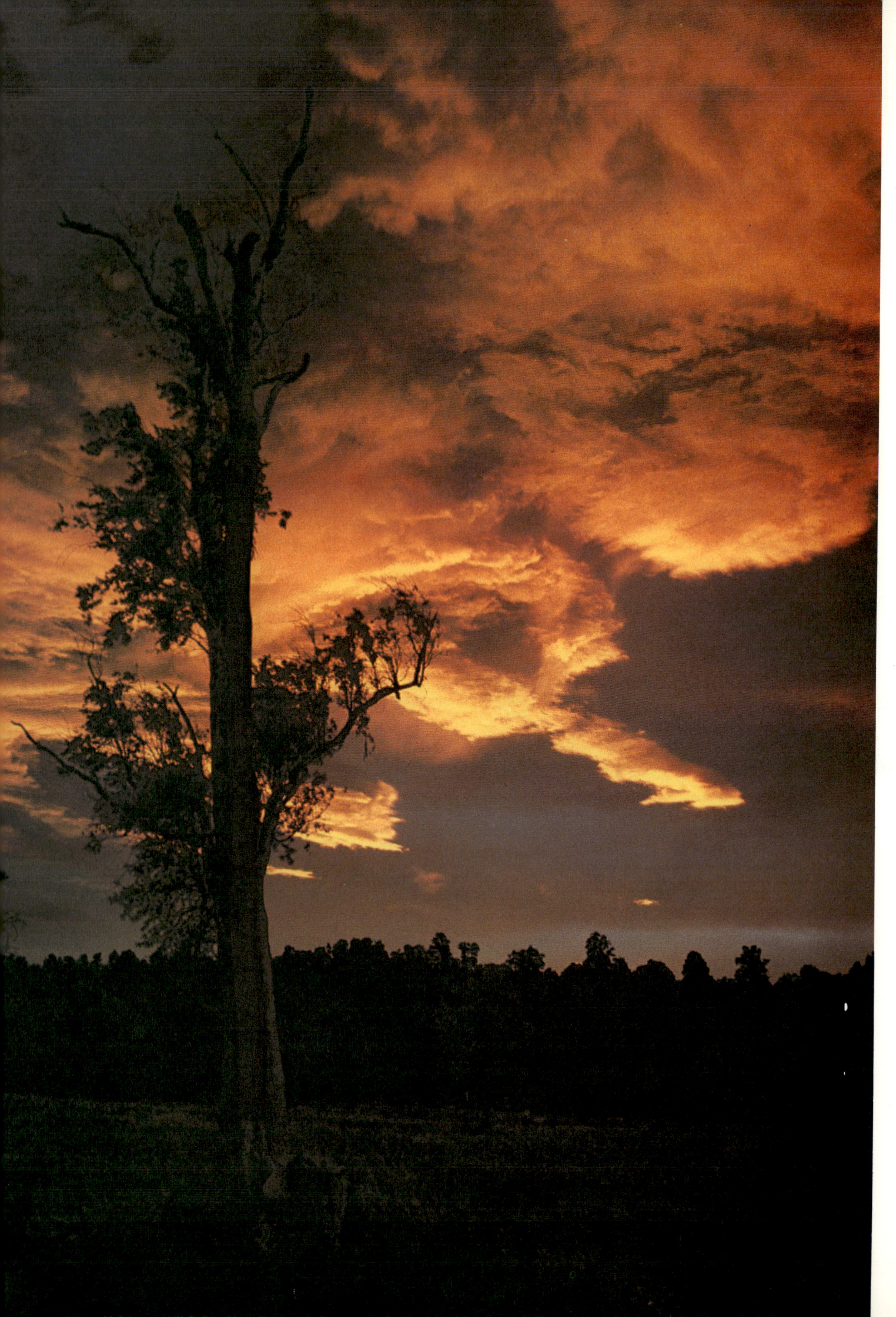

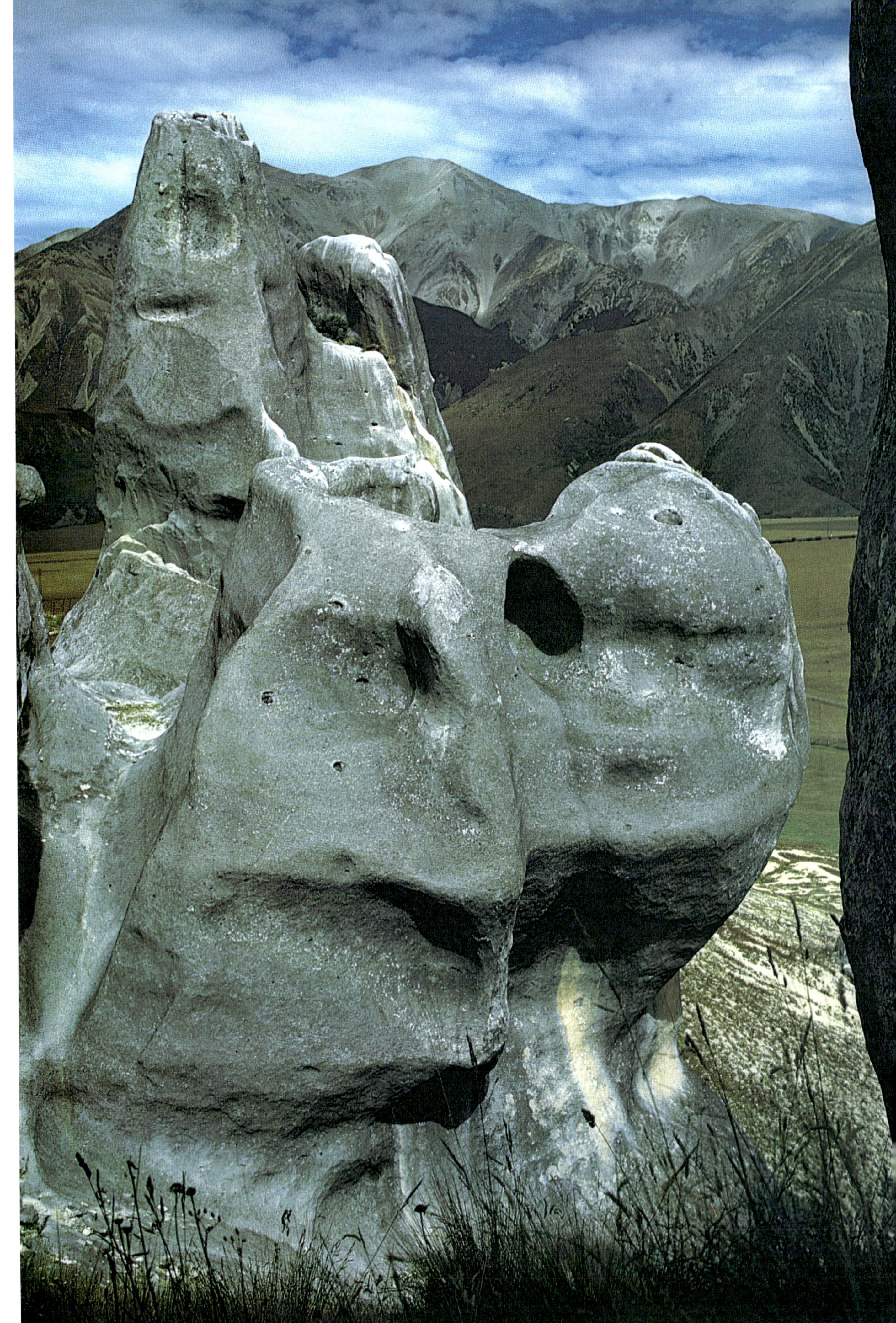

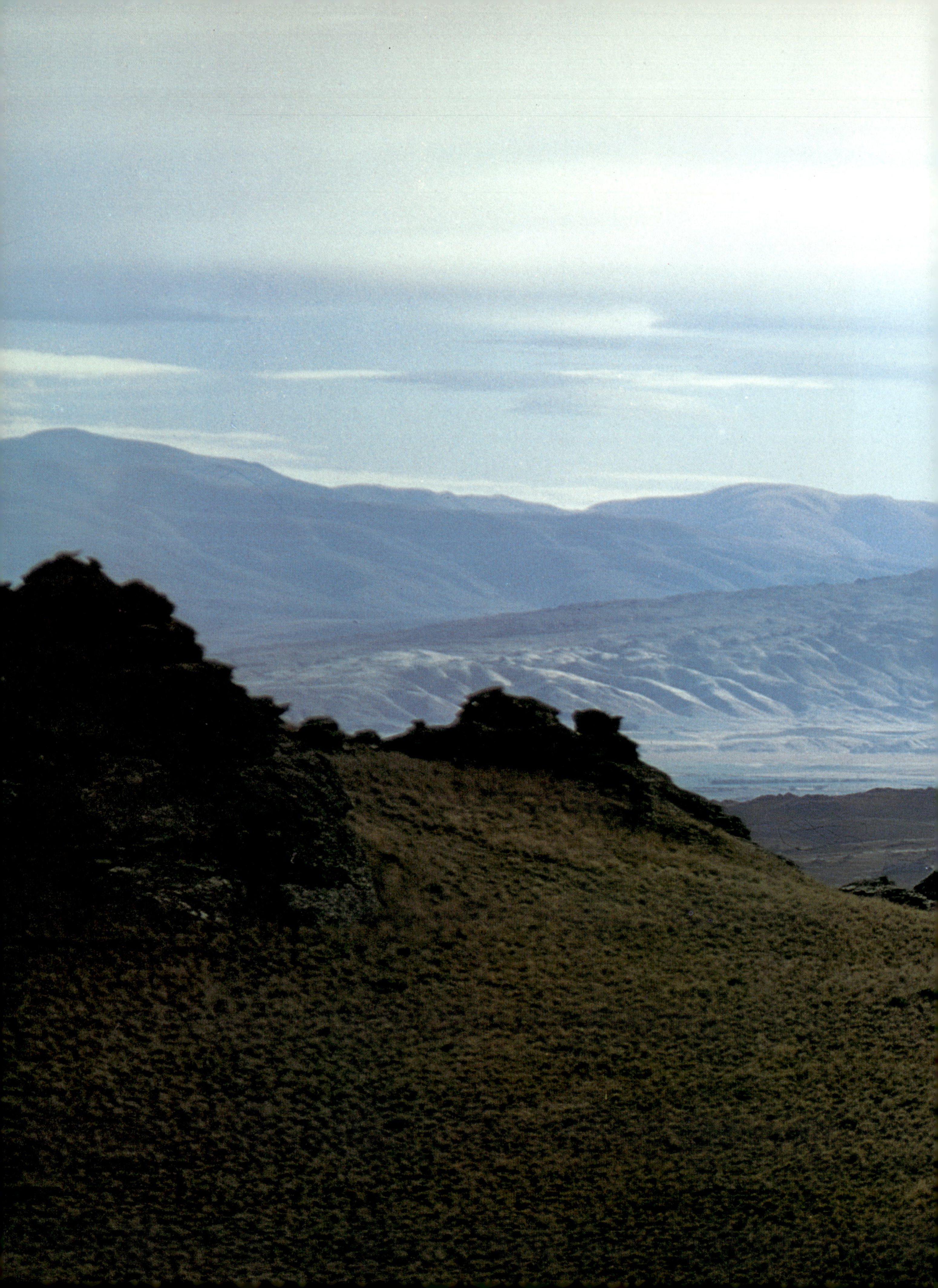

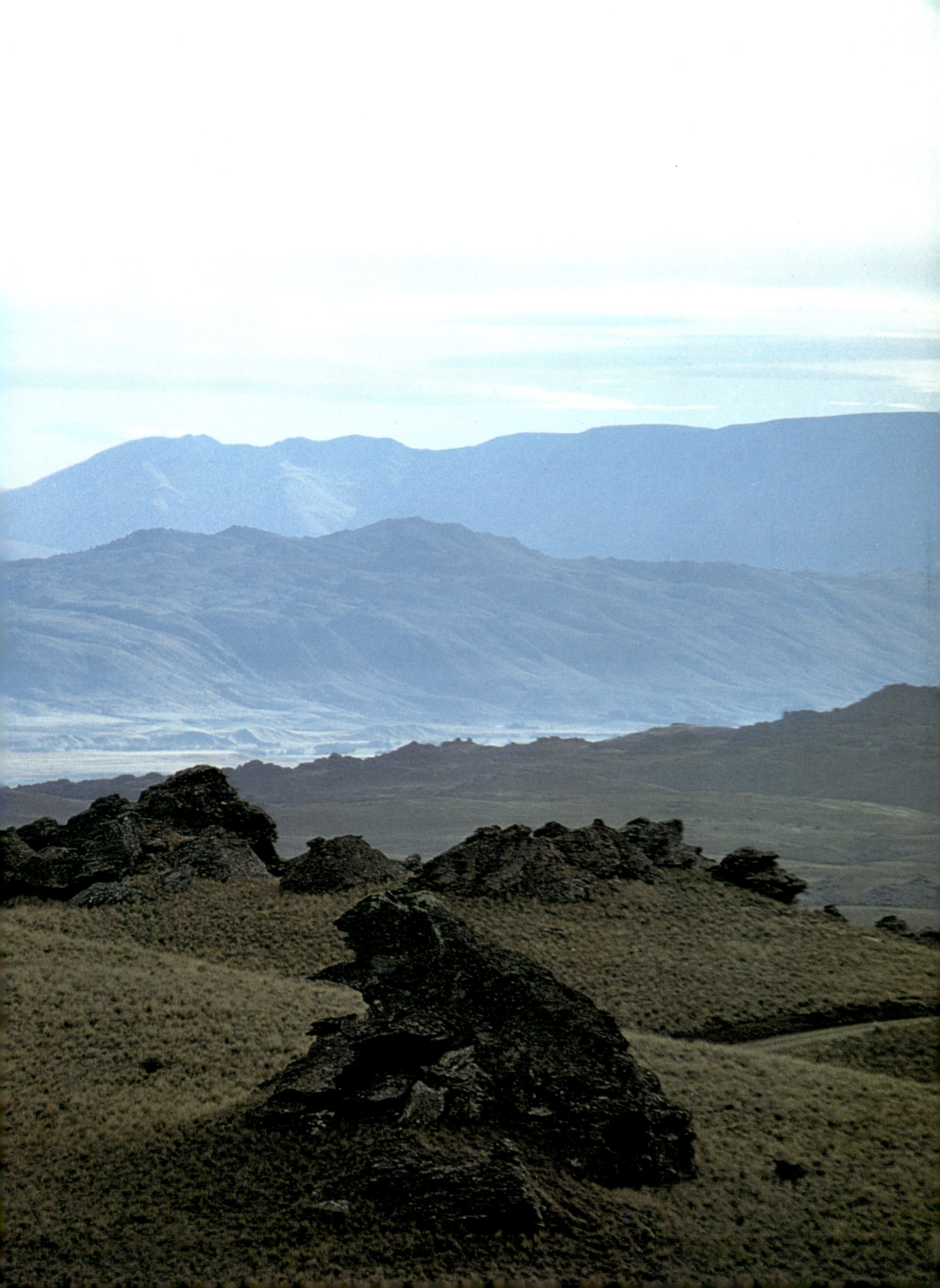

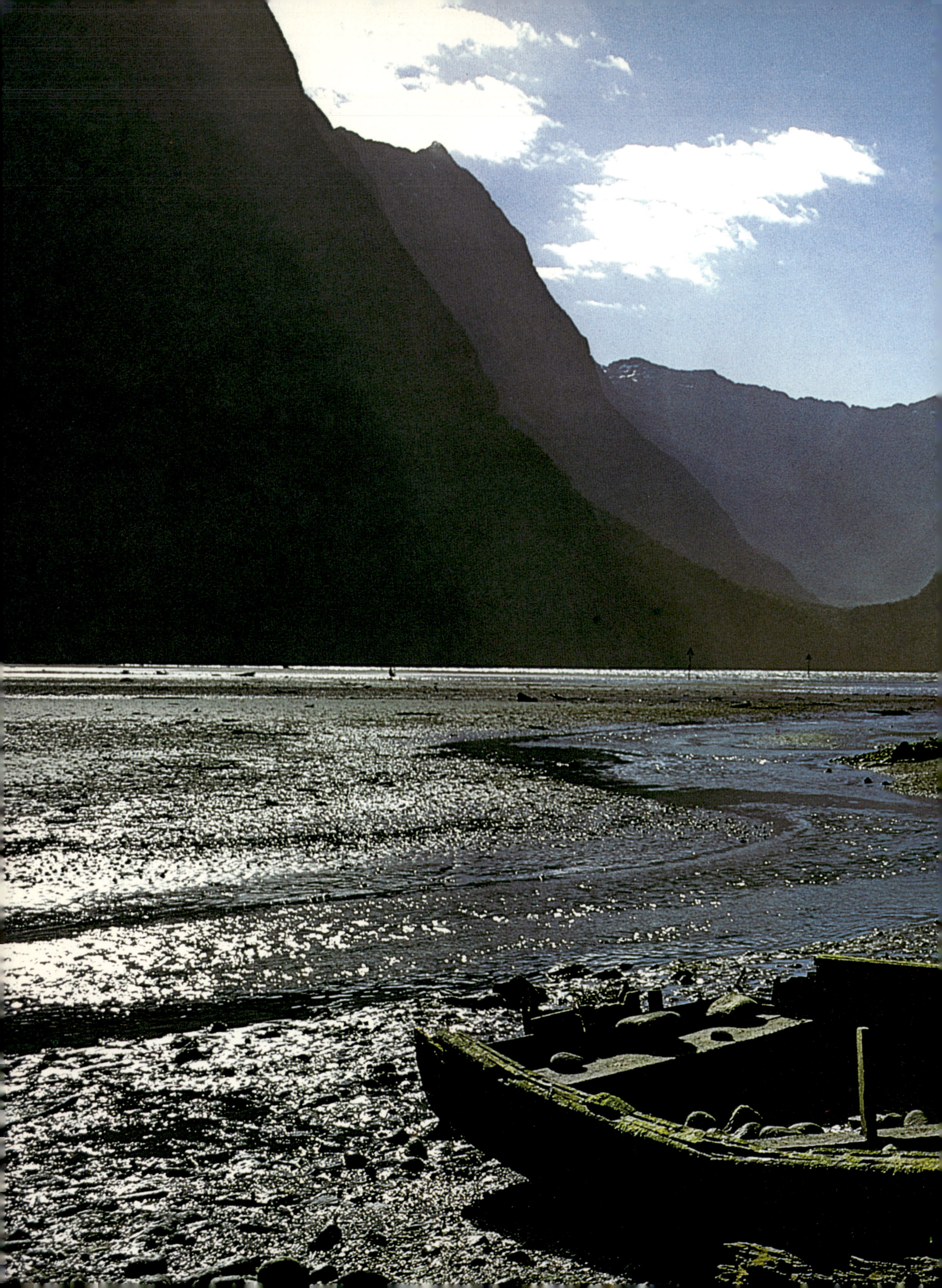

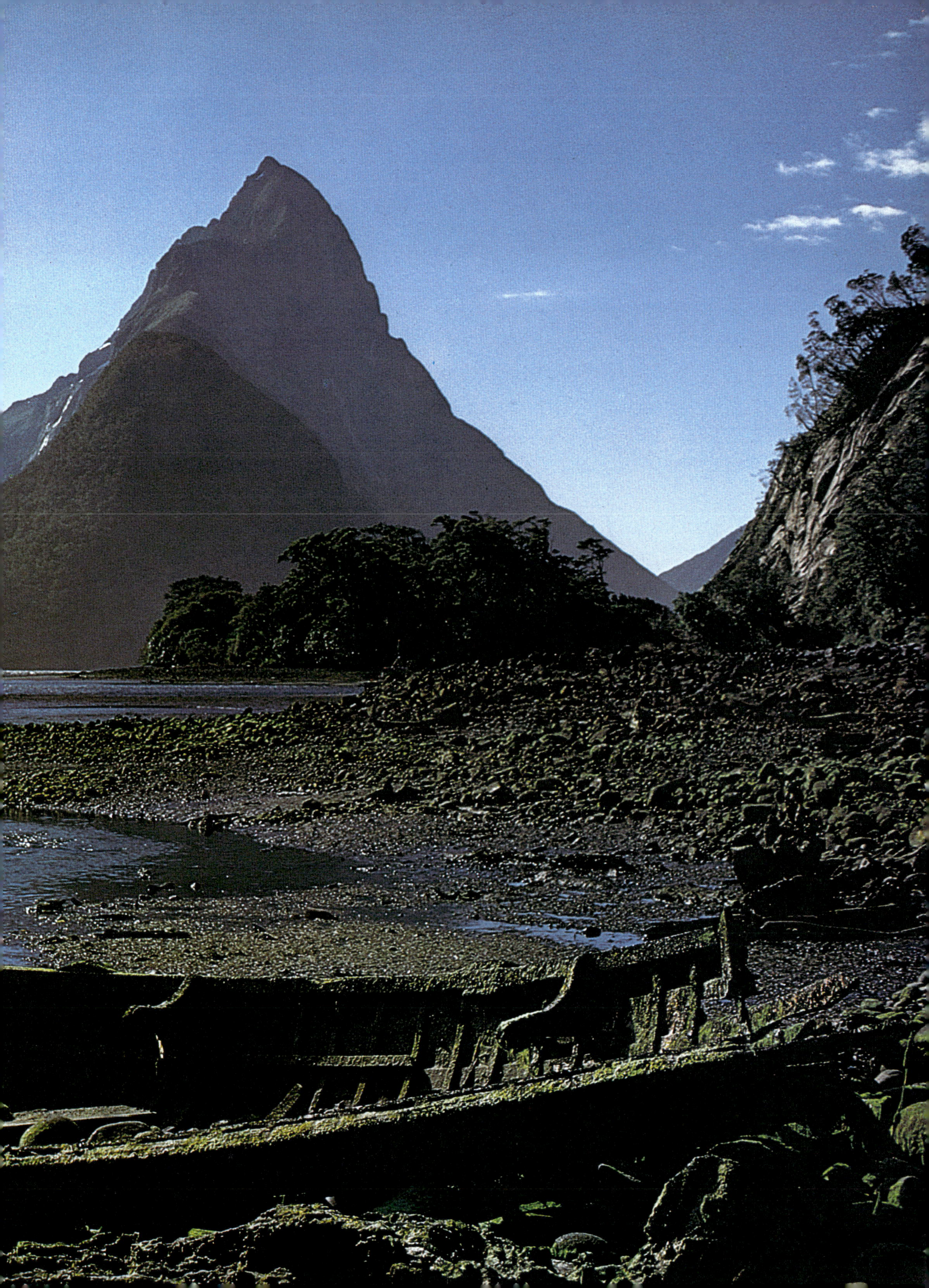

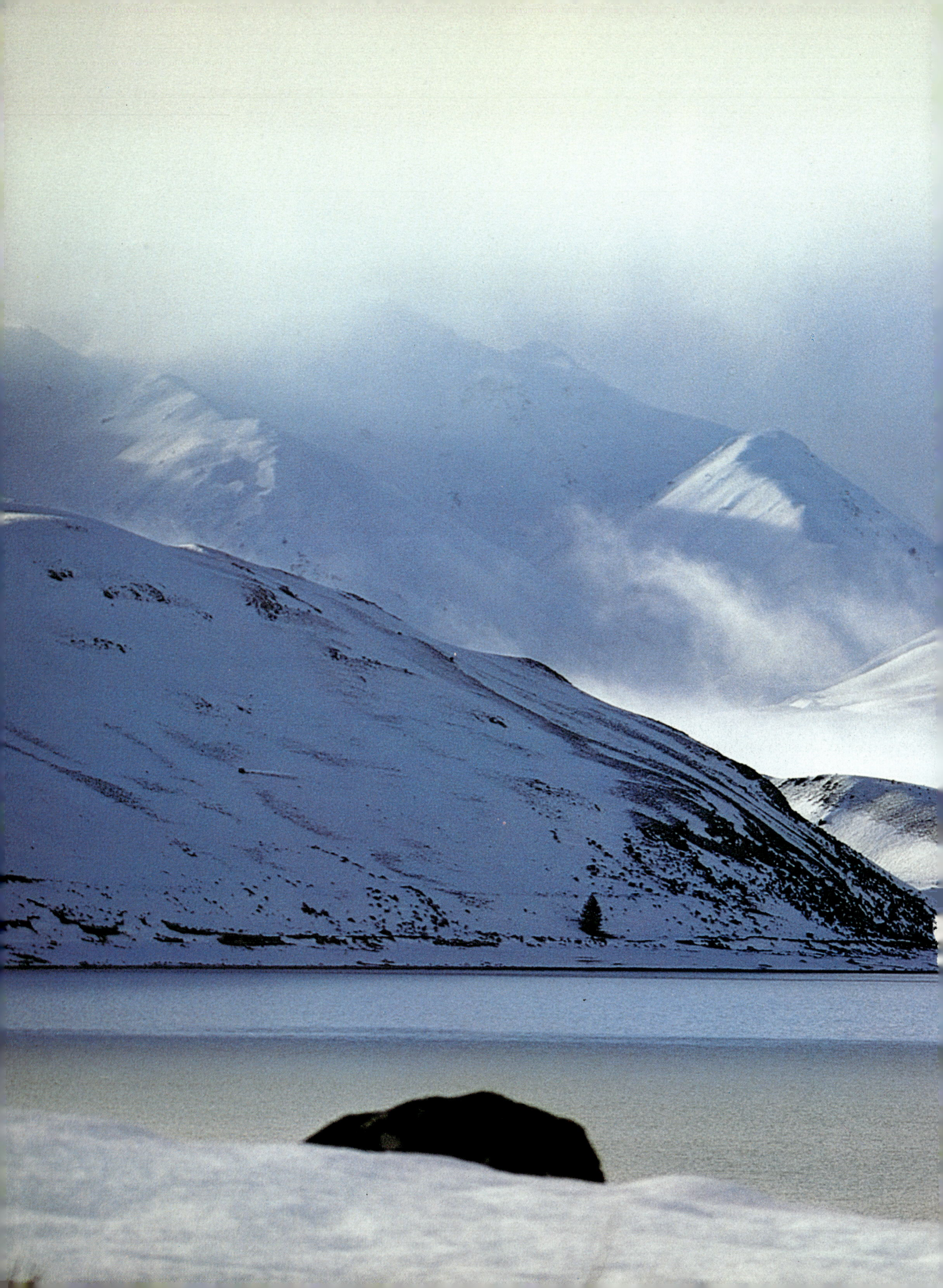

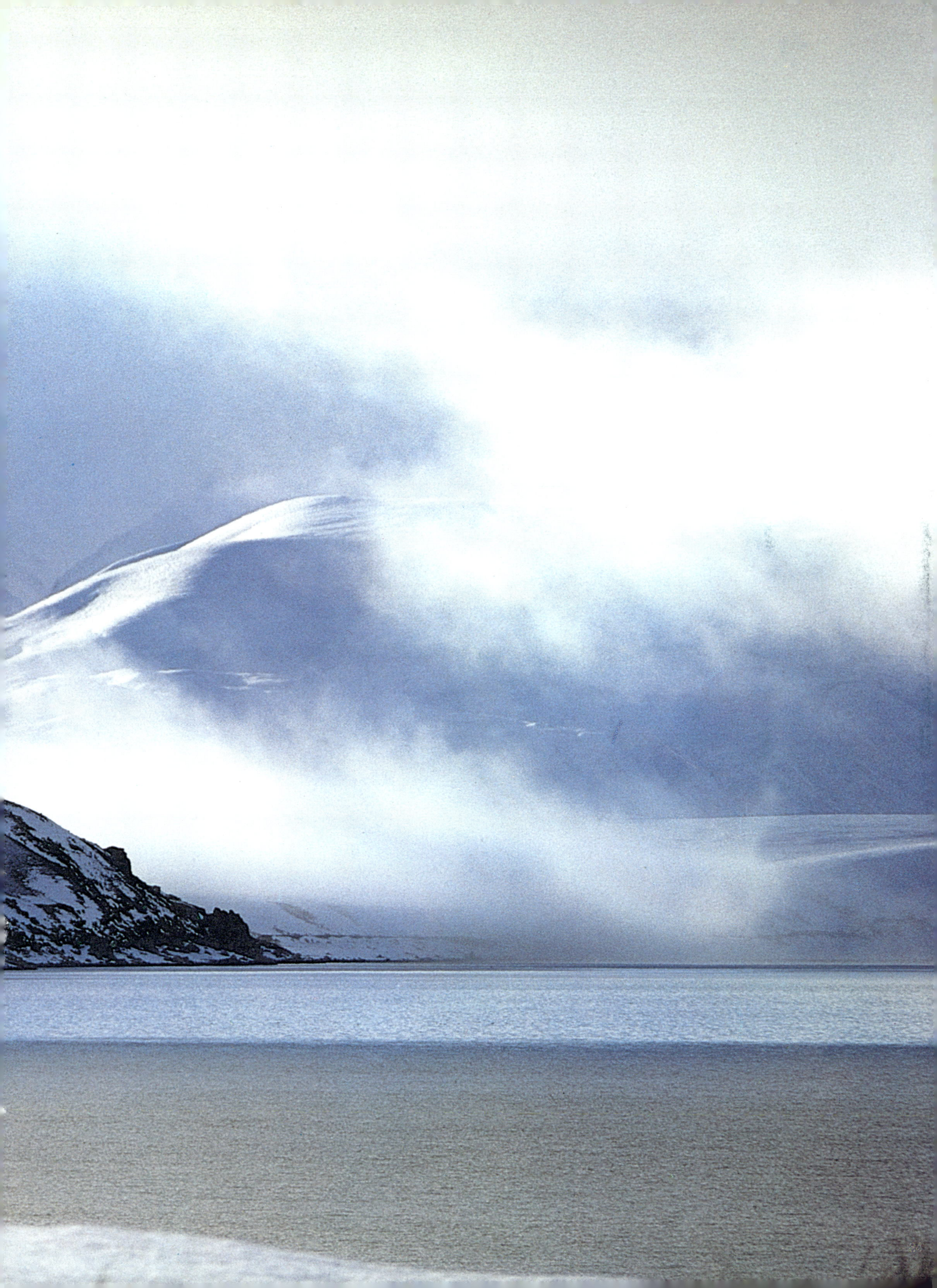

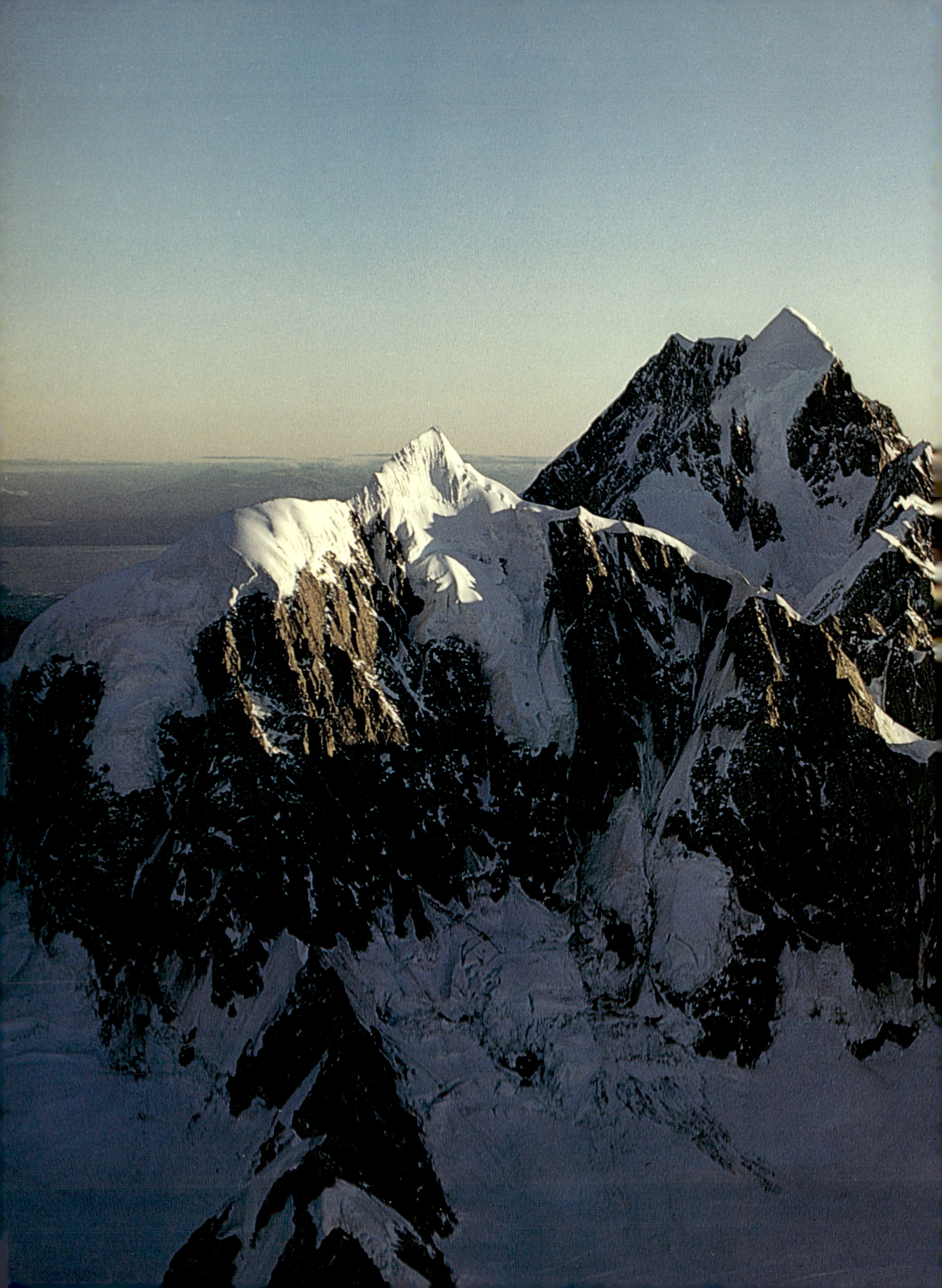

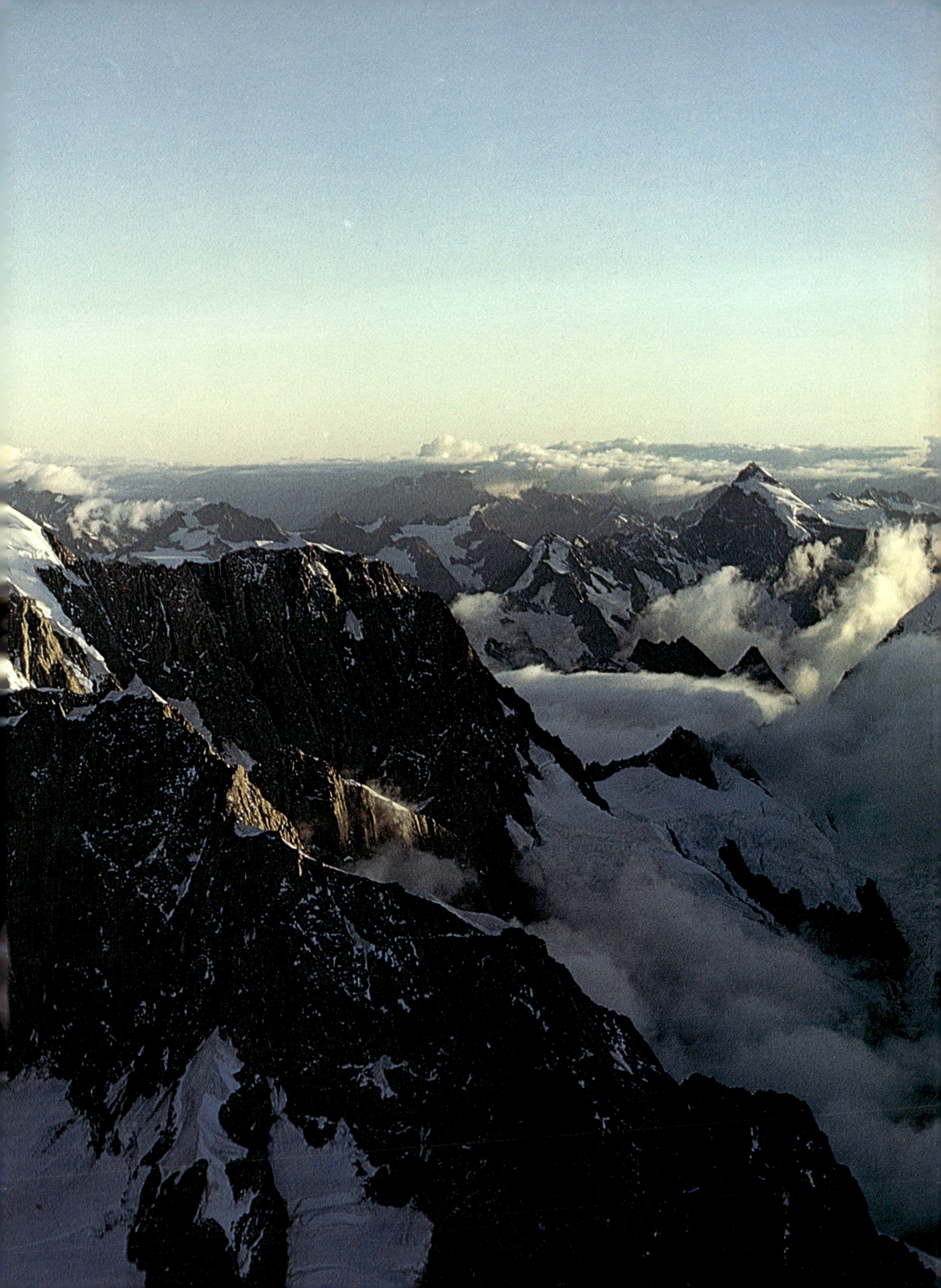

COMMENTARIES ON THE PHOTOGRAPHS

FRONT COVER. Sunset at Martin's Bay, South Westland, at the northern edge of Fiordland National Park. Attempts at settlement here and nearby Jamestown in 1870s largely failed through remoteness from main centres of population. Even today hunters, fishermen and trampers must reach the area by light plane or by foot-track and jetboat down the Hollyford River. The Hollyford Valley includes some of the finest stands of unspoiled lowland forest in New Zealand.

BACK COVER. First Church, Moray Place, Dunedin, opened in 1873, a tangible expression of the Presbyterian ideals which motivated the Otago Settlement in 1848.

ENDPAPERS. Wind patterns on a dune amid acres of shifting fine sand at Wharariki Beach, near Cape Farewell and Farewell Spit at the northern extremity of the West Coast.

1. Ruined stone cottages and isolated willows and poplars are all that remain of Logantown on barren slopes high above the upper Clutha Valley in Central Otago. Typical of gold rush towns, Logantown boasted a population of 400 in 1870 but by the turn of the century the people had gone with the gold.

2-3. Sunrise mists on Glacier Dome, 2453 m, beneath the eastern slopes of Mount Cook. A well-found alpine hut on its slopes provides a base for ascents of New Zealand's highest mountain. Pioneers on Mount Cook first crossed these slopes in 1882.

4-5. Power lines bringing power from the Manapouri hydro station to the Comalco aluminium smelter at Tiwai Point, Southland. Use of beautiful Manapouri as a storage lake caused a major conservation row in the early 1970s. Much of the South Island high country is decorated — or marred — by pylons and cables carrying electricity from lake power schemes to urban centres.

6. NZBC Symphony Orchestra concert in Christchurch Town Hall. Opened in 1972, the town hall complex provides the best concert facilities in the country. Designed, funded and built by Christchurch people.

8. Monument near Kaiapoi, North Canterbury, to mark site of Kaiapohia, major Ngaitahu pa destroyed by marauding North Island chief Te Rauparaha in 1832.

12-13. Morning run for trotting racehorse on beach near Kaka Point, South Otago. At the base of the bay beyond lies the mouth of the Clutha River which has the greatest cusec flow of any New Zealand river, deriving its water from the big mountain lakes of Wakatipu, Wanaka and Hawea.

14-15. Spring-shorn sheep in Makarora Valley beyond the head of Lake Wanaka. Once an important source of timber, the valley now supports sheep farms and is best known as the eastern approach to the lowest pass across the Southern Alps, the Haast Pass at 570 m.

16-17. Winter scene on the Ahuriri River near Omarama in the Mackenzie Country. This country, old glacial basins lying in the eastern shadow of the Southern Alps, was discovered by legendary sheep-stealer, James McKenzie, in 1855. Region of big sheep stations, hydro-electric schemes and tourism centred on Mount Cook, ski fields and lakes.

18-19. Looking west across Tasman Bay from city of Nelson. First settled by Europeans in 1842, this northern South Island colony prospered through wide diversity of pastoral and agricultural industries, favoured by mild and equable climate. Motueka-Riwaka district at far side of bay is sole source of New Zealand hops and tobacco, and coastal region as a whole is centre of apple and pear growing.

20. Northern aspect of main auditorium, Christchurch Town Hall. Designed by local architects M. Warren and M. E. Mahoney.

21. Southeastern aspect of First Church, Dunedin. Designed by R. A. Lawson.

22-3. Aerial view of Christchurch from the northwest, showing coastline at estuary of Avon and Heathcote rivers and northern edge of Banks Peninsula. Lyttelton harbour, port to the city, lies beyond the first range of hills. City centre at lower right. Planned Christchurch was founded in 1850 by English settlers of the Anglican Canterbury Association. At the edge of the rich Canterbury Plains, it has grown to become the largest city in the South Island and the third largest urban area in the country (after Auckland and Wellington). It is similarly placed as an industrial centre. Characterised by straight and level streets, but gardens and parks help to alleviate the monotony of its site. Closely identified with Canterbury farmlands, it retains much of the atmosphere of a market capital.

24-5. Limbs of a beech tree beside Lake Mackenzie on the Routeburn walking track, upper slopes of the Hollyford Valley. Much of the South Island high country, especially in the higher rainfall zones of the west, is still clothed in luxuriant native forest. Forests climb to as high as 1400 m on the Southern Alps and are characterised by *Nothofagus* beech species on the the east and mixed *Podocarpus* species on the west.

26-7.   The Geikie Snowfield at the head of the Franz
Josef Glacier, west of the Southern Alps Main Divide.
Heavy snows on the western slopes of the mountains
feed wide neves, and the icefalls of the Franz Josef
and Fox glaciers descend through narrow gorges to
within 200 m of sea level. This region, within the
Westland National Park, has become more accessible
to mountaineers and skiers with the increasing
employment of ski-planes and high-level huts.

42.   Suburbia: The Dunedin suburbs of South
Dunedin, St Kilda, Kew and Corstorphine on the
isthmus and hills between Otago Harbour and the
open Pacific coast.

43.   Industry: The industrial heart of Christchurch
beside the transport arteries of Moorhouse Avenue
and the main southern railway line.

44.   History in buildings: Detail of disused Union
Bank of Australia, Oamaru, built of local stone in
1878. Neglected harbour area of town contains many
fine but disfigured stone buildings dating from the
1860s and 1870s.

45.   Broadgreen, Stoke, Nelson, restored and
refurbished colonial homestead dating from 1855.

46.   View of Dunedin city from upper Stuart Street.
Spire of First Church is set against waters of Otago
Harbour. City wharves can be seen and suburban
homes round Anderson's Bay beyond. Dunedin was
founded by Scottish settlers of the Otago Association
in 1848. Divorced from extensive pastoral lands by
surrounding high hills, the city grew slowly until the
1860s gold boom in Central Otago when Dunedin
became the nation's commercial and industrial centre.
The finish of Otago gold production, awkward access
to hinterland and distance from main New Zealand
markets in North Island has braked Dunedin's
growth since World War I. A city of style and
character, with many fine buildings dating from the
last quarter of the nineteenth century, it owes much
of current life and activity to university and medical
school.

47.   Picturesque Port Chalmers, 15 km from
Dunedin, provides deepwater berthage for overseas
ships.

48.   Old homes off Nile Street, Nelson, contrast with
new Rutherford Hotel.

49.   Cathedral Square, Christchurch, provides an
open pedestrian area in the heart of the city. The
cathedral, consecrated in 1881, is seen as a church for
the entire city and is the embodiment of Anglican
ideals in the original plan of settlement.

50-1.   Summer Friday night, Cashel Street, in the
shopping centre of Christchurch. Bridge of
Remembrance in background.

52.   Memorabilia of Otago's early European history
are held in the Otago Early Settlers Association
museum in Dunedin. Walls are filled with portraits of
men and women who arrived on ships during the first
thirty years of settlement — a constant reminder of
ancestry to present-day citizens.

53.   Sunday afternoon strollers in Queen's Park,
Invercargill, New Zealand's southernmost city. It is
the market and service centre for the rich pastoral
province of Southland.

54.   Group of youths in Cathedral Square,
Christchurch.

55.   Choir of Christchurch Cathedral. The city is
noted for the strength and quality of its choirs, the
Royal Christchurch Musical Society receiving its
charter in 1920.

56-9.   People of the cities: 56 *top*— Students listening
to visiting speaker in Student Union Building,
Dunedin. 56 *bottom*— Friends in the Octagon, centre
of Dunedin. 57 *top*— Spectators at Lancaster Park,
home of Canterbury rugby. 57 *bottom*— Group
outside Christchurch Cathedral on occasion of
memorial service, Battle of Britain Day. 58 *left*—
Scene at Addington Raceway, Christchurch. 58-9
centre— Beside the Avon River, Christchurch. 59
right— In Cathedral Square.

60.   Otago Boys High School, Dunedin, one of the
South Island's older traditional secondary schools,
established in 1863.

61.   Pupils at Burnside High School, Christchurch,
the largest secondary school in the country with a roll
of nearly 1700.

62.   New residential quarters for students in
Dunedin. The first university in New Zealand, opened
in 1869, Otago University exerts a major influence on
the character and life of Dunedin.

63.   Students at Otago Medical School, until recently
the only one in New Zealand, world renowned for the
quality of its training and research.

64-5.   City work and industry based on primary
produce: 64 — Logs for export to Japan, Port Nelson.
65 *top left*— Cutting beef carcase, Belfast freezing
works, North Canterbury. 65 *top right*— Curing sheep
skins at Belfast. 65 *bottom left*— Beef on the hoof,
Addington Saleyards, Christchurch. 65 *bottom right*—
Fish filleting, Nelson.

66-7: City work and secondary industry: 66 — Boatbuilding, Port Nelson. 67 *top left* — Production line at Hamilton jetboat factory, Christchurch. 67 *top right* — Research, Otago Medical School. 67 *bottom left* — Quilt manufacture at Arthur Ellis and Co., Dunedin. 67 *bottom right* — Bottling New Zealand whisky, Dunedin.

68. Dunedin Railway Station (1904), architecture in the grand manner and the culmination of Victorian building in the city's heyday.

70. Summer croquet at Rangiora, North Canterbury.

71. Winter rugby at Lancaster Park, Christchurch. Canterbury *(right)* and Otago provincial teams clash in one of their fiercely contested annual fixtures.

72-3. Christchurch punters at Riccarton racecourse *(left)* and Addingon Raceway. Addington, with lavish facilities, is the home of New Zealand trotting and Riccarton remains the venue for the N.Z. Cup and the Grand National steeplechase.

74-5. The stadium at Queen Elizabeth II Park, Christchurch, was built for the 1974 Commonwealth Games and provides the only world-class athletics facilities in New Zealand.

76. New Year holidaymakers taking part in a housie game at Caroline Bay, Timaru, a popular family holiday resort.

77. Practice session, City of Dunedin Ladies Pipe Band. Misleadingly Dunedin has been called the 'Edinburgh of the South', though traditions and pastimes of the first Scots settlers persist.

78. One of the South Island's leading painters, Philip Trusttum, at work in his Christchurch studio.

79. Nelson is well known for its potters and weavers; this weaver was photographed in her studio in the city centre.

80-1. The spring brings nets out of winter storage as that prized delicacy, whitebait, make their annual migration up tidal rivers and creeks. A fisherman studies his catch from the Waihopai Stream, at the northern edge of Invercargill.

88-9. Droving cattle through the township of Murchison, Buller district.

90-1. The high valleys and basins of the eastern slopes of the Southern Alps are sheep station country; merinos and other hardy breeds range over the wide acres of native tussock to heights of 1600 m on the mountains. With first winter snows on the tops, sheeps are here mustered down to safer pastures at Mesopotamia in the upper Rangitata Valley. This station was first established by *Erewhon* author Samuel Butler in 1860.

92. Venison hunters recover red deer carcases from a high basin in Fiordland National Park. Introduced deer, without natural enemies, burgeoned in South Island forests, creating havoc with vegetation unadapted to browsing animals. Government deer-culling operations have been largely taken over by professional meat-hunters who have established a profitable venison export industry.

93. Shearers in action on the board at Cattle Flat Station near Lake Wanaka. Itinerant shearing gangs following seasonal work are a colourful and lively feature of high-country life.

94-5. Ripening barley on the Waihao Downs, South Canterbury. Canterbury is well termed the 'granary of New Zealand', producing two-thirds of the nation's wheat crop and over half its crops of barley and oats.

96-7. Trimming logs for a mill near Tuatapere, Southland *(left)* and a skidder dragging out a newly felled tree in coastal forest near Harihari, Westland. While exotic timbers are harvested from Nelson plantations, largely for export to Japanese pulp and paper industries (see page 64), native timbers from the West Coast and Southland are in heavy demand for local building.

98. Sheep on overgrazed pastures in drought-afflicted country near Seddon in Marlborough.

99. Takaka Hill country between Tasman and Golden bays. Burning and felling of native forest were essential in the early days of European settlement to make a way for a farming economy; but indiscriminate or uncontrolled burning destroyed much valuable forest cover needed for soil and watershed protection.

100-1. Workers at the Strongman coal mine, Buller. The Buller fields are the country's only source of bituminous coal and coal mining has been a prime source of income for the region for the past century.

102. Pink brine of evaporating ponds at Lake Grassmere solar saltworks, Marlborough. High sunshine rate and low rainfall make this site ideal for the production of most of the country's industrial and domestic salt.

103. The Canterbury Plains, looking towards Christchurch and Banks Peninsula from Bottle Hill above the Ashley River gorge — a familiar pattern of chequerboard fields planted for crops or grazing and sheltered by belts of introduced macrocarpa or pine trees.

104-5. Country Crafts: Men at the wheels of Waimea Pottery, Richmond, Nelson. Kobi Bosshard, one of New Zealand's leading jewellers, in his workshop at Akaroa, Banks Peninsula.

106-7. Rural work and produce: 106 — Apples from Nelson orchards. 106-7 — Launching a fishing boat at Kaimataitai, South Otago. Small fishing fleets operate from many ports, harbours and estuaries, chiefly on the northern and eastern seaboards. 107 *bottom* — Drainage pipe ready for firing at pottery works based on local clay deposits at Glentunnel, Mid-Canterbury. 107 *top right* — Manufacture of linen fibre in New Zealand's only linen flax factory at Geraldine, South Canterbury. 107 *bottom right* — Picking tobacco near Riwaka in Nelson's Motueka district.

108-9. As distance from pioneer beginnings increases, South Islanders become more conscious of the need to preserve relics of early history. Near Queenstown there is a re-creation of a gold town street *(left)* of the 1860s with museum-style exhibits within reconstructed buildings. Brayshaw Park, Blenheim *(right)*, has become the graveyard for scores of drays, traps and buggies which recall life before the motorcar.

110-11. Rural buildings that have survived from the colonial era: 110 — Homestead in the Takaka Valley, Golden Bay. 111 *top left* — The old post office at St Bathans, Central Otago. 111 *top right* — Derelict home at Owaka, South Otago. 111 *bottom* — Farm homestead near Middlemarch, Otago.

112. Abandoned gold mine, Waiuta, Buller. Quartz mining persisted here until the early 1950s but when the gold ran out, the mine and a thriving township were quickly deserted. All that remain are a few crumbling homes and the poppet head and battery building shown here.

114. Fishing boats and visiting yacht in the small estuary harbour of Waitapu, Takaka.

115. Launches and lake steamer *Earnslaw*, Queenstown waterfront. Queenstown, on Lake Wakatipu, is the most popular high-country resort, a centre for lake excursions, skiing and exploration of a region which was a focus of the 1860s Otago gold rushes.

116. Bather on the Picton foreshore. Picton, the 'capital' of the Marlborough Sounds, is the South Island terminus for Cook Strait ferries and popular as a base for fishing and boating enthusiasts.

117. The bare and rounded foothills of the Southern Alps provide many ideal skiing basins in winter. This skier was photographed in competition on Mount Hutt, Mid-Canterbury.

118. Fairy and queen on procession float for Alexandra Blossom Festival held every September to mark flowering of apricot, peach, plum and cherry trees which provide much of the district's economic wealth.

119. Singer and audience at Country and Western Carnival held each New Year at Fairlie, centre for the Mackenzie Country.

120-1. Scenes from country carnivals and shows: *Top left* — Harness trotters racing at Okains Bay, Banks Peninsula. *Top centre* — World coal-shovelling contest, Reefton Agricultural and Pastoral Show, Buller. *Top right* — Traction engine demonstration, Fairlie carnival. *Bottom left* — Beauty contest, Okains Bay. *Bottom right* — Sheep shearing competitors and spectators, Reefton.

122. Prizewinning calves at Reefton A. & P. Show. District shows are a highlight of country life, displaying the best of local produce and livestock and providing an occasion for competition in such rural activities as riding and shearing, as well as family outing and entertainment.

123. Three-legged race at school picnic, Raupo Bay, Banks Peninsula. Rural schools often provide a focus for community gatherings.

124. Coes Ford, Selwyn River, Mid-Canterbury. The countryside is easily accessible to most city dwellers and summer Sunday picnics are a popular form of relaxation.

125. Jetboat and water-skier, Blue Lake, St Bathan's. Boating on lake, sea or river is the pastime of many holidaymakers. Blue Lake was formed after goldminers created an enormous crater from sluicing in this rich corner of Central Otago.

126-7. A fisherman's evening, Mahau Sound, Marlborough.

129. Rain-soaked forest and hills of the Moeraki River valley, South Westland.

130-1. The wild West Coast at Twelve Mile Bluff, north of Greymouth.

132. Golden sands of Totaranui beach, Abel Tasman National Park, named for the first European discoverer of New Zealand who made his abortive attempt to land near here in 1642.

133. Makarora River, flowing down from the Haast Pass to Lake Wanaka.

134. Bush and bluffs of Kenepuru Sound, Marlborough.

135. Sutherland Falls, near the Milford Track, Fiordland. The highest falls in New Zealand and third highest in the world — 580 m in three jumps.

136-7. A typical Westland lake, Mahinapua, between Hokitika and Ross. The wreck is of a paddle steamer that once plied between the two townships in the district's golden heyday.

138. Sunset reflected on nor'west cloud, Peel Forest, South Canterbury.

139. Weather-sculpted limestone outcrops on Castle Hill, close to the main highway between Christchurch and the West Coast via Arthur's Pass.

140-1. Raggedy Range and the Dunstan Mountains from Rough Ridge, Central Otago. This way came the diggers in the 1860s, searching for gold in a barren, unpopulated landscape.

142-3. Mitre Peak above Milford Sound, grandest of the southern fiords.

144-5. Winter snows at Lake Tekapo, 708 m high in the Mackenzie Country.

146-7. The roof of New Zealand. Mounts Tasman, 3498 m *(left)*, Cook, 3764 m *(centre)*, and Sefton, 3157 m *(far right)*, at the apex of the Southern Alps, the chain of mountains that dominates the landscape of the South Island.

All the author's photographs were taken with Asahi Pentax 35 mm single lens reflex cameras, using Super Takumar 35 mm, 55 mm, 105 mm and 85-210 mm (zoom) lenses. Skylight filters were used for all colour work and extensive use was made of yellow and orange filters in black and white photography. Thanks is extended to Roy Sinclair for his work with black and white film.

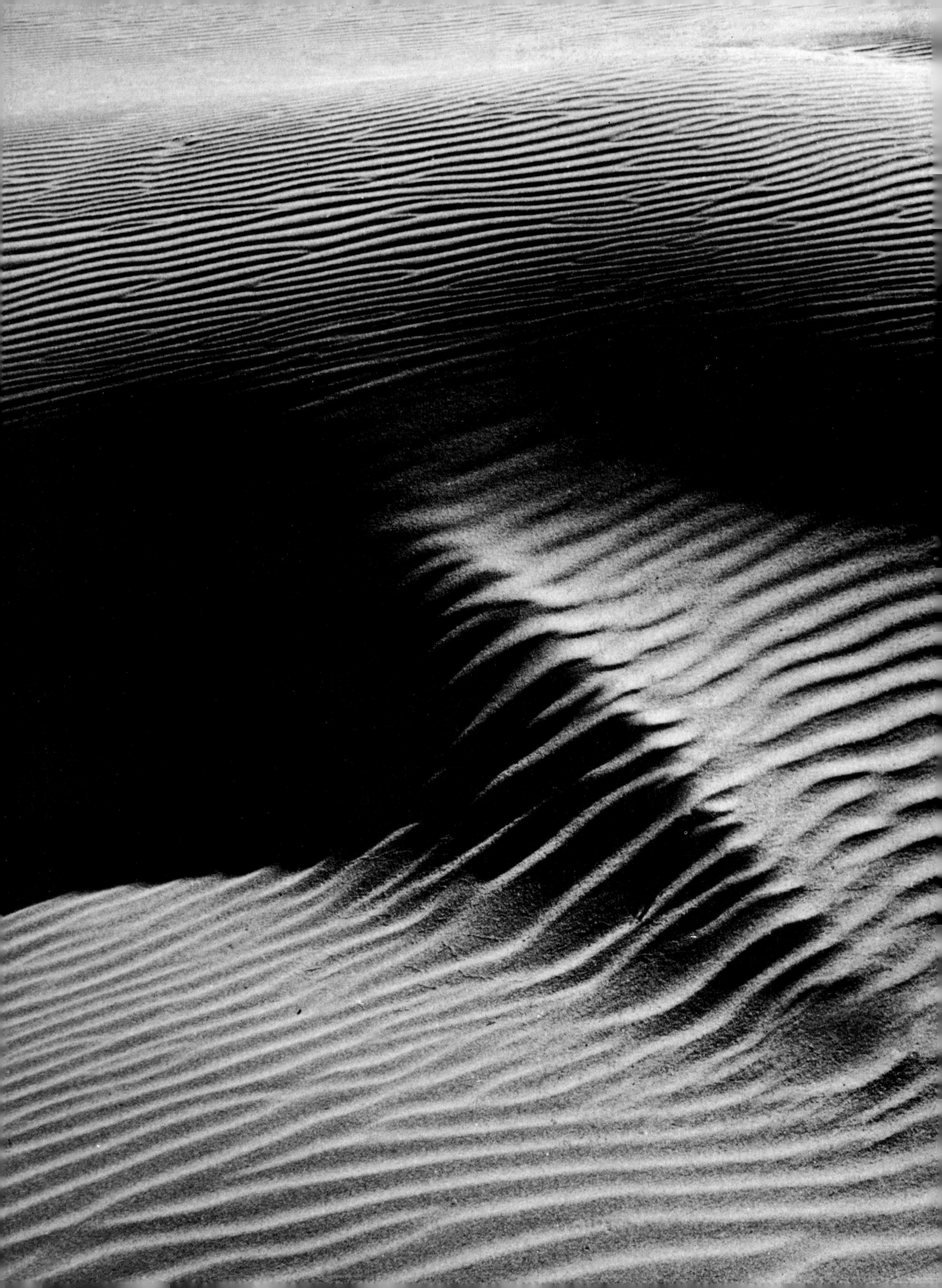